Microsoft® Office PowerPoint 2003

fast&easy™

Microsoft® Office PowerPoint 2003

fast&easy™

Lois Lowe

Premier Press™

SVP, Retail Strategic Market Group: Andy Shafran
Publisher: Stacy L. Hiquet
Senior Marketing Manager: Sarah O'Donnell
Marketing Manager: Heather Hurley
Manager of Editorial Services: Heather Talbot
Associate Marketing Manager: Kristin Eisenzopf
Project Editor/Proofreader: Megan Belanger
Technical Reviewer: Marc Spoto
Retail Market Coordinator: Sarah Dubois
Copy Editor: Sean Medlock
Interior Layout: Danielle Foster
Cover Designer: Mike Tanamachi
Indexer: Kelly Talbot

ISBN: 1-59200-081-9
Library of Congress Catalog Card Number: 2003105358
Printed in the United States of America
04 05 06 07 08 BH 10 9 8 7 6 5 4 3 2 1

Premier Press, a division of Course Technology
25 Thomson Place
Boston, MA 02210

Acknowledgments

A big thanks to the top-notch staff at Premier Press for another job well done.

Contents at a Glance

Contents

PART III
JAZZING UP THE PRESENTATION 95

Introduction

This *Fast & Easy* guide from Premier Press will help you master Microsoft Office PowerPoint 2003 so you can create and deliver informative and effective presentations. PowerPoint is a presentation design program that makes it easy to design a slide show to fit any need. It has been popular with users for many years, and new features have been added to each new version of the program to make it more user-friendly and Web-compatible.

Anyone can use PowerPoint, not just artists and professional presenters. With PowerPoint, you can create multimedia-rich presentations complete with graphics, sounds, animations, voice-overs, and slide transitions. PowerPoint presentations can be delivered on a computer, through a projector, in a kiosk, or as part of a Web site.

Who Should Read This Book?

This book is for the novice computer user in need of a hands-on approach. The generous use of illustrations makes this book ideal if you've never used a presentation design program before. This book is also useful if you're familiar with previous versions of PowerPoint and want to quickly apply your skills to this newest version.

This book is organized so you can quickly look up tasks to help you complete a job or learn a new trick. You may need to read an entire chapter to master a subject, or you may only need to read a certain section to get your creative juices flowing.

Becoming a Presentation Wizard

You'll notice that this book keeps explanations to a minimum to help you learn faster and get up to speed with PowerPoint quickly. Other features of this book provide more information on how to work with PowerPoint.

> **TIP**
>
> Tips offer PowerPoint hints that make your job a little easier and help you create presentations efficiently.

> **NOTE**
>
> Notes offer additional information about PowerPoint to enhance your learning experience with the software.

The appendix lists shortcut keys to help you make the transition from the mouse to the keyboard. You'll also find that using shortcut keys can increase your productivity and help you complete a presentation in less time.

Have fun with PowerPoint, and make your next presentation a smashing success!

PART I

Getting Acquainted with PowerPoint

1

Understanding the Basics

Every project needs a starting point, and if you're using PowerPoint for the first time, you'll want to start with a quick exploration of the program. Start up the application, look around the program window, and open a few menus. If you're upgrading from a previous version of PowerPoint, a quick look around will reveal some new features that you may find useful. In this chapter, you'll learn how to:

- Start and exit PowerPoint
- Switch between PowerPoint views
- Work with the task pane
- Display and hide toolbars
- Turn off the Personalized Menus feature

Starting PowerPoint

One easy way to start PowerPoint is to select it from the Start menu. Depending on your Windows version and the way Windows is set up, PowerPoint may appear at the top of the Start menu, or it may require you to open the All Programs (or Programs) menu to find it.

1. **Click** on **Start**. The Start menu will appear.
2. **Click** on **Microsoft Office PowerPoint 2003** if it appears on the Start menu's top level. PowerPoint will open, and you can skip the rest of these steps. Otherwise, continue to step 3.
3. **Move** the **mouse pointer** to **All Programs** (or **Programs**). The Programs menu will appear.

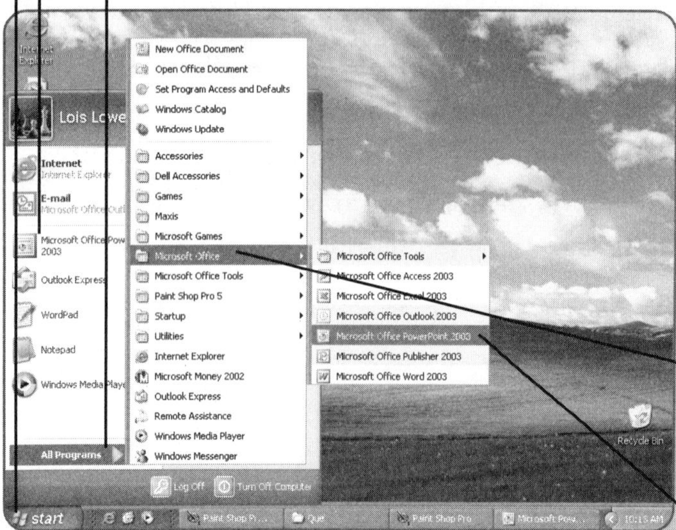

NOTE

The difference in wording in step 3 is due to the Windows version. Windows XP uses All Programs; all other versions use Programs.

4. **Move** the **mouse pointer** to **Microsoft Office**. A menu of Microsoft Office applications will appear.
5. **Click** on **Microsoft Office PowerPoint 2003**. PowerPoint will open and will display a new, blank presentation.

TIP

You can force PowerPoint to always appear at the top of the Start menu by "pinning" it there. In step 4, instead of clicking on Microsoft PowerPoint, right-click it and choose Pin to Start menu. From then on, a shortcut to PowerPoint will appear at the top of the Start menu, and you'll never have to open the All Programs menu again to locate it.

Creating a Desktop Shortcut for PowerPoint

If you use PowerPoint often, you might want to put a shortcut to it on the desktop. You can double-click it to start PowerPoint instead of going through the Start menu each time.

1. **Click** on **Start**. The Start menu will appear.
2. **Move** the **mouse pointer** to **All Programs** (or **Programs**). The Programs menu will appear.
3. **Move** the **mouse pointer** to **Microsoft Office**. A menu of Office applications will appear.

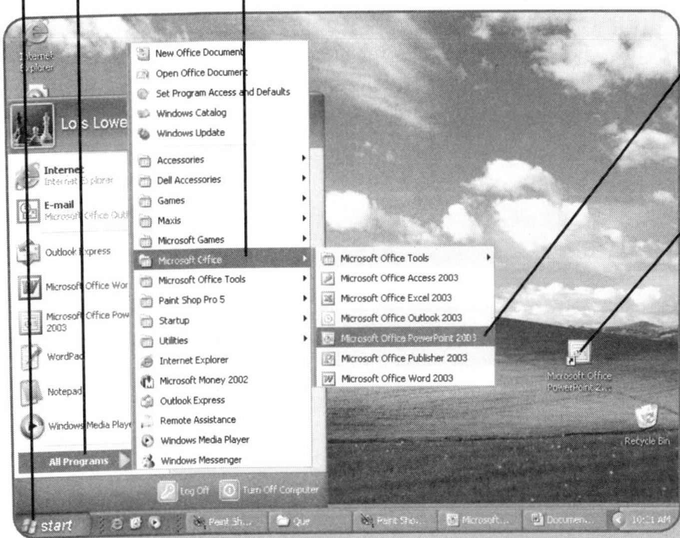

4. **Move** the **mouse pointer** to **Microsoft Office PowerPoint 2003**. PowerPoint will be highlighted.
5. **Hold** down the **Ctrl key** and **drag Microsoft Office PowerPoint 2003** to the desktop. A shortcut to Microsoft PowerPoint will appear on the desktop.

TIP

You can use these steps to create a desktop shortcut for any program that is installed on the computer.

Starting PowerPoint and Opening a Saved File

If you already have a PowerPoint presentation started, you can start PowerPoint by opening that file. PowerPoint files have a .ppt extension, and the icon matches the PowerPoint 2003 icon (orange).

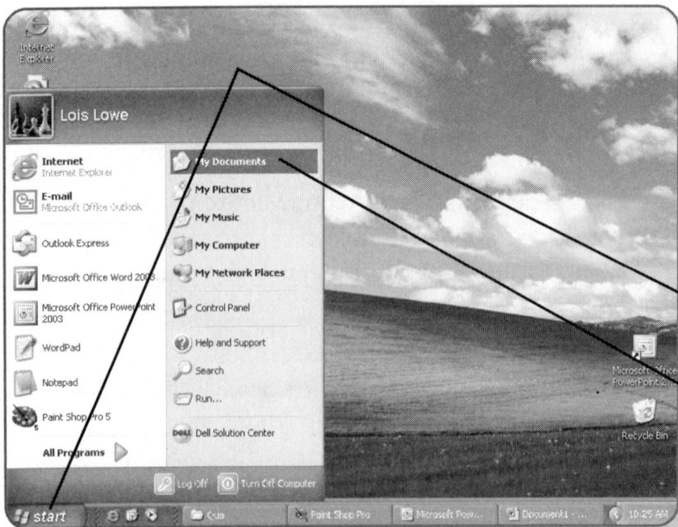

The following steps are for Windows XP, and they assume that your existing file is stored in the My Documents folder. If you have an earlier version of Windows, or if your file is located somewhere else, see the notes following the steps.

1. **Click** on **Start**. The Start menu will appear.
2. **Click** on **My Documents**. The My Documents folder will appear.

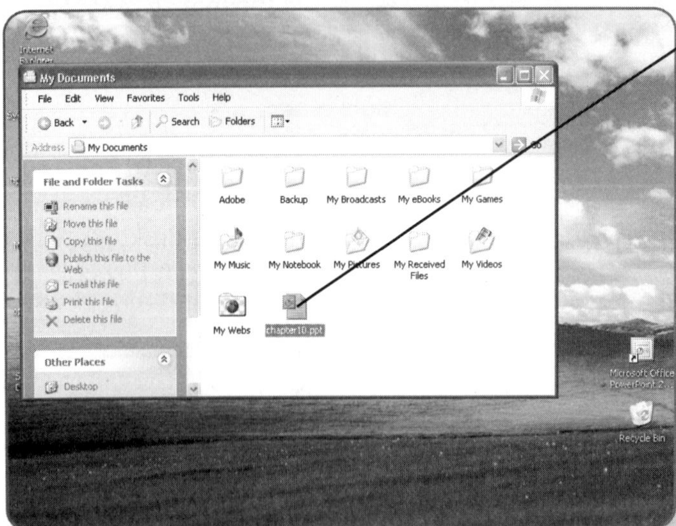

3. **Double-click** on the **presentation file**. PowerPoint will start, and that presentation will open within PowerPoint.

> **NOTE**
>
> Don't have Windows XP? Then double-click the My Documents icon on the desktop instead of performing steps 1 and 2.

NOTE

File stored in some other location? Open My Computer and browse for it. In Windows XP, click Start and then click My Computer. In all other Windows versions, double-click the My Computer icon on the desktop.

Exiting PowerPoint

When you're finished working with PowerPoint, you'll want to exit the program to free up the system for other tasks, and to make your screen more tidy.

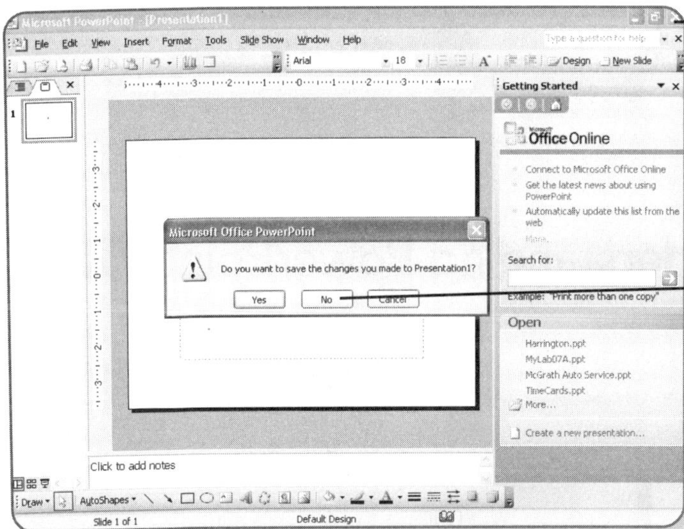

1. **Click** on **Close** in the upper-right corner of the PowerPoint window. If there are no unsaved changes, PowerPoint will close immediately. If there are changes, a Save dialog box will appear.
2. **Click** on **No** to discard your changes. PowerPoint will close.

NOTE

Notice that there are several X buttons near the upper-right corner of the window. The topmost button closes PowerPoint itself. The button directly beneath that closes the open presentation only. The button about one inch below those two closes the task pane.

Minimizing and Restoring PowerPoint

If you don't want to close PowerPoint but simply want to move it out of the way temporarily, minimize it. Minimizing a window shrinks it down to an icon on the Taskbar. You can then click that icon to reopen—restore—the window when you're ready to use it again.

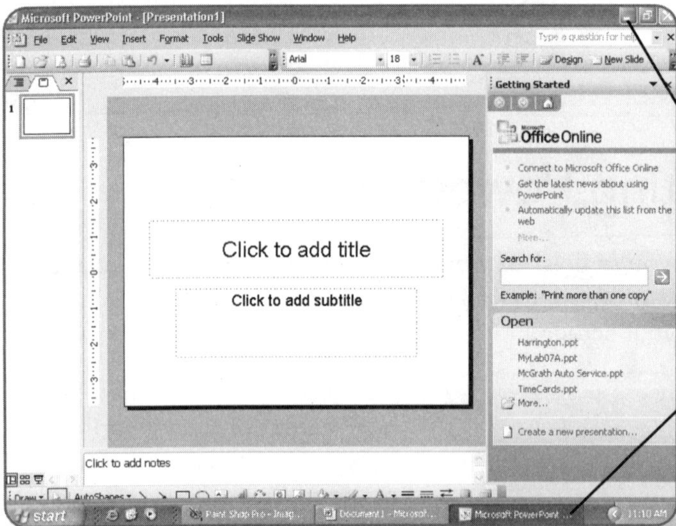

1. **Click** on the **Minimize button** in the upper-right corner of the PowerPoint window. PowerPoint will disappear except for its icon in the Taskbar.

2. **Click** on the **PowerPoint icon** on the Taskbar. The PowerPoint window will appear again.

Understanding PowerPoint Views

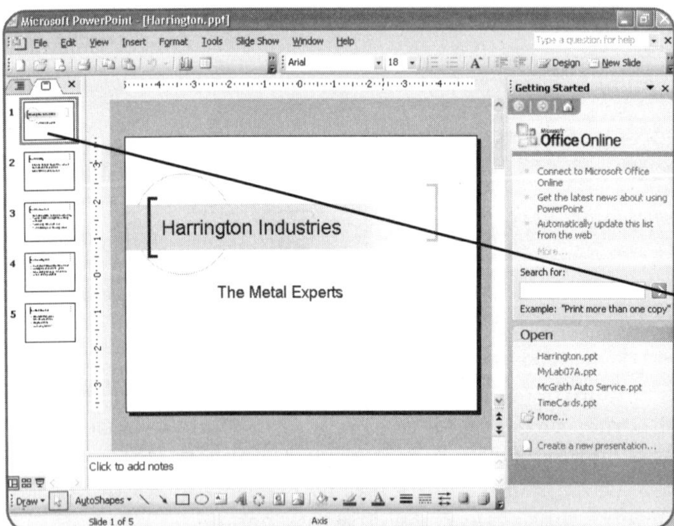

PowerPoint operates in several different views. Each view is useful for a different type of activity.

Normal view is the default view. In Normal view, you'll see the following panes:

- **Slides pane**. Thumbnail images of the slides in the presentation appear here. The other tab at the top of this pane is for the Outline pane, discussed in Chapter 4, "Organizing the Presentation Outline."

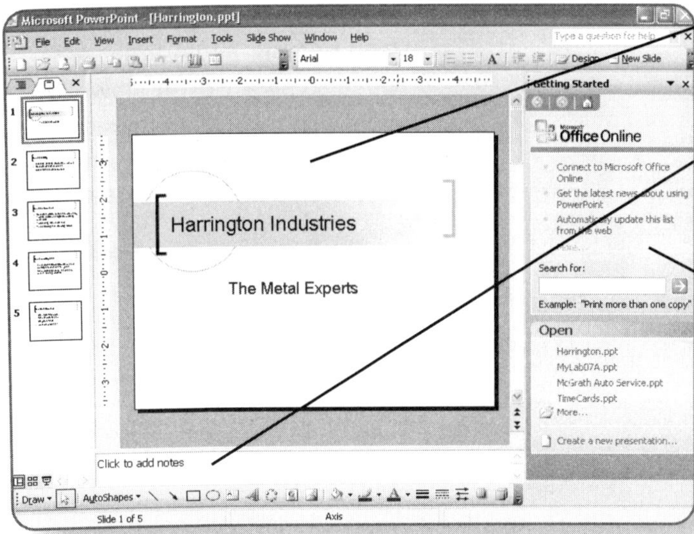

- **Current slide**. A single slide at a time appears here. It's enlarged so you can work on it.
- **Notes pane**. Any speaker notes you type for the slide appear here. These notes aren't visible to the audience.
- **Task pane**. This pane changes depending on what you're doing. You can also **click** its **Close (X) button** to give you more room.

> **NOTE**
>
> A presentation file containing several slides is shown here for example purposes. You'll learn how to open and create presentations of your own starting with Chapter 3, "Learning About Presentations."

Changing to a Different View

There are two other views: Slide Sorter and Slide Show. Slide Sorter view shows thumbnail images of all the presentation slides at once. Slide Show view shows full-screen images of each slide.

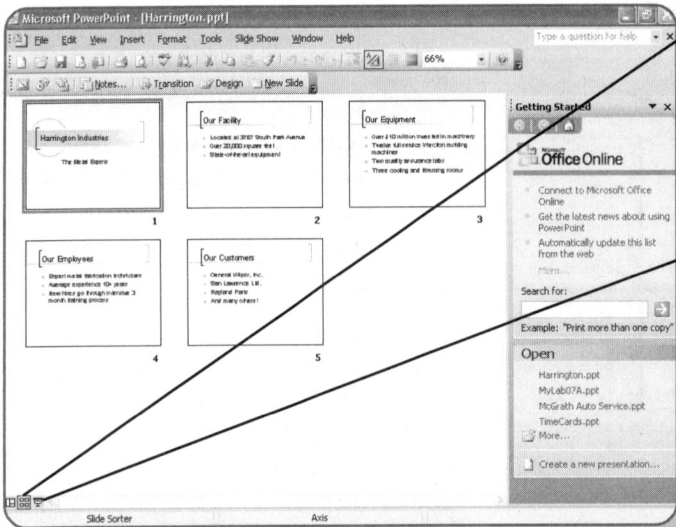

1. Click on the **Slide Sorter View button**. PowerPoint will switch to Slide Sorter view. You might use this for a bird's-eye view of the presentation, or to rearrange the slides more easily.

2. Click on the **Slide Show View button**. PowerPoint will switch to Slide Show view.

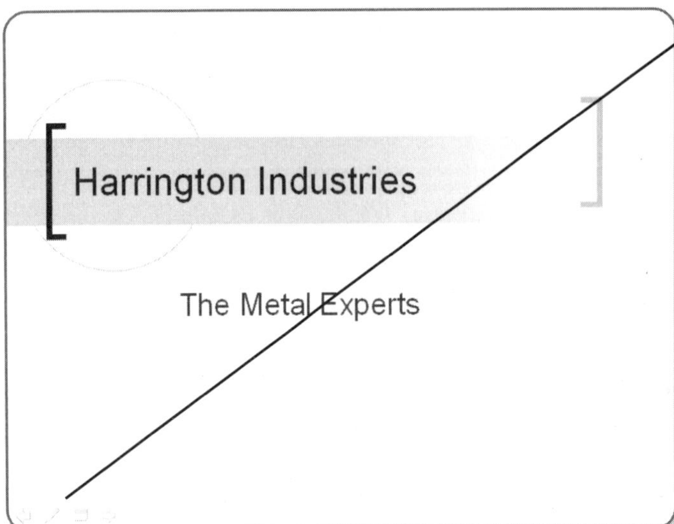

In Slide Show view, there is nothing you can edit. You can only view the slides. You would use this view for giving a presentation. Navigation buttons appear in the corner.

3. Press the **Esc key**. Slide Show view will close and the screen will return to Slide Sorter view.

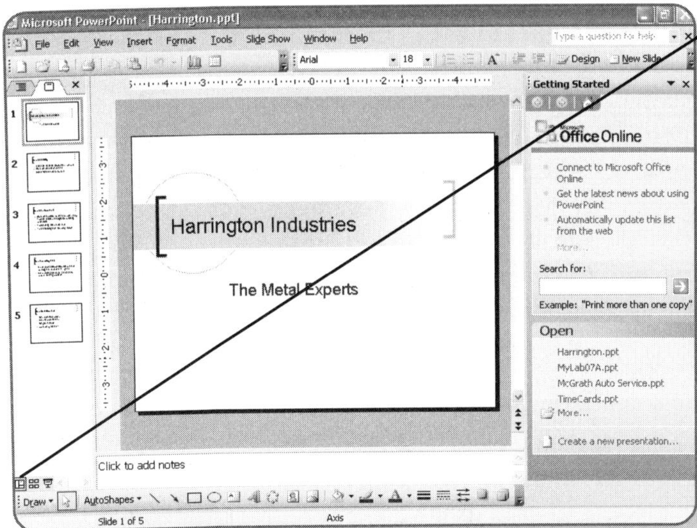

4. Click on the **Normal View button**. PowerPoint will switch back to Normal view.

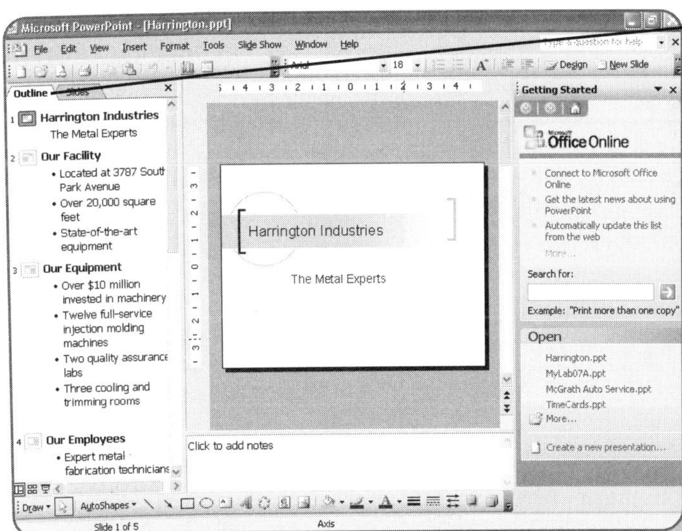

5. Click on the **Outline tab**. The presentation outline will come to the front.

NOTE

You'll learn how to create an outline in Chapter 4, and you'll learn how to rearrange the slides in Chapter 5, "Organizing and Improving the Presentation."

Working with the Task Pane

The task pane is an area that appears to the right of the other PowerPoint panes. There are actually many different task panes, each one containing tools and options appropriate for a certain activity. Most of the time, the correct task pane will appear automatically when needed. For example, if you select the command to change a slide's layout, the Slide Layout task pane will appear automatically.

Many people prefer to work with the task pane hidden so they have more space onscreen. You can redisplay it when you need it.

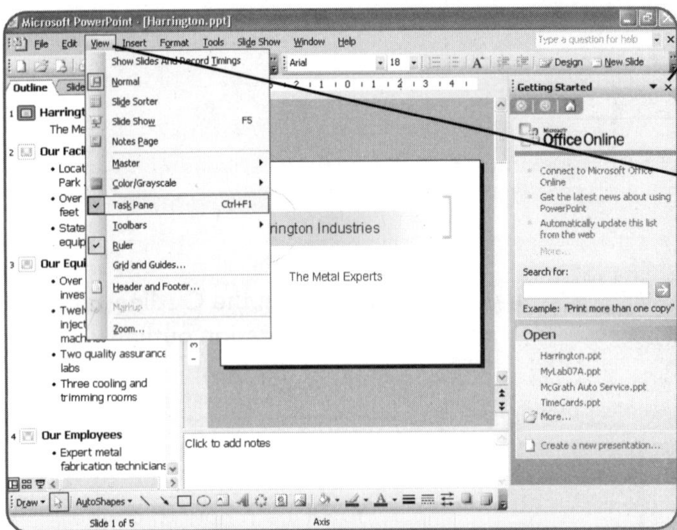

1. **Click** on the **Close button** on the task pane. The task pane will disappear, and the current slide will have more space available.

2. **Click** on the **View menu**. The View menu will appear.

3. Pause for a few seconds if there is a down-pointing arrow at the bottom of the menu. The full menu will appear after a brief delay.

> **NOTE**
>
> Step 3 may be necessary if the Personalized Menus feature is turned on. You will learn how to turn it off later in this chapter.

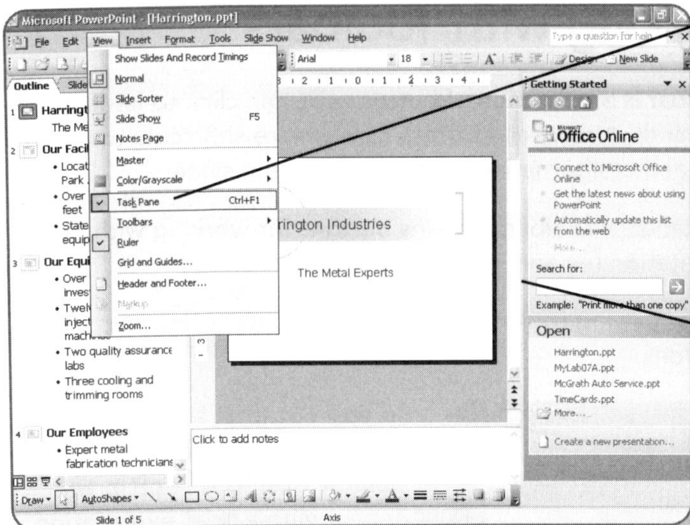

4. Click on **Task Pane**. The task pane will reappear.

> **TIP**
>
> Instead of steps 2 through 4, you can press Ctrl+F1.

5. Move the **mouse pointer** over the border between the current slide's pane and the task pane. The mouse will become a two-headed arrow. Then **drag** to the left or right to resize the task pane.

Choosing a Different Task Pane

PowerPoint will often display a certain task pane based on what you're doing. You can also choose which task pane you want to see at any given moment.

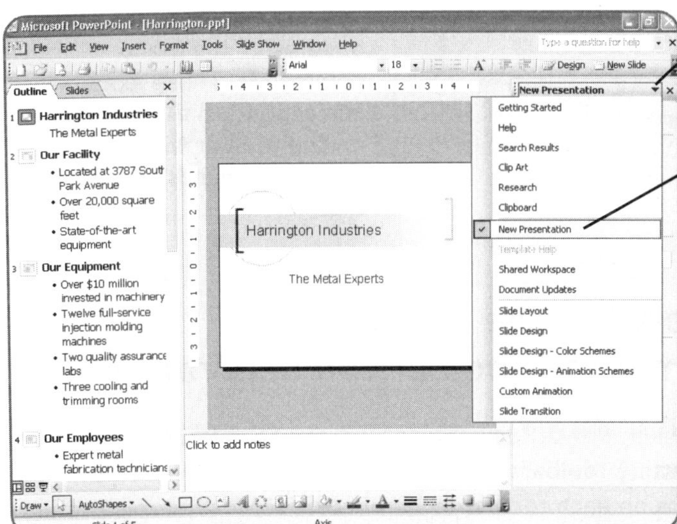

1. Click on the **Task Pane down arrow**. A list of available task panes will appear.

2. Click on a **task pane**. The selected task pane will appear.

> **TIP**
>
> The task pane has its own Back and Forward arrows, just like a Web browser window. You can click the Back (left) arrow to return to a previously used task pane.

Working with Toolbars

A toolbar is a collection of buttons you can click to issue commands. Nearly all of these buttons are shortcuts to menu commands—alternatives to using the menu system.

The Standard toolbar contains buttons for working with the presentation file and its content.

The Formatting toolbar contains buttons for formatting text and slides.

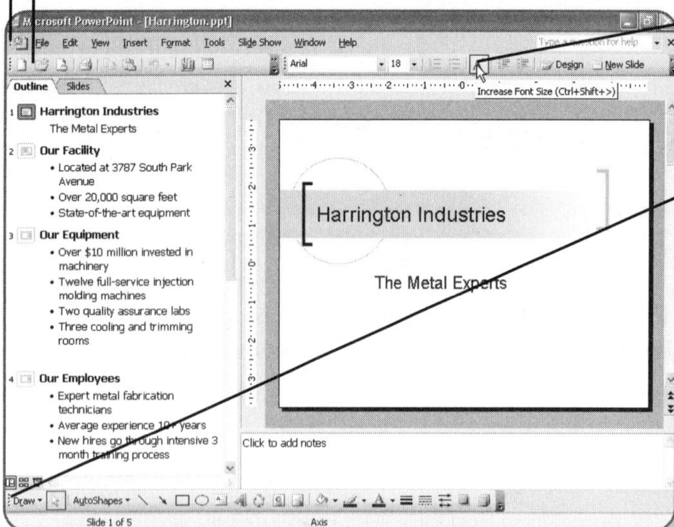

To find out what a particular button does, **move** the **mouse pointer** over it. A ToolTip will appear with a brief explanation.

The Drawing toolbar contains buttons for creating or inserting artwork.

> **TIP**
>
> When you open a menu, you'll see icons to the left of some of the menu commands. These icons correspond to the buttons on the toolbar that match those commands.

Displaying the Standard and Formatting Toolbars on Separate Rows

By default, PowerPoint shows both the Standard and Formatting toolbars on the same row. This causes some buttons on each toolbar to be obscured. Most people prefer to display these toolbars on separate rows. (That's how they're shown in most of the figures in this book.)

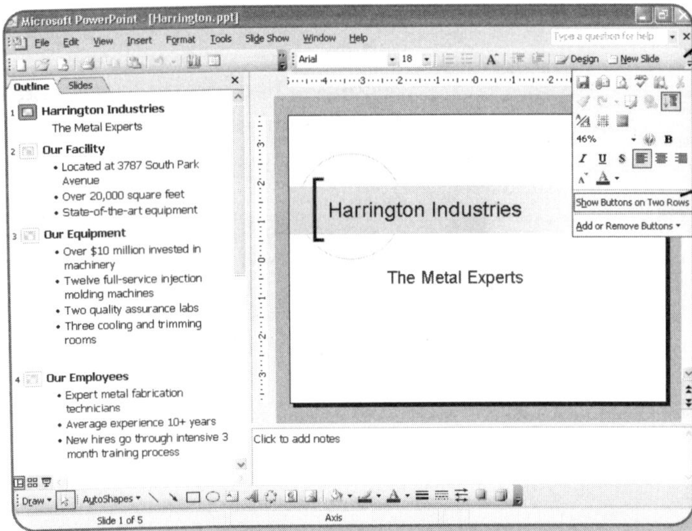

1. Click on the **down-pointing arrow** at the end of the Standard or Formatting toolbar. A menu will appear.

2. Click on **Show Buttons on Two Rows**. The Formatting toolbar will move to a new row below the Standard toolbar.

Moving a Toolbar

You may find that the location of toolbars is inconvenient for the way you work. Toolbars can be moved to any location on the screen that's convenient for you. A toolbar may be docked (attached to other toolbars), or it may float all by itself.

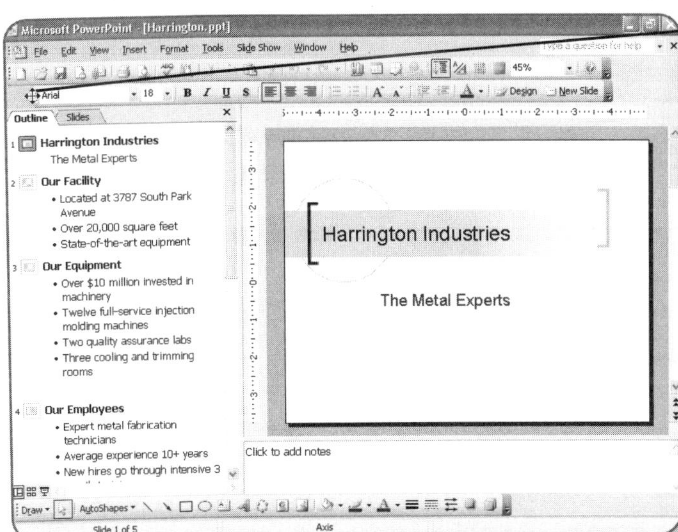

1. Move the **mouse pointer** over the toolbar handle (the set of dots at its left edge). The mouse pointer will change to a four-pointed arrow.

2. Drag the **toolbar handle** to another location on the PowerPoint window. The toolbar will move with the mouse.

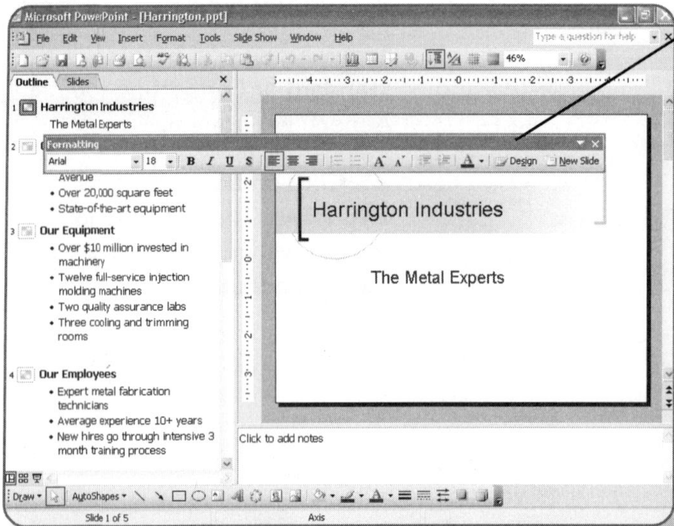

If you **drag** the **toolbar** into the middle of the window, it will become a floating toolbar. **Drag** it back to an edge of the screen to dock it again.

Hiding or Displaying a Toolbar

There are many toolbars available in PowerPoint. Some of them appear automatically when needed; others must be displayed manually.

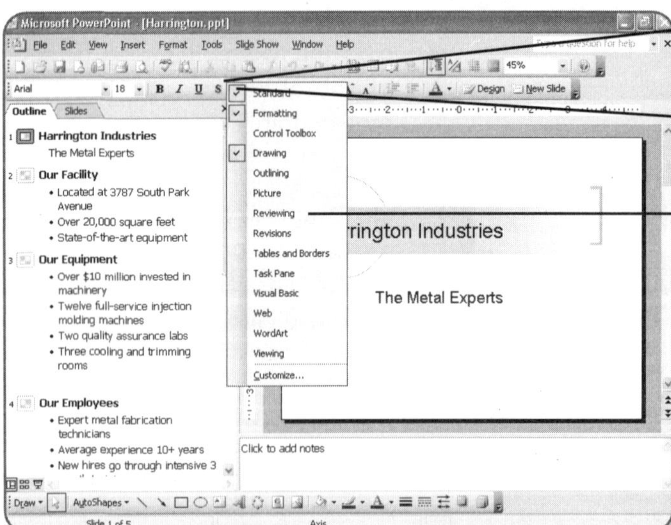

1. Right-click on a **toolbar**. A shortcut menu appears.

Each currently displayed toolbar has a check next to its name.

2. Click on the **name of the toolbar** you want to display (if it's not already checked) or hide (if it's already checked).

> **NOTE**
>
> What if no toolbars are displayed? In that case, open the View menu, point to Toolbars, and then click the name of the toolbar you want.

Turning Off the Personalized Menus Feature

By default, the Personalized Menus feature is turned on in PowerPoint. When you open a menu, only a few of the available commands appear. PowerPoint monitors your usage, and if you've used a certain command before, it's on that short, initial list. The rest of the commands appear after a few seconds, or when you click the down arrow at the bottom of the menu.

The figures in this book have this personalized menu feature turned off to avoid inconsistency between the book's pictures and your screen. To follow along more closely with the figures in this book, we recommend that you turn this feature off, too.

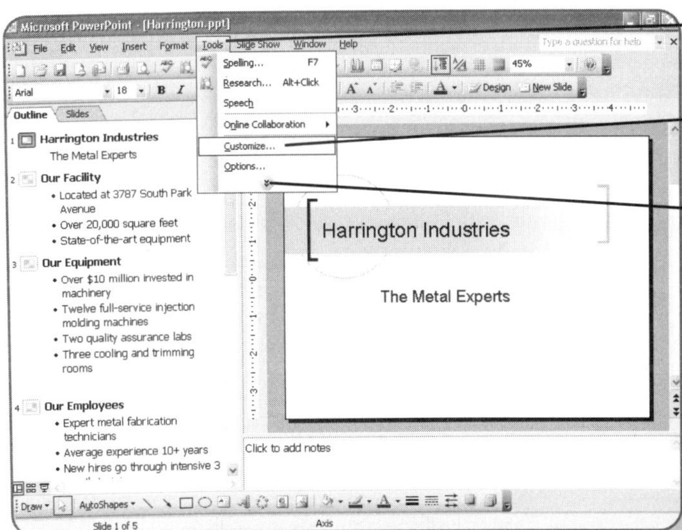

1. **Click** on **Tools**. The Tools menu will appear.

2. **Click** on **Customize**. The Customize dialog box will open.

Notice the down-pointing arrow at the bottom of the menu. This indicates that more commands are available than are currently shown.

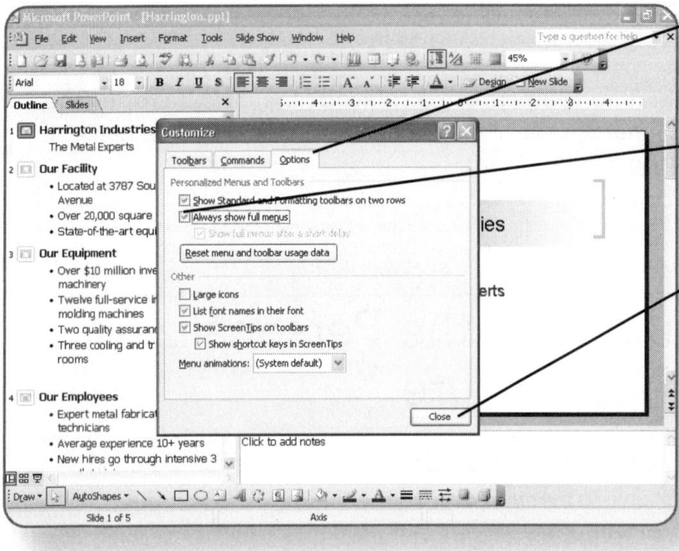

3. **Click** on the **Options tab**. The Options tab will come to the front.

4. **Click** on the **Always show full menus check box**. A check will be placed in the check box.

5. **Click** on **Close**. Your new setting will be applied.

2

Asking for Help

As you work on a presentation, you may find that every now and then you need a quick reminder on how to perform a task or some help learning an unfamiliar program feature. You have several choices. You can refer back to books that you've read, you can get on the Internet and do some research, or you can use the built-in PowerPoint help system. In this chapter, you'll learn how to:

- Use the Ask a Question feature
- View and print Help topics
- Find help on the Internet
- Get program updates

Asking a Question

The Ask a Question box, in the top-right corner of the screen, provides quick access to the Help system.

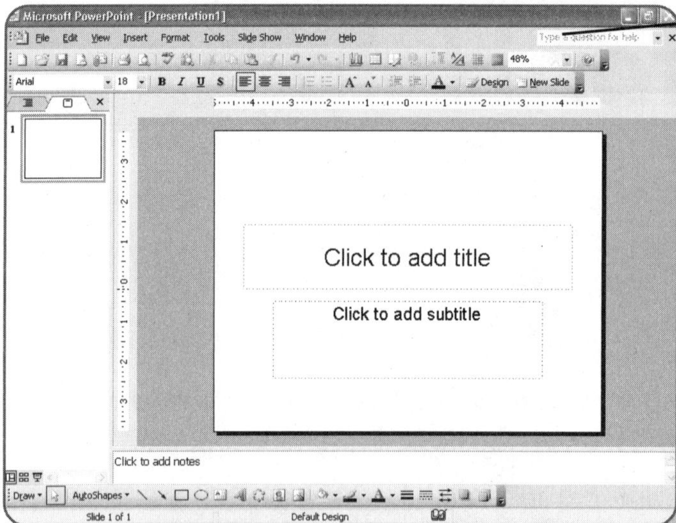

1. **Click** in the **Ask a Question text box**. The cursor will appear in the box.

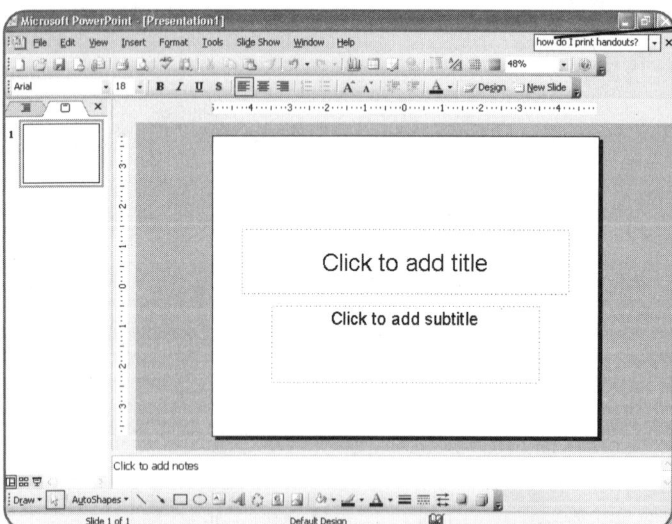

2. **Type** a **question** and **press Enter**. The Help task pane will appear, and the help system will be searched.

> **NOTE**
>
> If you are connected to the Internet, the search for Help topics will include topics available through Microsoft's Web site.

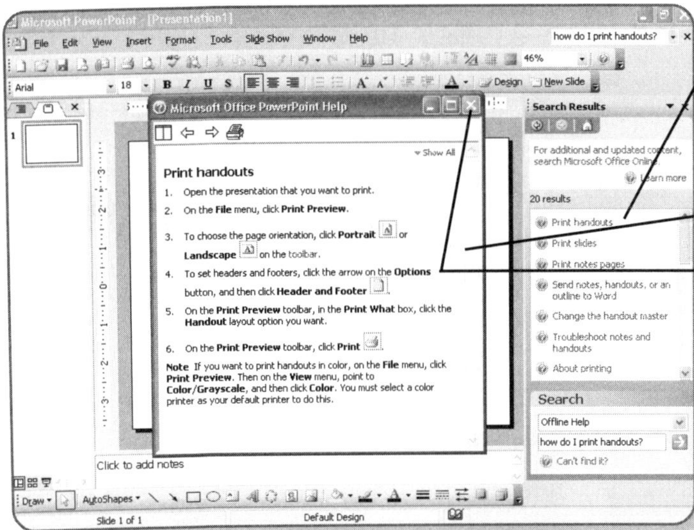

3. **Click** on the **topic** that most closely answers your question. The Help topic will appear in the Microsoft PowerPoint Help window.

4. **Read** the **Help topic**.

5a. **Click** on the **Close button** to close the Help window

OR

5b. See the following steps to print it.

Printing a Help Topic

Printing a Help topic enables you to refer to it easily after you have closed its window onscreen.

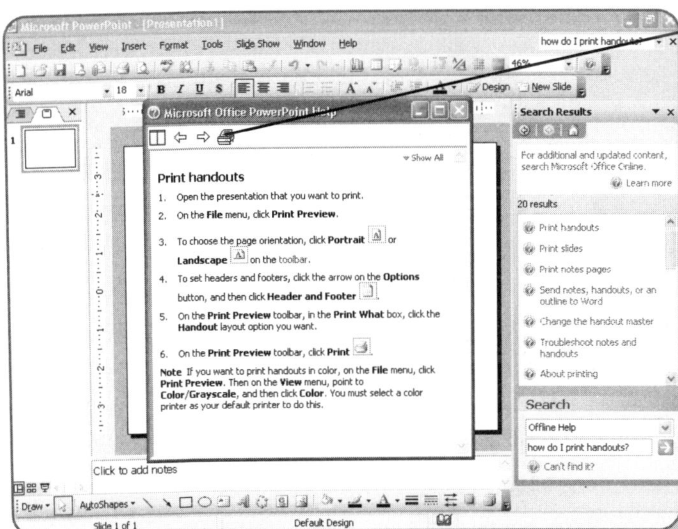

1. **Click** on the **Print button** in the Help window. The Print dialog box will open.

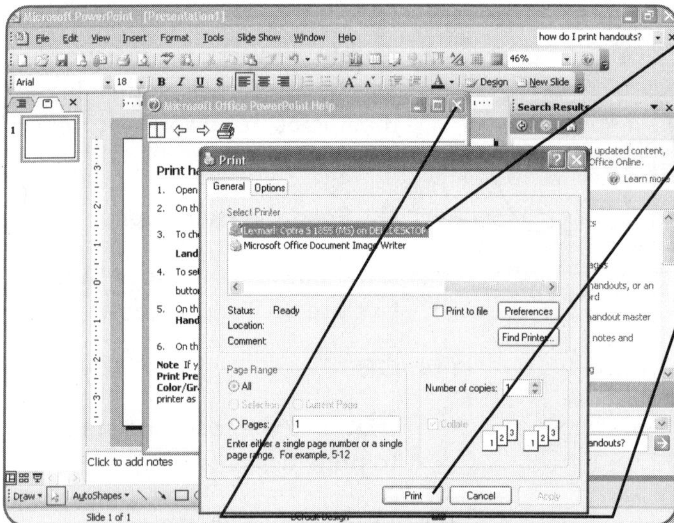

2. **Click** on the **desired printer**. It will be selected.

3. **Click** on **Print**. The Help article will print.

4. **Click** on the **Close button** to close the Help window.

Getting Help on the Internet

When you use PowerPoint while connected to the Internet, PowerPoint automatically integrates online help into its own Help system. You can also visit the Office Online site to browse for additional downloads and information not related to a specific question.

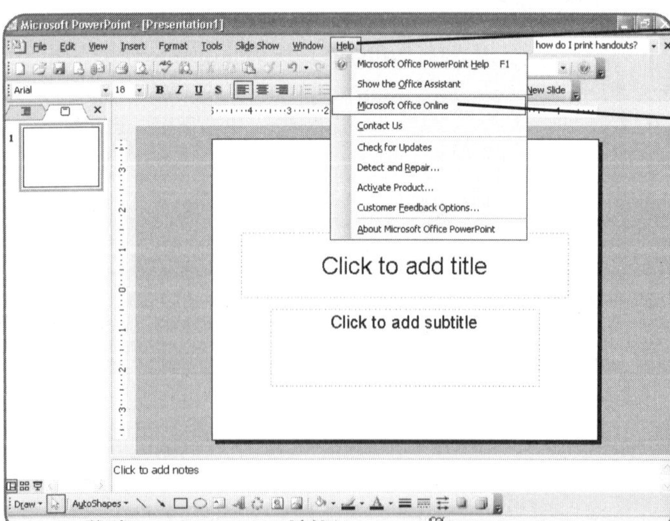

1. **Click** on **Help**. The Help menu will appear.

2. **Click** on **Microsoft Office Online**. Your default Web browser will start and you will be connected to the Internet.

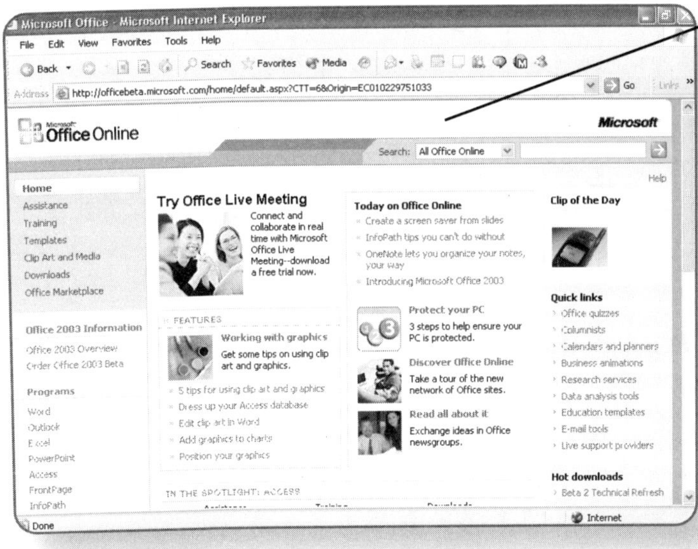

3. Explore the **Office Online** site.

Getting Program Updates

Microsoft periodically releases fixes and enhancements for PowerPoint and other Office products. You can download them through the Internet.

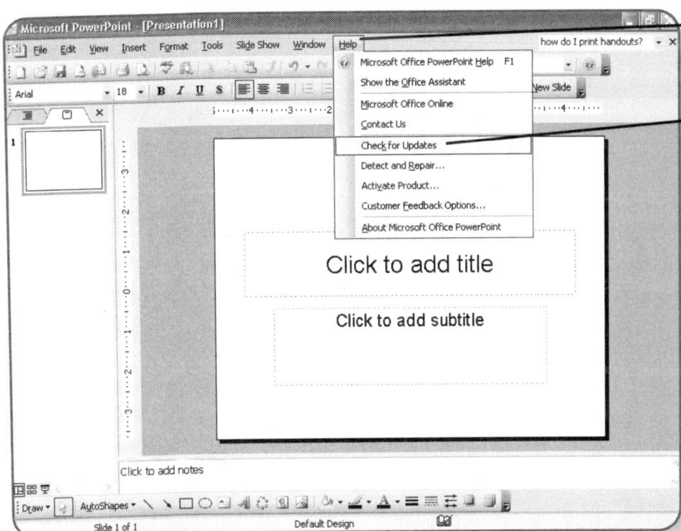

1. Click on **Help**. The Help menu will appear.

2. Click on **Check for Updates**. Your default Web browser will start and you will be connected to the Internet.

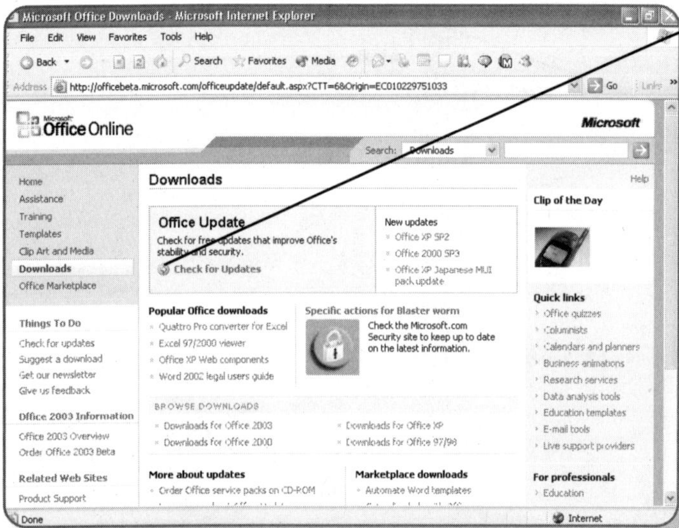

3. Click on **Check for Updates**.

4. Follow the onscreen prompts to download and install any needed updates.

3

Learning About Presentations

It's time to get started on your first presentation, but you don't know where to begin. Don't worry, PowerPoint contains a number of tools to help you take that first step. You'll find wizards and templates that help you design professional-looking presentations. You can use these wizards and templates as a learning tool or as a start for your presentation. In this chapter, you'll learn how to:

- Start a fast and easy presentation with the AutoContent Wizard
- Use templates to develop a uniform design
- Save a presentation
- Print a presentation

Using the AutoContent Wizard

PowerPoint contains many sample presentations that can give you a quick start. You can use these samples to learn how an effective presentation is built or as a starting place for your own. All of them can be changed to suit your needs.

1. **Click** on the **File menu**. The File menu will appear.

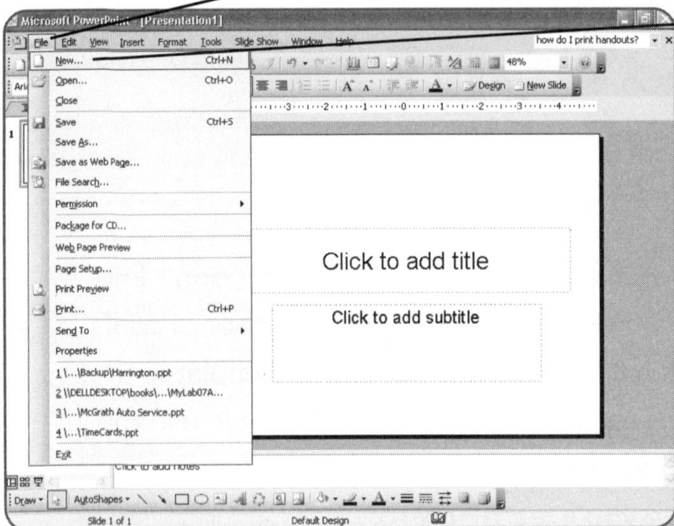

2. **Click** on the **New command**. The New Presentation task pane will appear.

> **NOTE**
>
> The New button on the toolbar starts a new, blank presentation, which is not what we want right now.

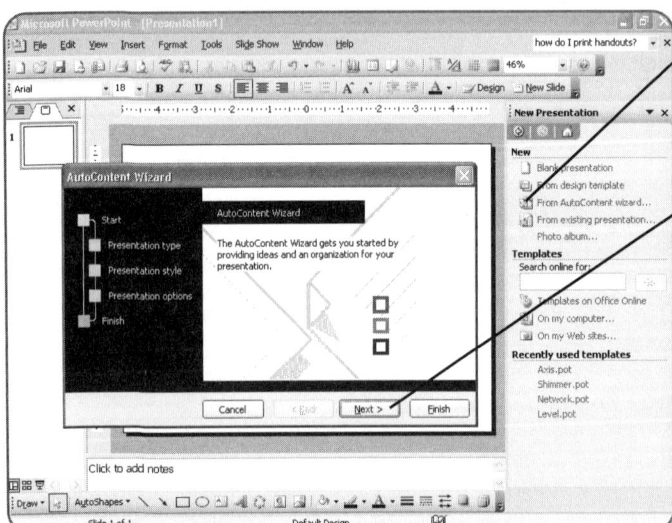

3. **Click** on **From AutoContent wizard** in the New Presentation task pane. The AutoContent wizard will start.

4. **Click** on **Next**. The Presentation type page of the wizard will appear.

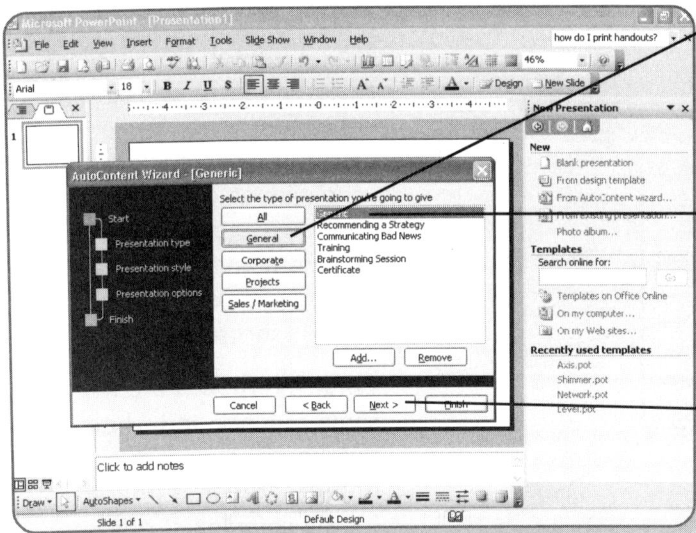

5. **Click** on the **button** for the category of presentation that you want to create. A list of presentation types will appear on the right side of the dialog box.

6. **Click** on a **presentation type** that closely matches the information that you want to use in your presentation. The presentation type will be selected.

7. **Click** on **Next**. The Presentation style page of the wizard will appear.

8. **Click** on the **option button** for the method you will use to display the presentation. The option will be selected. Select from one of these options:

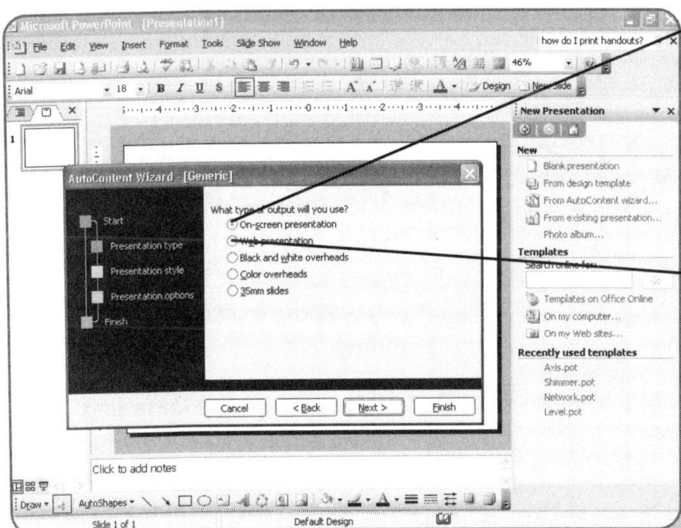

- An **On-screen presentation** is displayed on a computer monitor or on a projector connected to a computer. The computer must have either the PowerPoint program or the PowerPoint viewer installed.
- A **Web presentation** is one that is formatted in HTML and can contain hyperlinks and other Web page elements. This type of presentation can be viewed on the Internet or on a corporate intranet.

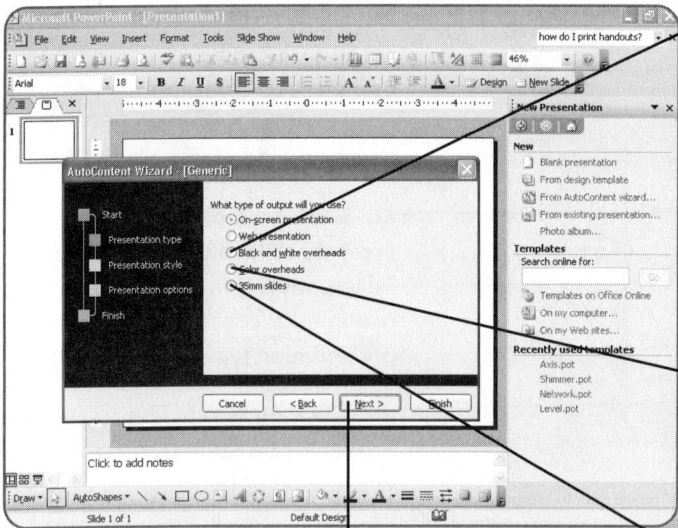

- **Black and white overheads** can be printed from a black-and-white laser printer on either transparencies or paper. Transparencies can be used with an overhead projector to deliver the presentation. These presentation slides are 8.5 x 11 inches in size.
- **Color overheads** are the same as black-and-white overheads, except this type of presentation is printed from a color inkjet printer.
- If you want to deliver a presentation using a slide projector, select the **35mm slides** option.

9. **Click** on **Next**. The Presentation options page of the wizard will appear.

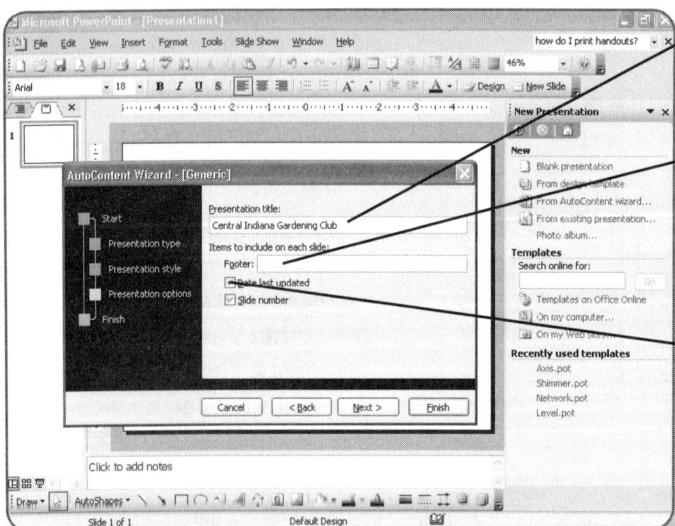

10. **Click** in the **Presentation title text box** and **type** a **title** for your presentation.
11. **Click** in the **Footer text box** and **type** the **text** that you want to appear in the footer area at the bottom of each slide, if any.
12. **Click** in the **Date last updated check box** if you do not want to display the date when you last made updates to the presentation. (This information is found in the footer area of a slide.) The check box will be cleared.

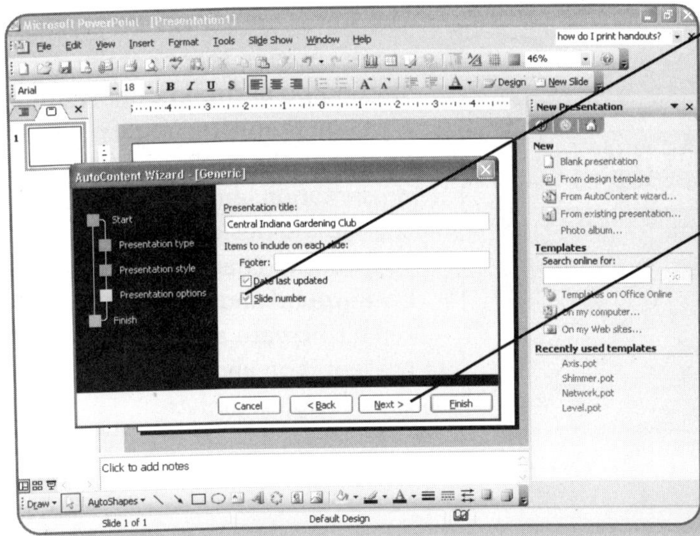

13. Click in the **Slide number check box** if you do not want to show the slide number in the footer area. The check box will be cleared.

14. Click on **Next**. The Finish page of the wizard will appear.

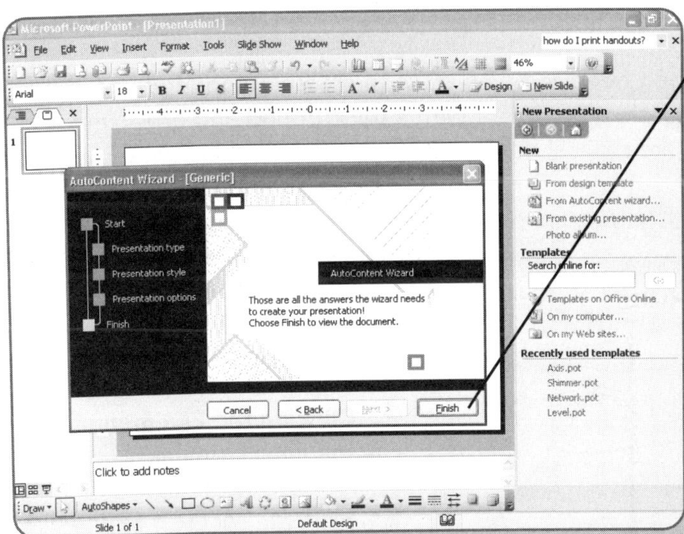

15. Click on **Finish**. The presentation will appear in the PowerPoint window.

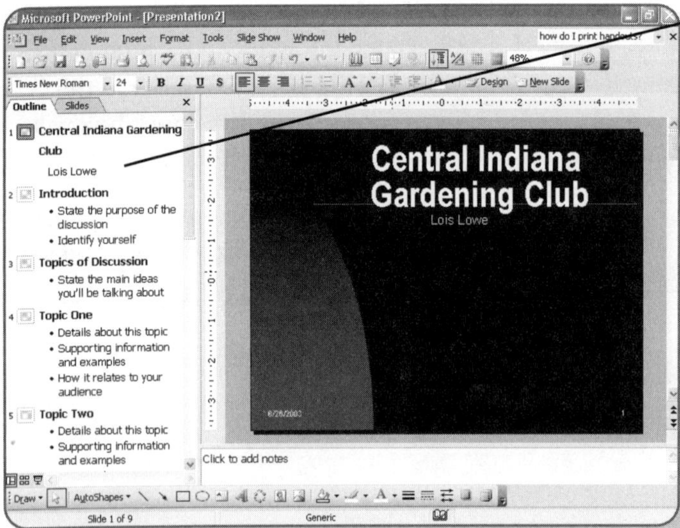

The AutoContent wizard creates a presentation that contains a starting point for an outline and a design template. You'll need to modify the outline to fit your presentation, and you'll need to change the design template if you want to change the slide background and text font. You can also create a blank presentation and create your own design template.

Starting a New Presentation Using a Template

You don't need to be an artist to create a good-looking presentation, complete with a background and other images. There are several design templates bundled in PowerPoint that will be pleasing to both you and your audience. Take a look at some of the design templates from which you can choose, and see if any of them suit your needs.

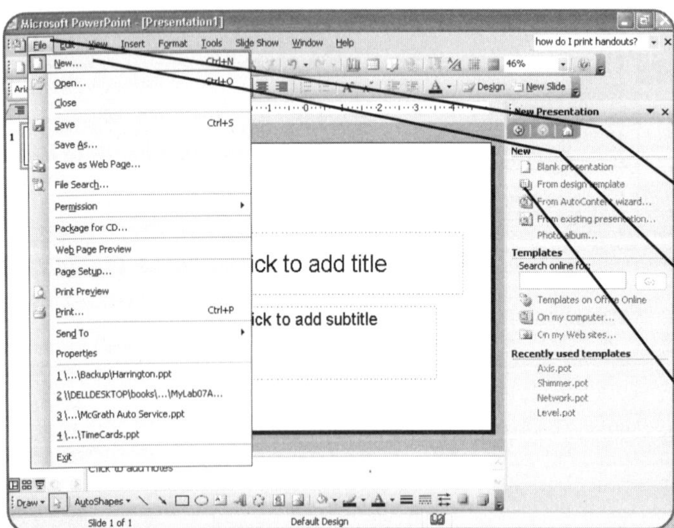

1. **Click** on the **File menu**. The File menu will appear.
2. **Click** on the **New command**. The New Presentation task pane will appear.
3. **Click** on the **From design template hyperlink**. The Slide Design task pane will appear.

4. Click on a **design**. It will be applied to the slide, so you can see what it looks like.

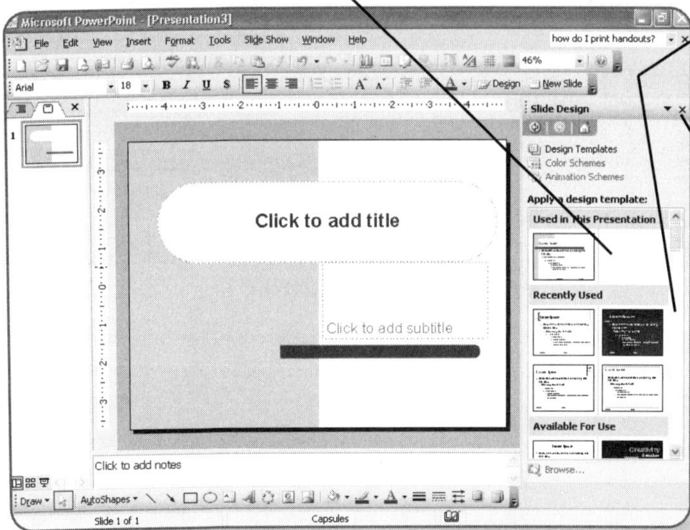

Scroll through the list with the scroll bar.

5. Repeat step 4 until you find the design you want.

6. Click on the **Close button** for the task pane. The task pane will close.

Starting a Blank Presentation

If you are not sure what design or content you want, you might wish to start with a completely blank presentation with no text and no formatting.

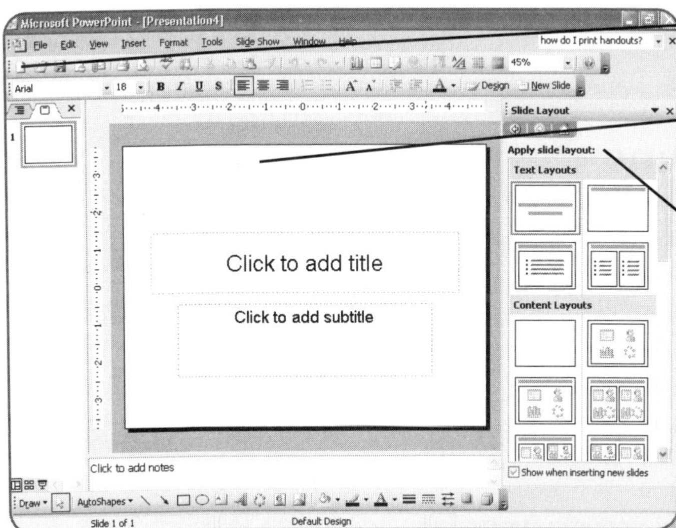

1. Click on the **New button** on the toolbar.

A new presentation will appear. It will have a single slide with a Title layout.

The Slide Layout task pane will appear, so you can specify a different layout for the slide, if desired.

Previewing the Presentation Onscreen

As you're working on a presentation, you may want to see how each slide will look when displayed onscreen in Slide Show view.

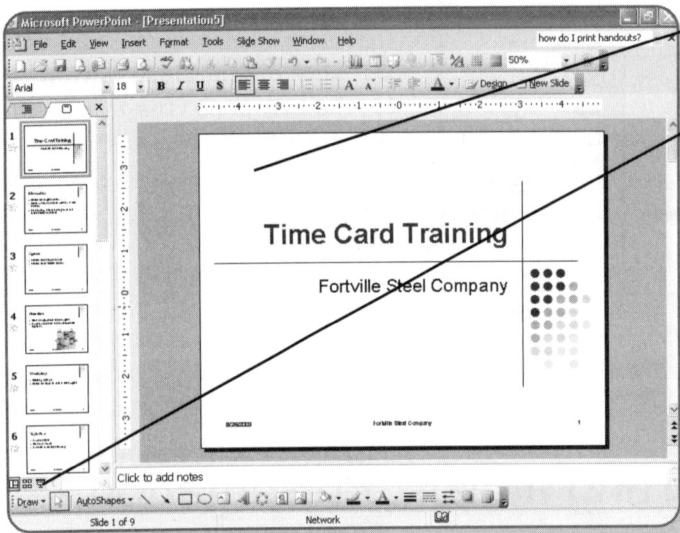

1. Display the **slide** you want to preview.

2. Click on the **Slide Show View button**.

> **NOTE**
>
> In step 2, you can also use the View, Slide Show View command or the Slide Show, View Show command, or you can just press F5. The only difference is that they all start with the first slide rather than the currently displayed one.

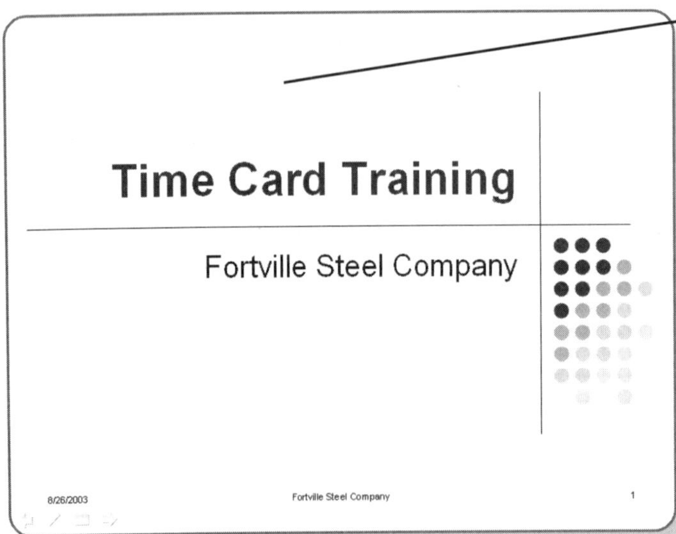

The current slide will appear full-screen, as it will look during a show.

3a. Click the **left mouse button** to move to the next slide. Continue through the presentation.

OR

3b. Press the **Esc key** to return to PowerPoint.

Printing the Presentation

When you want a paper copy of a presentation, send the file to a printer. Later in the book, especially in Chapter 17, "Creating Audience Handouts," you will learn more about printing. For now, let's just print a single copy of the presentation with each slide on a separate page.

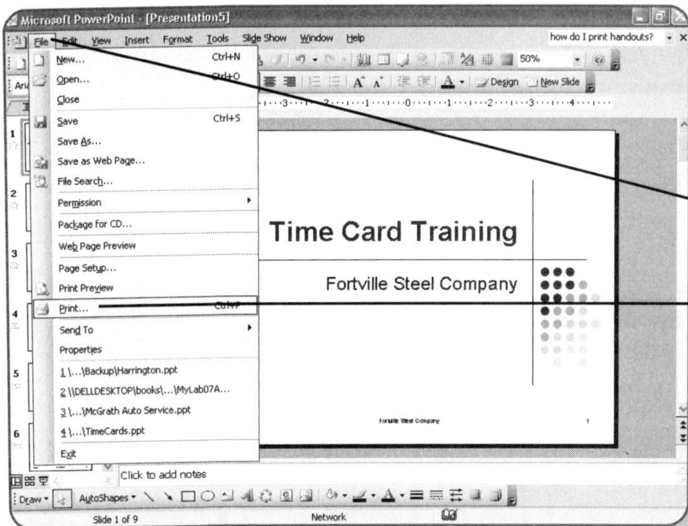

1. **Click** on **File**. The File menu will appear.

2. **Click** on **Print**. The Print dialog box will open.

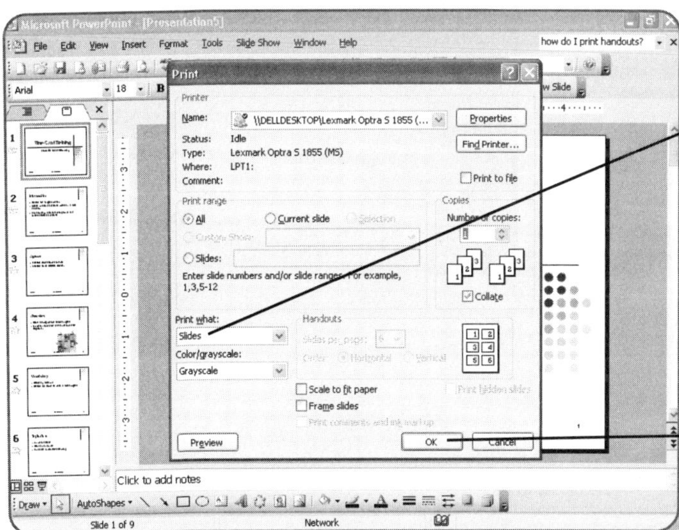

> **NOTE**
>
> For a new presentation, the default view to print is Slides. If you have previously printed handouts or notes pages, that might be the default and you might need to **change** the **Print what setting**.

3. **Click** on **OK**. The presentation file will be sent to the printer using the default print settings.

Working with Presentation Files

Before you get too involved in developing a presentation, you'll need to save the presentation file. Remember to save the file often so that you don't lose your valuable efforts. Then, once you've started on the presentation, you'll want to see how you are progressing. You can easily preview the presentation or print it.

Saving Your Presentation

It can never be stressed enough that you must save your work often while you are working on a presentation. Also, you may want to back up the presentation file to a floppy disk, a Zip disk, or a recordable CD, in case you run into a computer problem.

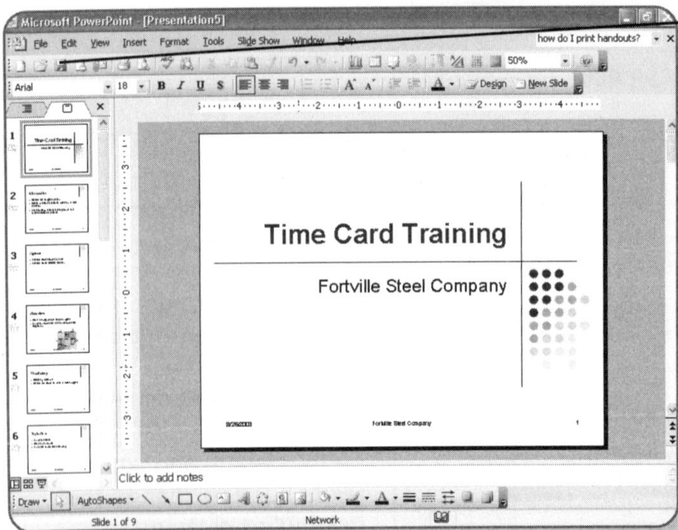

1. **Click** on the **Save button** on the Standard toolbar. The Save As dialog box will open.

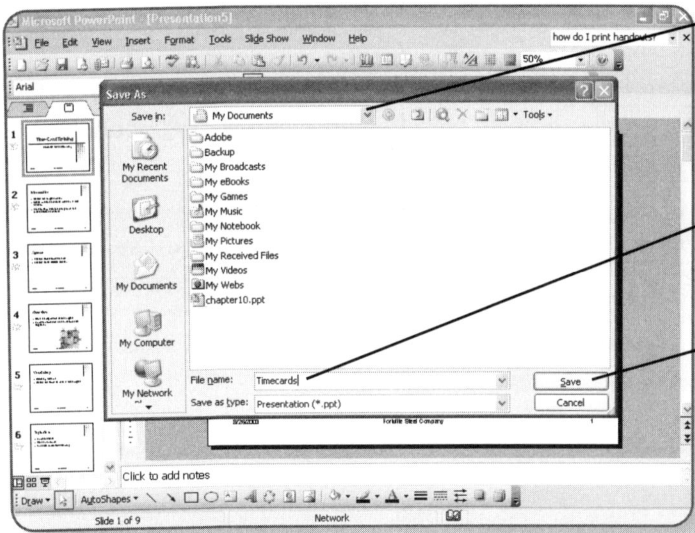

2. **Click** on the **Save in drop-down list arrow** and **select** the **folder** in which you want to store the file. The folder will be selected.

3. **Click** in the **File name text box** and **type** a **name** for the presentation.

4. **Click** on **Save**. The presentation file will be stored in the designated folder, and the file name will appear in the title bar of the PowerPoint window.

> **NOTE**
>
> After you've saved the presentation file the first time, you can save your changes by clicking on the Save button.

Closing the Presentation

When you've finished working on a presentation, close the presentation file. You can close a presentation file without closing the PowerPoint program, or you can close both at once.

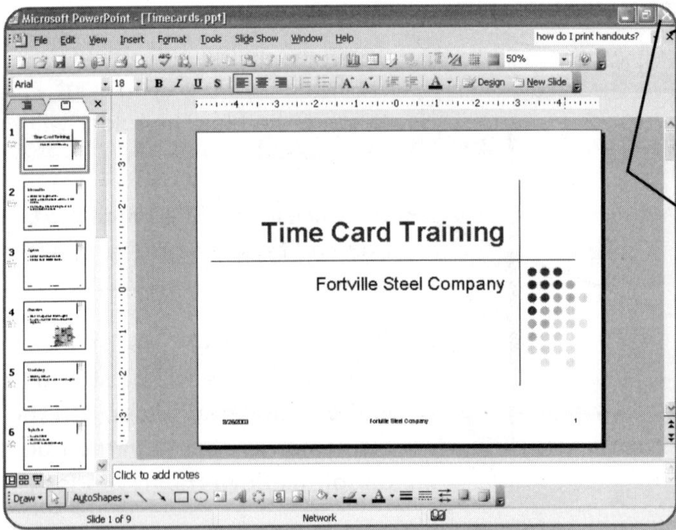

1a. **Click** on the **Close button** for the presentation. The presentation file will close and PowerPoint will stay open.

OR

1b. **Click** on the **Close button** for the PowerPoint program. The program will close.

Opening a Recently Used Presentation

PowerPoint keeps a list of the saved files you've worked with recently. This list is found at the bottom of the File menu.

1. **Click** on **File**. The File menu will appear.

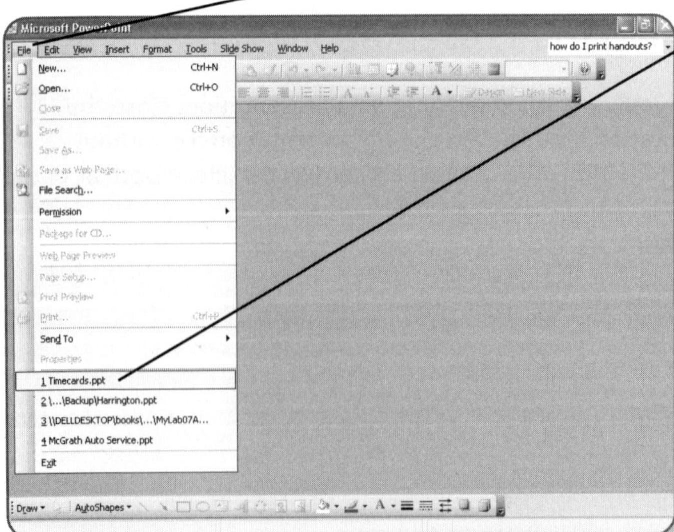

2. **Click** on the **presentation file** in the recently used file list. The presentation will appear in the PowerPoint window.

Opening Any Saved Presentation

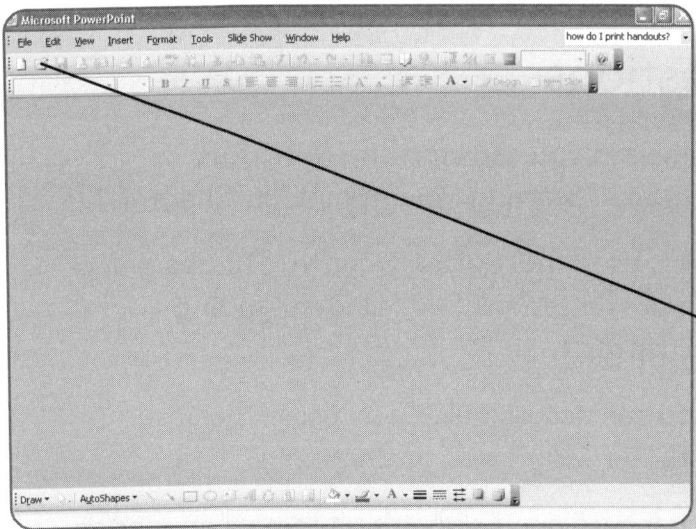

If the presentation you want to open does not appear at the bottom of the File menu, you can use the Open dialog box to select and open it.

1. **Click** on the **Open button** on the toolbar. The Open dialog box will appear.

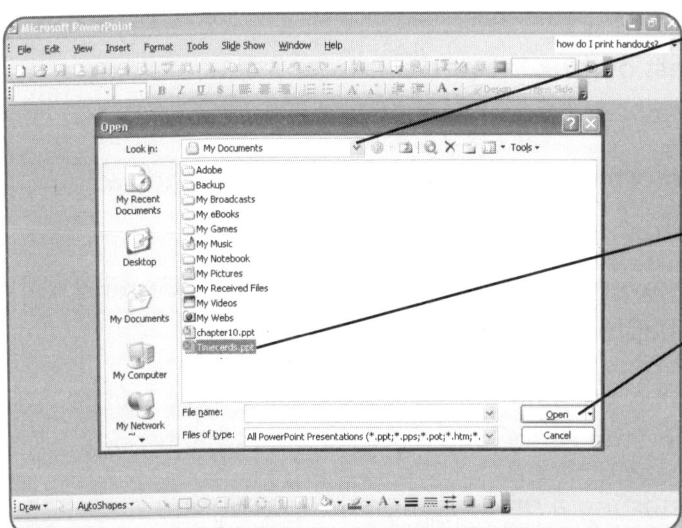

2. **Click** on the **Look in drop-down list arrow** and **select** the **folder** in which you want to look for the file. The folder will be selected.
3. **Click** on the **file name** for the presentation.
4. **Click** on **Open**. The presentation file will open in the PowerPoint window.

NOTE

You can also open a presentation file and start PowerPoint at the same time by double-clicking the presentation file in a Windows file management window.

Part I Review Questions

1. What are three different ways you can start the Microsoft PowerPoint application? See "Starting PowerPoint" in Chapter 1.
2. Which PowerPoint view is used most often when you're designing the individual slides in a presentation? See "Understanding PowerPoint Views" in Chapter 1.
3. Name two tasks that you can access quickly by using the Task Pane. See "Working with the Task Pane" in Chapter 1.
4. How do you make the Standard and Formatting toolbars appear on separate rows at the top of the screen? See "Displaying the Standard and Formatting Toolbars on Separate Rows" in Chapter 1.
5. Where is the Ask a Question box located onscreen? See "Asking a Question" in Chapter 2.
6. How do you print the information found in a Help topic window? See "Printing a Help Topic" in Chapter 2.
7. How do you check for PowerPoint program updates? See "Getting Program Updates" in Chapter 2.
8. Where will you find existing presentation content that you can edit to fit your needs? See "Using the AutoContent Wizard" in Chapter 3.
9. What is the benefit of starting a presentation using a design template? See "Starting a New Presentation Using a Template" in Chapter 3.
10. What function key can you press to view the presentation in Slide Show view? See "Previewing the Presentation Onscreen" in Chapter 3.

PART II

Developing an Effective Presentation

4

Organizing the Presentation Outline

In the first part of this book, you learned how presentations work by looking at the presentation and design templates. You also learned how to use some of PowerPoint's features to design a presentation. Now it's time for you to fly on your own and start a presentation from scratch. In this chapter, you'll learn how to:

- Develop a presentation outline
- Insert slides from another presentation
- Use a Microsoft Word outline in PowerPoint
- Edit slide text
- Print the outline

Displaying Outline View

Much of the activity in this chapter takes place in the Outline pane. If it does not appear in Normal view already, you can display it easily.

1. Click the **Normal View button**. If any other view is in use, it will be replaced by Normal.

2. Click on the **Outline tab**. The presentation outline will appear.

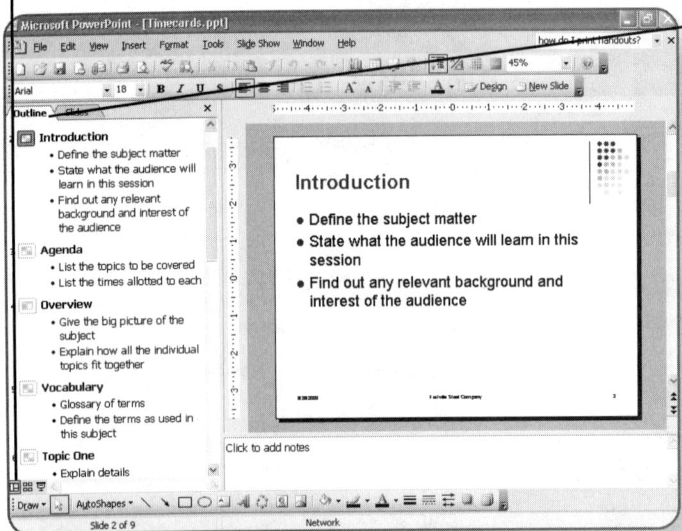

> **NOTE**
>
> If the Outline tab is not already showing, it will not have the word "Outline" on it. Instead, it will have some horizontal lines representing text.

Displaying the Outlining Toolbar

The Outlining toolbar can be useful when you're working with outlines. If it does not appear automatically, you can enable it.

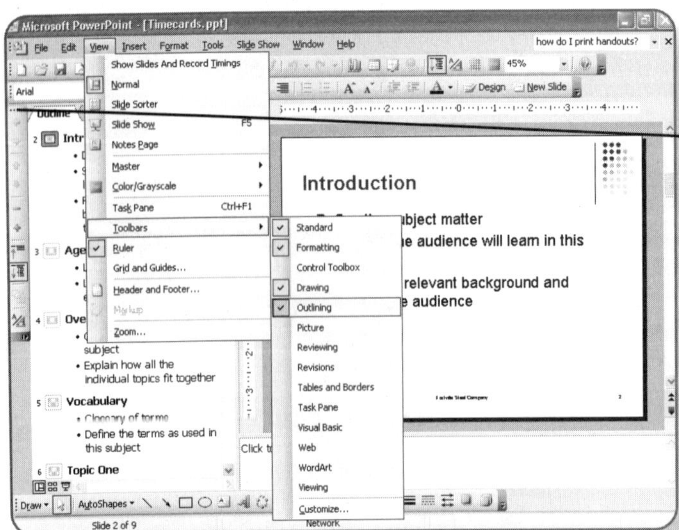

1. Click on **View**. The View menu will appear.

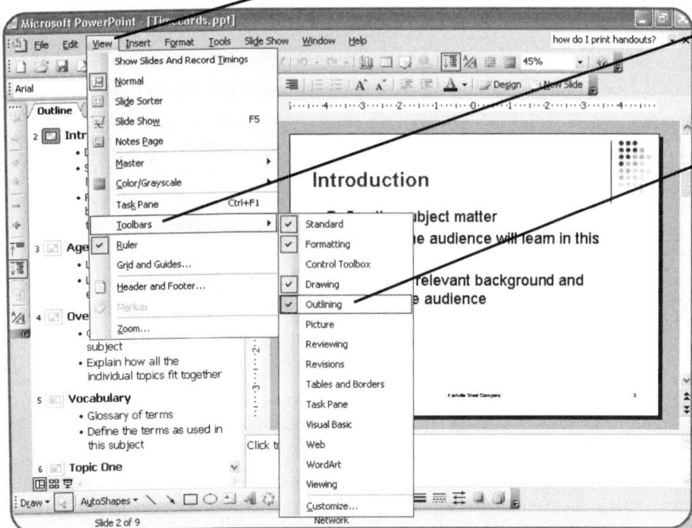

2. Move the **mouse pointer** to **Toolbars**. A list of available toolbars will appear.

3. Click on **Outlining**. The Outlining toolbar will appear along the left side of the PowerPoint window.

The Outlining toolbar can be used to:

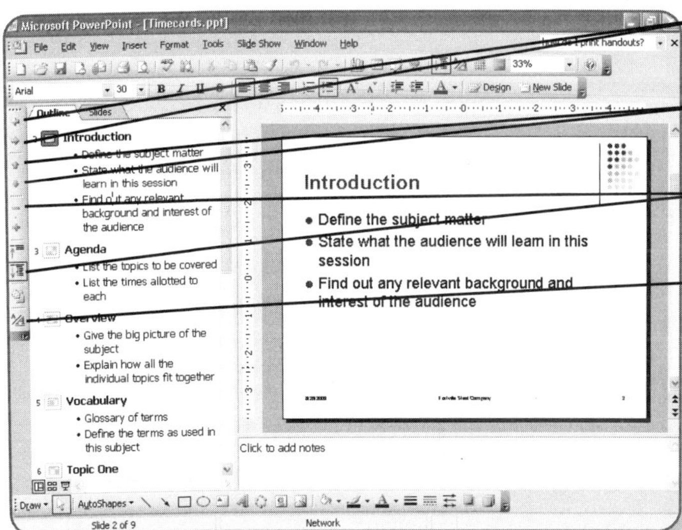

- Promote and demote text within the outline
- Change the order of slides within the presentation
- Collapse and expand the outline
- Display the same text formatting on the outline that is used on the slides

Outlining a Presentation

The most important part of a presentation is the outline, which will keep your presentation organized and on track. Before you start adding graphics, animations, and transitions, make sure you have a solid foundation for your presentation.

NOTE

If you've created an outline in Microsoft Word, you can import it into PowerPoint. To learn how, see the "Sharing Outlines with Microsoft Word" section later in this chapter.

Creating Slides in the Outline Pane

If you used the AutoContent Wizard to start your presentation, an outline has already been started for you (as shown in the preceding figures). It is a simple matter of editing the outline by changing a few words or adding a few new slides. If you started with a blank presentation, you'll need to create each new slide by adding text to the outline.

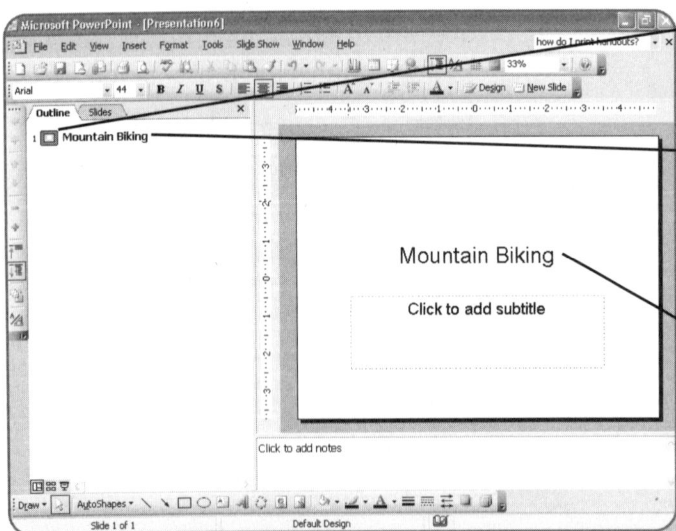

1. **Click** to the **right of the slide icon**. The cursor will move there.
2. **Type** the **text** that you want to appear as the title of the first slide.

NOTE

Notice that the text also appears on the slide in the Title area.

3. **Press** the **Enter key**. A new slide icon will appear on a new line.

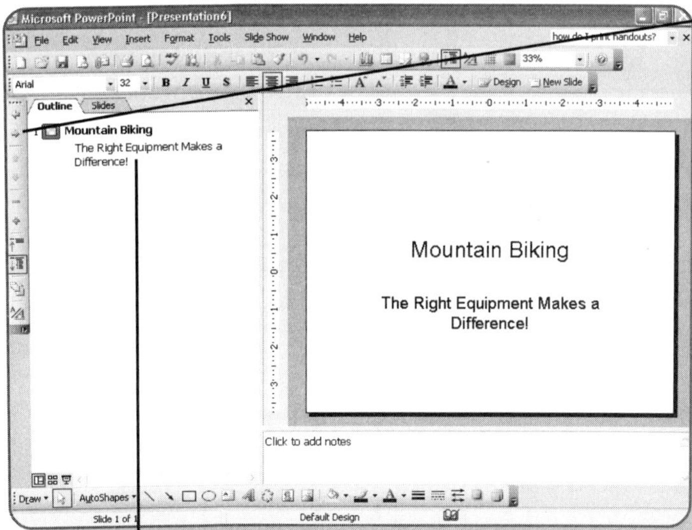

4. Click on the **Demote button** on the Outlining toolbar, or **press Tab**. The new line will be demoted in importance so that it represents text on the preceding slide.

> **NOTE**
>
> Each time you press Enter, a new line appears at the same outline level as the previous line. Since you were typing title text in step 2, pressing Enter in step 3 started a new slide. Demoting the line makes it part of the preceding slide.

5. Type additional text for the slide.

6. Press the **Enter key**. Another line on the same slide will appear for typing.

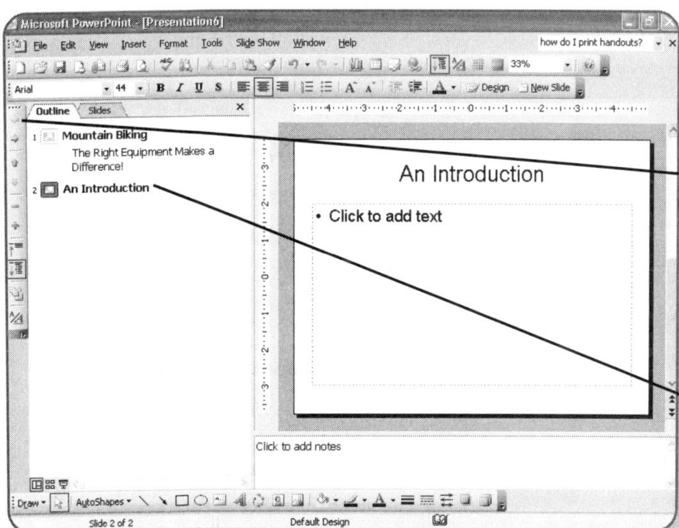

7a. Return to **step 5** to type additional text.

OR

7b. Click on the **Promote button** on the Outlining toolbar, or **press Shift+Tab**. The new line will be promoted in importance so that it represents a new slide title.

8. Type the **text** for the title of the second slide and **press Enter**.

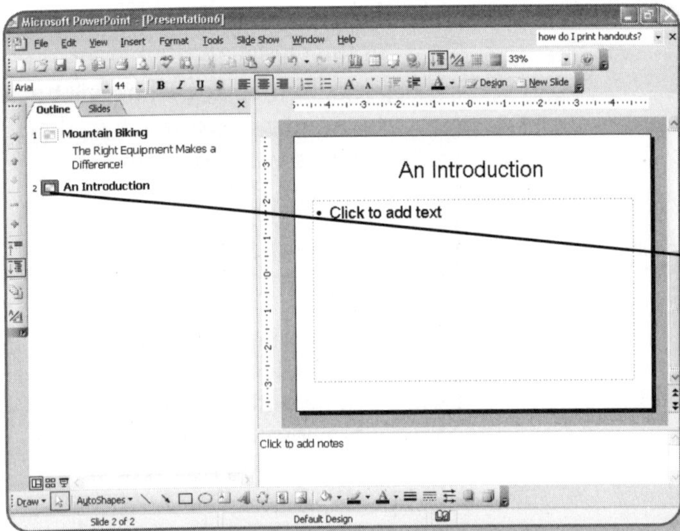

9. **Continue adding text** until all the topics that you want to cover in the presentation appear in the outline.

> **NOTE**
>
> To delete a slide, **click** on the **slide icon** and **press Delete**.

Promoting and Demoting Lines

Once you've added the topics that you want to cover in the presentation, you may want to change the level at which some outline items appear.

1. **Click** on the **line** that you want to promote or demote. The insertion point will appear in it.

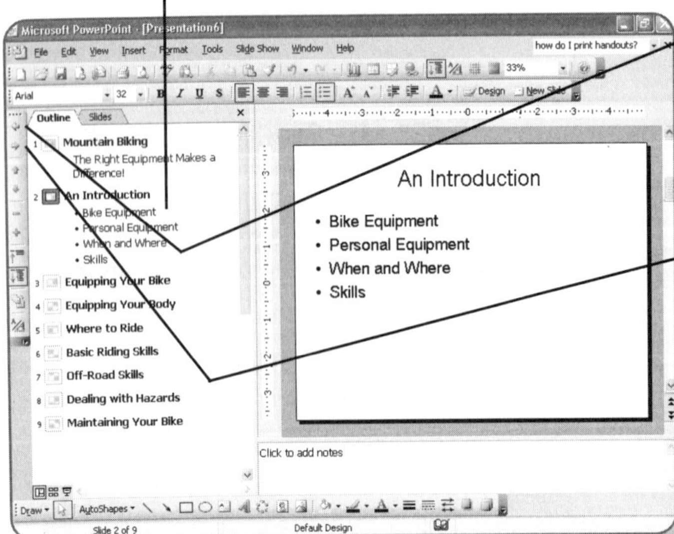

2a. **Click** on the **Promote button** or **press Shift+Tab**. The text will be promoted to a higher outline level.

OR

2b. **Click** on the **Demote button** or **press Tab**. The text will be demoted to the next outline level.

Promoting to the highest level makes the text into slide title text on a separate slide. Demoting a slide title makes it a bullet point on the previous slide.

Rearranging Outline Text

Each paragraph in the outline is either a slide title or a bullet point on the body of a slide. You can move individual paragraphs or groups of them up or down in the outline.

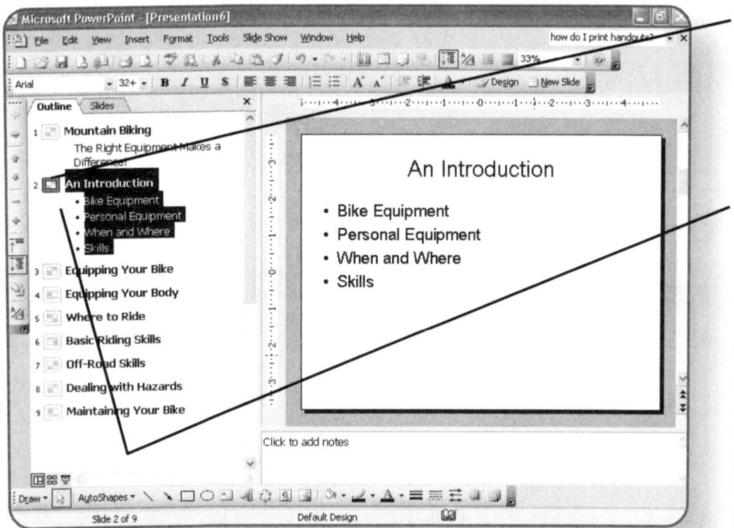

1a. Click on a **slide icon**. The entire slide and all its subordinate text will be selected.

OR

1b. Click to the **left of an individual paragraph**. Only that paragraph will be selected.

> **NOTE**
>
> To select multiple slide icons or multiple paragraphs, hold down Shift as you click on additional ones.

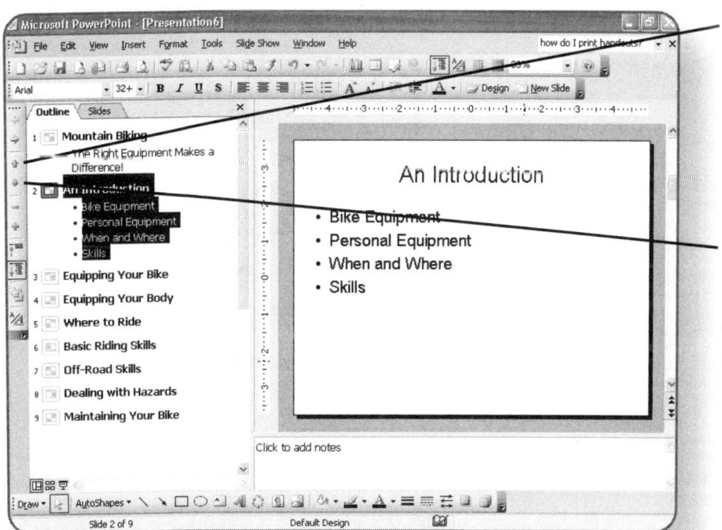

2a. Click on the **Move Up button** or **drag** the selection **upward**. The selection will move higher in the outline.

OR

2b. Click on the **Move Down button** or **drag** the selection **downward**. The selection will move lower in the outline.

Inserting Slides from Another Presentation

If you want to add an existing presentation to a presentation you're working on right now, just insert the slides from the existing presentation. You can insert the entire presentation or just a group of slides.

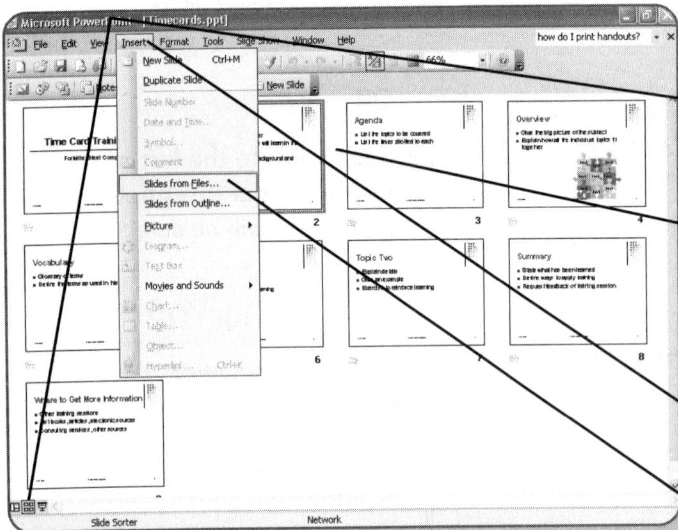

1. **Click** on the **Slide Sorter View button**. The display will change to Slide Sorter view.
2. **Click** in the **space** where you want the slides from the other presentation to appear. The insertion bar will appear in the selected location.
3. **Click** on **Insert**. The Insert menu will appear.
4. **Click** on **Slides from Files**. The Slide Finder dialog box will open.

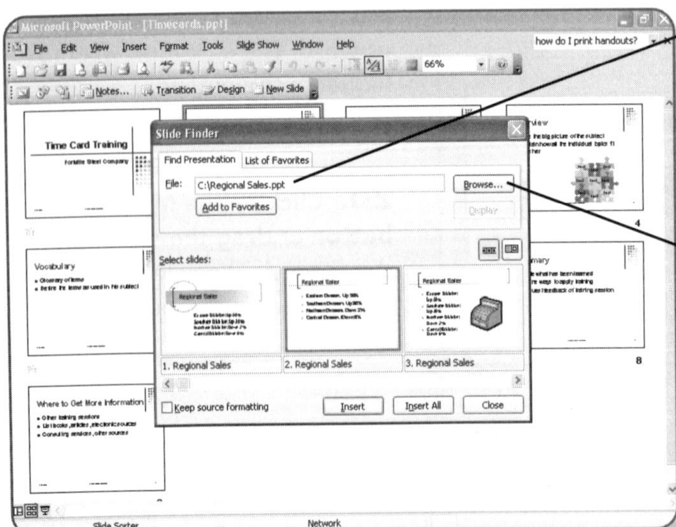

5. **Type** the **path and file name** of the presentation that contains the slides that you want to add to the open presentation.

> **NOTE**
>
> If you don't know the path or file name, **click** on **Browse** to open the Browse dialog box. Navigate to the folder that contains the presentation and select the presentation file.

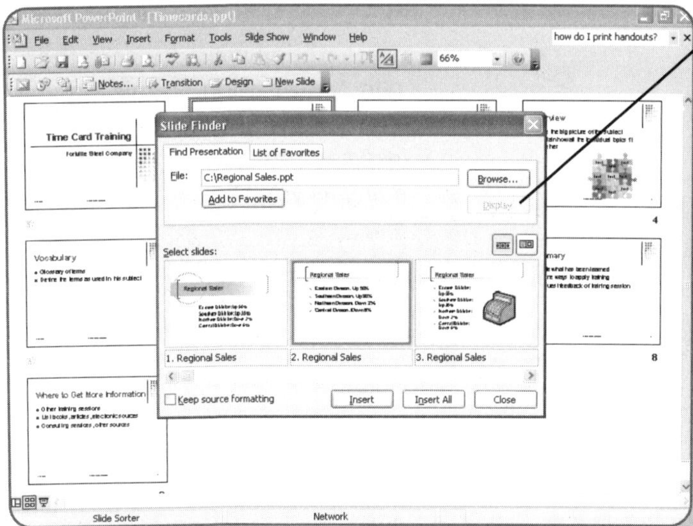

6. **Click** on **Display** if the slides do not appear automatically. A preview of the presentation slides will appear in the Select slides area.

7. **Click** on the **slides** that you want to insert into the presentation. The slides will be selected.

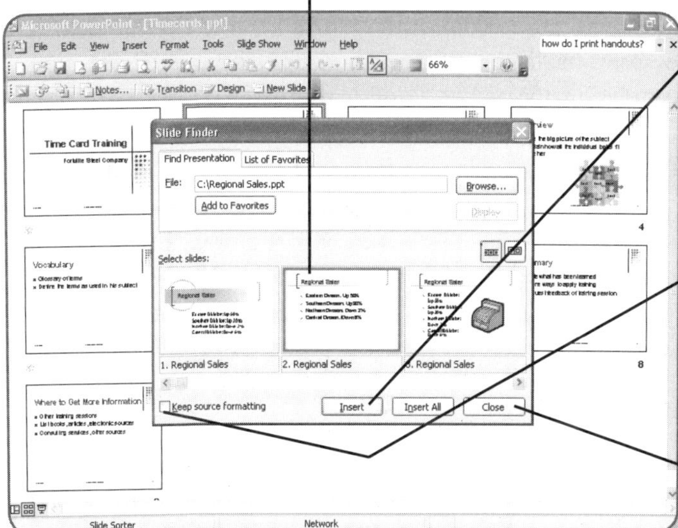

8. **Click** on **Insert**. The selected slides will be inserted into the open presentation.

> **NOTE**
>
> If you want the slides to retain the original slide design, **click** on the **Keep source formatting check box.**

9. **Click** on **Close**. The Slide Finder dialog box will close.

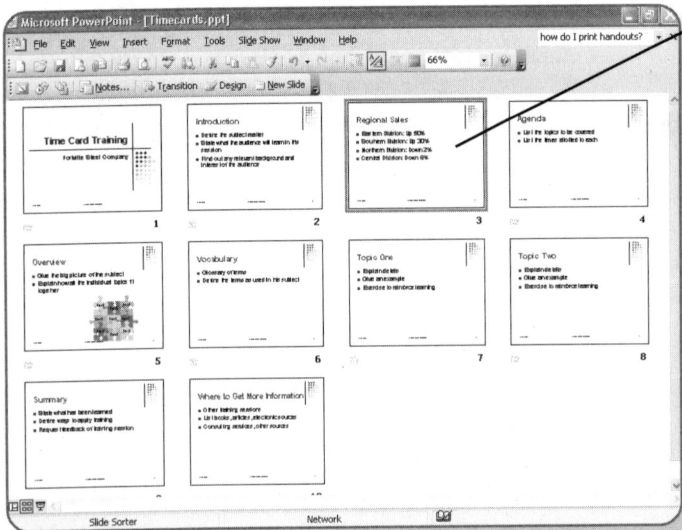

The slides from the existing presentation will appear in the selected position. In this example, only one slide was inserted, but you can insert as many as you like.

Sharing Outlines with Microsoft Word

If you use the outlining feature in Microsoft Word, you may find it easier to create the outline in Word and then import it into PowerPoint. If you started an outline in PowerPoint, you can export it into Word and edit it there.

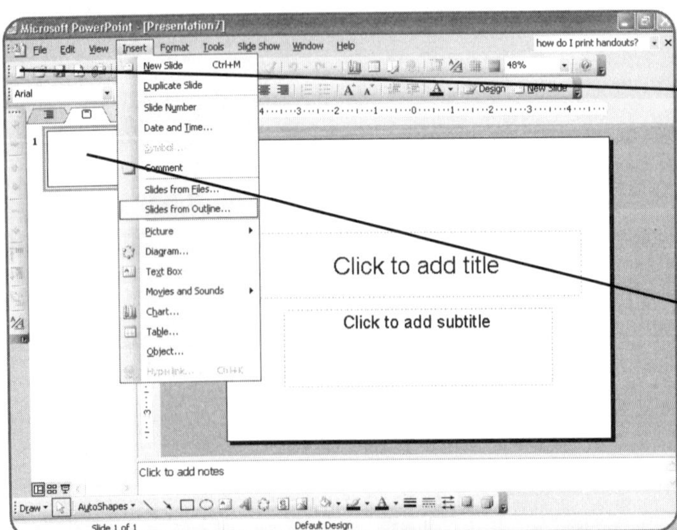

Importing an Outline

1a. Start a **new, blank presentation**. A new presentation with a single Title slide will appear.

OR

1b. Select the **slide** after which the imported outline text will appear.

2. Click on **Insert**. The Insert menu will appear.

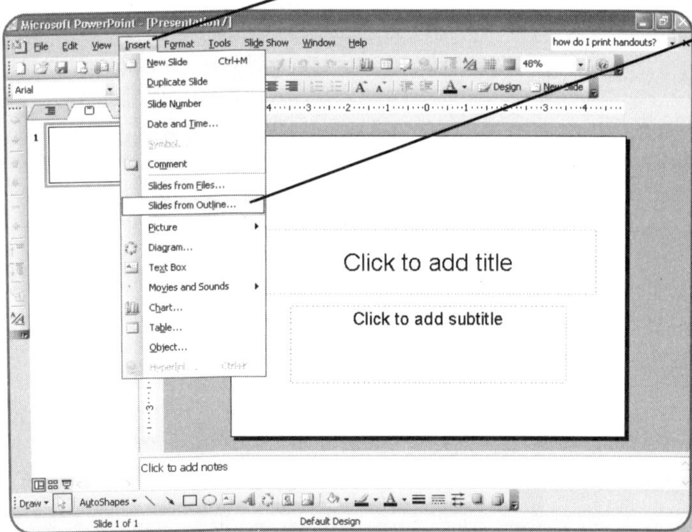

3. Click on **Slides from Outline**. The Insert Outline dialog box will appear.

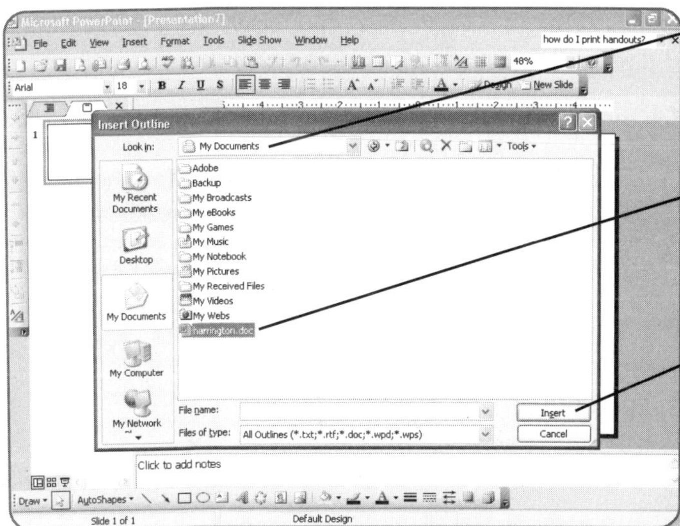

4. Display the **folder** in which you've stored the Word outline file. The folder will appear in the Look in list box.

5. Click on the **file** that contains the outline that you want to add to the presentation. The file will be selected.

6. Click on **Insert**.

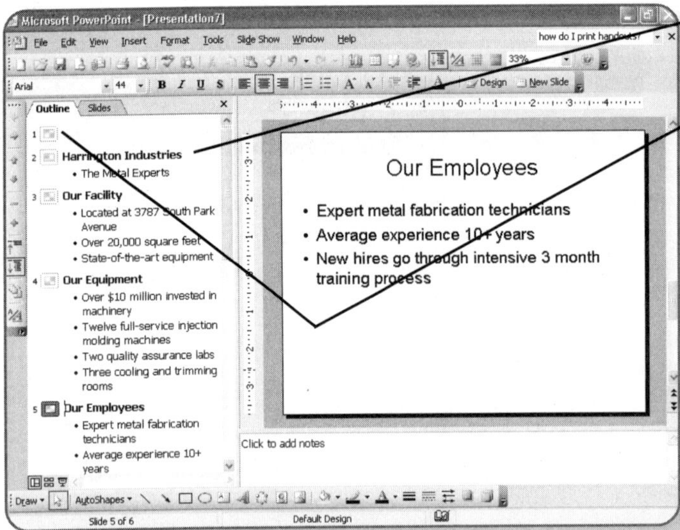

The outline will be inserted into the presentation.

If you started with a blank presentation, you will need to delete the blank slide at the beginning.

Exporting an Outline

You can also send a PowerPoint outline to Word and save it as a Word document.

1. **Click** on **File**. The File menu will appear.

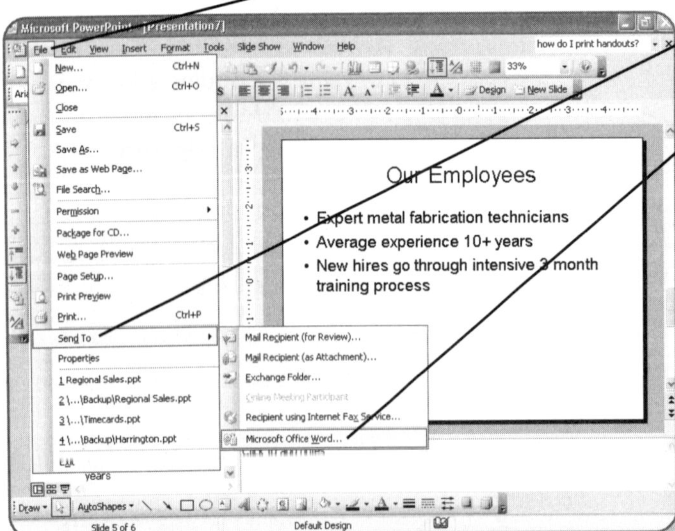

2. **Click** on **Send To**. The Send To submenu will appear.

3. **Click** on **Microsoft Office Word**. The Send To Microsoft Word dialog box will open.

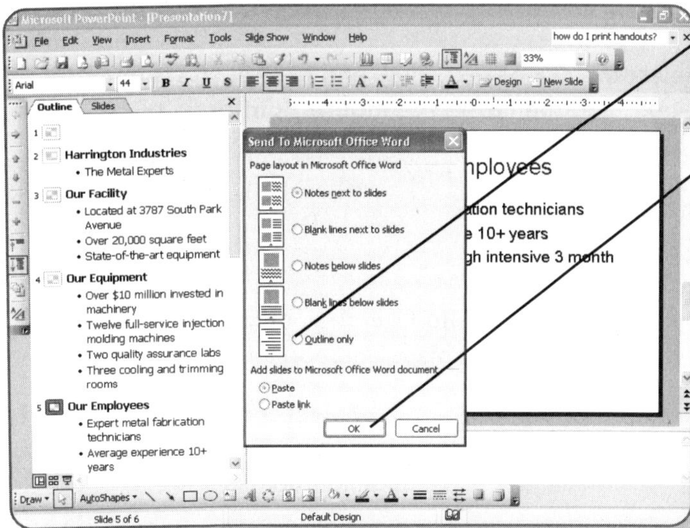

4. **Click** on the **Outline only option**, if it is not selected already.

5. **Click** on **OK**. The outline will open in Microsoft Word.

From Word, you can edit or save the outline normally.

Editing Text

Once the basic outline structure is in place, you can make any changes you want to the outline. You may need to change a few words or add a few new words.

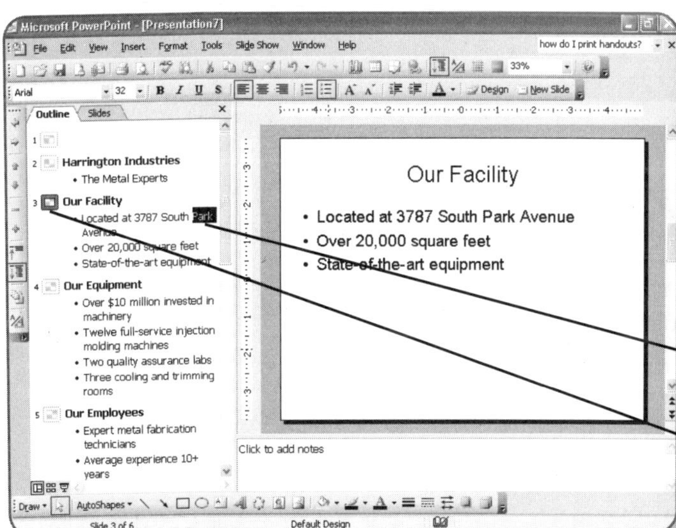

Selecting Text

Before you can edit or format text, you'll need to select the text. Selected text appears inside a boxed background. The selected text can be a single letter or word, or several words. Here are a few tips for selecting text.

- To select a word, **double-click** on the **word**.
- To select an entire slide, **click** the **slide icon**.
- To select a paragraph, **triple-click** it.

- To select the entire outline, **press Ctrl+A**.
- To select a block of text, **click and hold** at the **beginning of the text**, and then **drag** the **mouse pointer** to the **end of the text**. **Release** the **mouse button**.

Revising Text

When you need to revise items in the outline, select the words that you want to replace and add a few of your own.

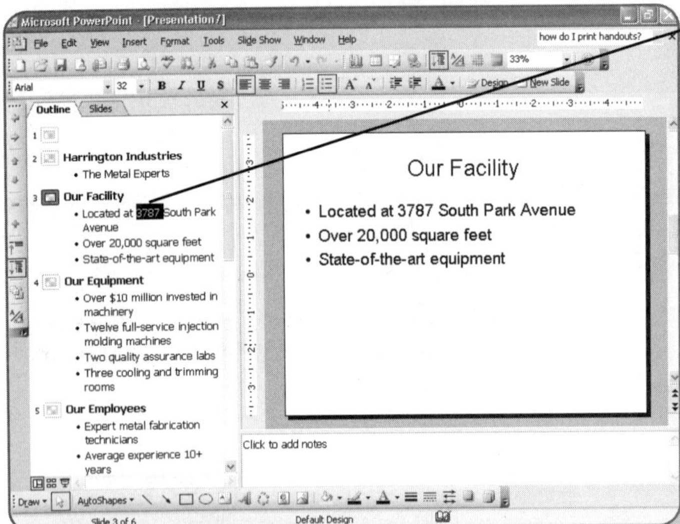

1. Select the **text** that you want to replace. The text will be highlighted.

2. Type the **new text**. The selected text will be deleted and replaced with the new text.

Adding Text to a Placeholder

If you have created some slide titles in the outline with no subordinate text beneath them, you'll notice that on the slide is a "Click to add text" placeholder.

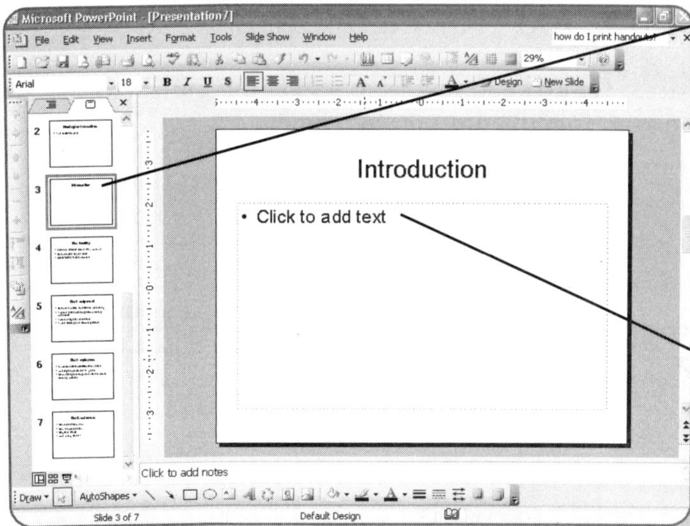

1. Display a **slide** that contains a text placeholder. The slide will appear in Normal view.

NOTE

Click the slide you want in the Slides or Outline pane.

2. Click on the **text** in the placeholder. The placeholder text will disappear, and the cursor will appear in the text box.

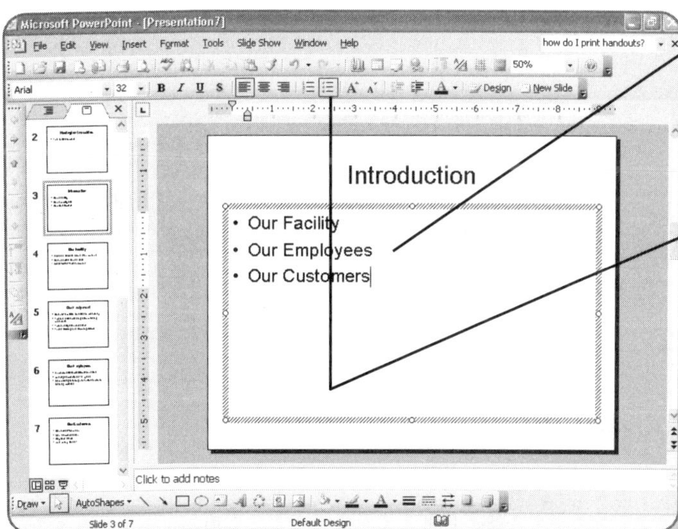

3. Type the **text** that you want in the placeholder.

TIP

The bullets can be removed. **Select** the **bulleted items** and **click** on the **Bullets button** on the Formatting toolbar.

Deleting Text from a Slide

The process for deleting text from a slide is identical to deleting text from the presentation outline.

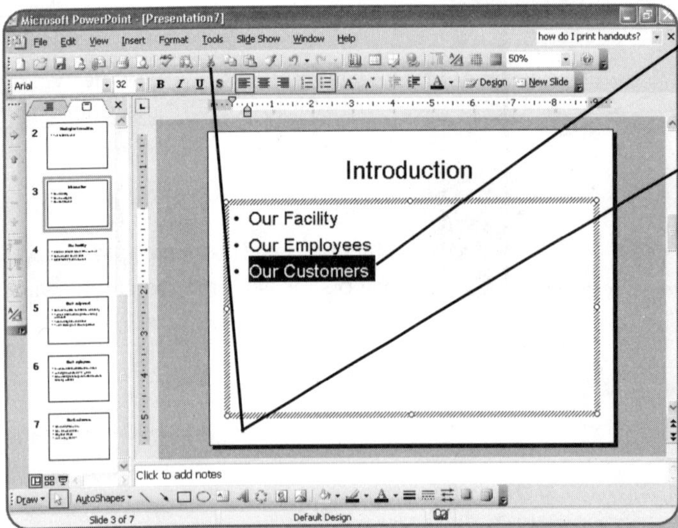

1. **Select** the **text** that you want to delete. The text will be highlighted.
2. **Click** on the **Cut button** or **press Delete**. The text will be removed from the slide.

> **NOTE**
>
> Cutting and deleting are actually two different things. Cutting moves text to the Clipboard; deleting simply deletes it. If you do not subsequently paste the text from the Clipboard, however, the overall result is the same.

Using the Replace Feature

You can use the Replace feature to search for text, such as individual words, phrases, or characters in a presentation, and then replace it with some other text.

1. **Click** on **Edit**. The Edit menu will appear.

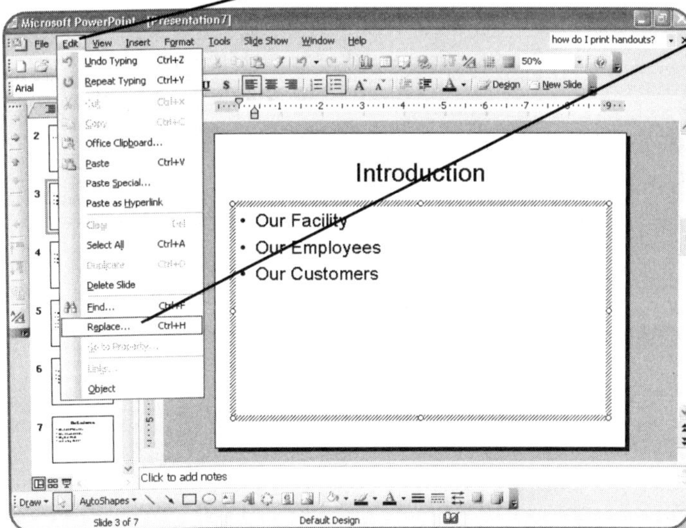

2. **Click** on **Replace**. The Replace dialog box will open.

3. **Type** the **text** that you want to locate in the Find what text box.

4. **Type** the **text** to be used as the replacement in the Replace with text box.

The **Match case check box** allows you to limit the replacement to certain capitalization.

The **Find whole words only** check box allows you to limit the replacement to whole words.

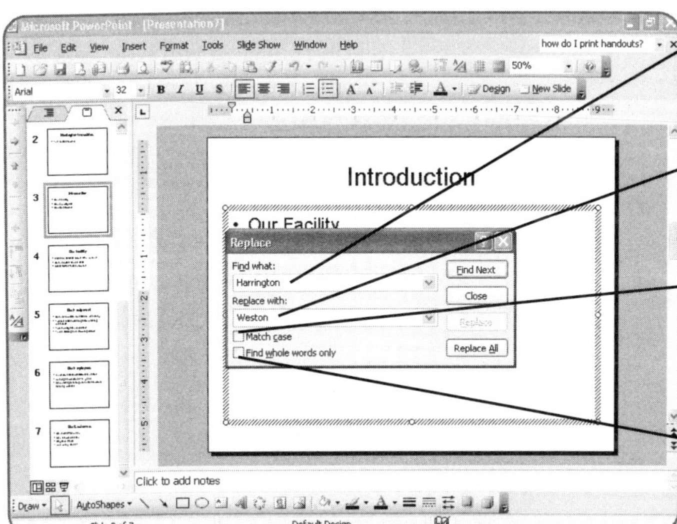

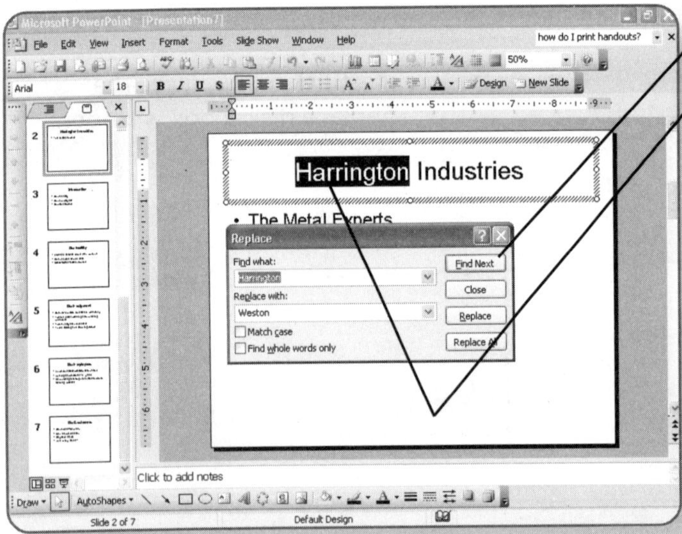

5. Click on **Find Next**.

The first occurrence of the word(s) for which you are searching will be highlighted on the slide.

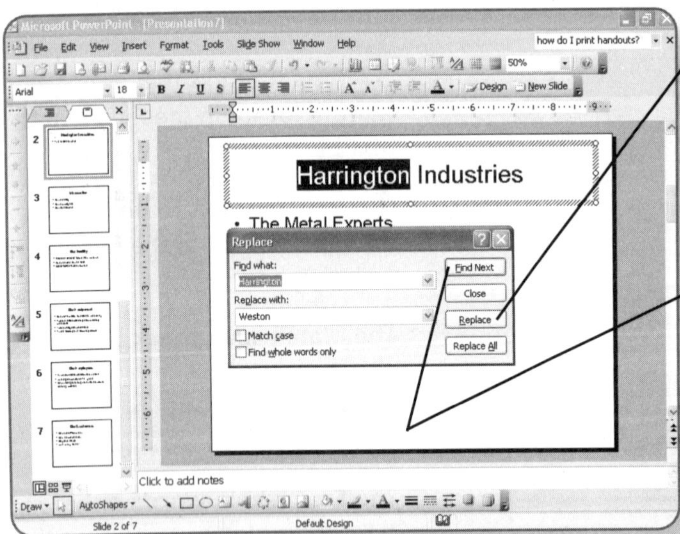

6a. Click on **Replace**. The text that is highlighted on the slide will be replaced with the text specified in the Replace with text box.

OR

6b. Click on **Find Next** to skip that occurrence.

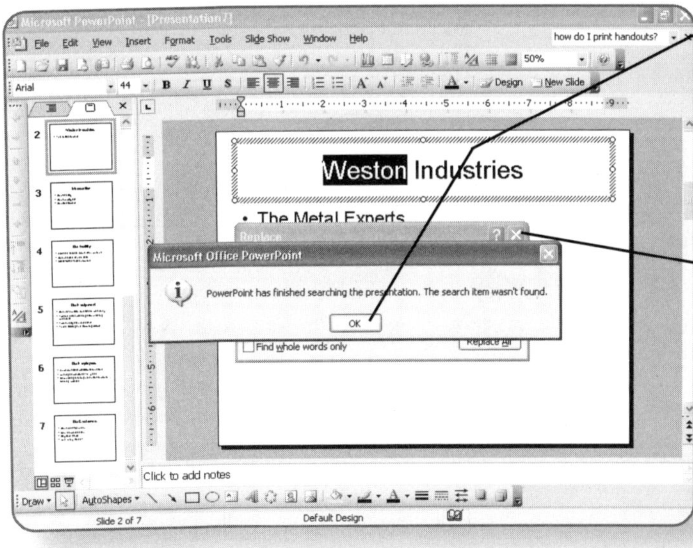

7a. Repeat steps 5 and 6 until all instances have been found. A dialog box will appear stating that it is finished. Then **click** the **OK button**.

OR

7b. Click on **Close** to end the search early.

Printing the Outline

Before you print a presentation outline, display the items in the Outline tab that you want to print. If an item is collapsed (that is, hidden), it will not print. Use the Outlining toolbar to expand and collapse the outline.

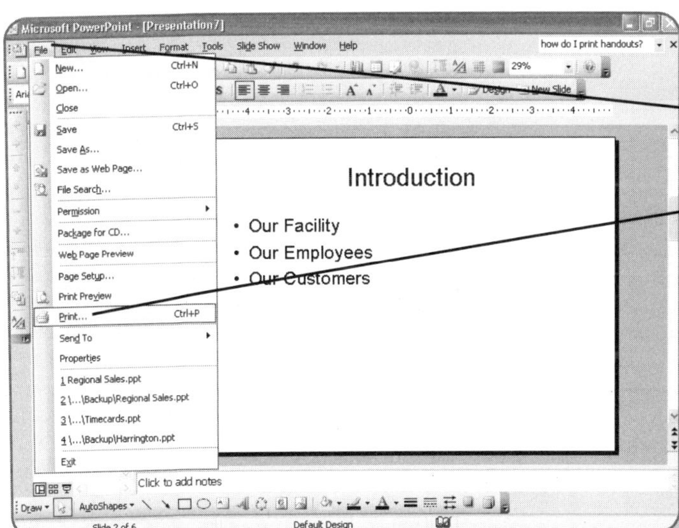

1. Click on **File**. The File menu will appear.

2. Click on **Print**. The Print dialog box will open.

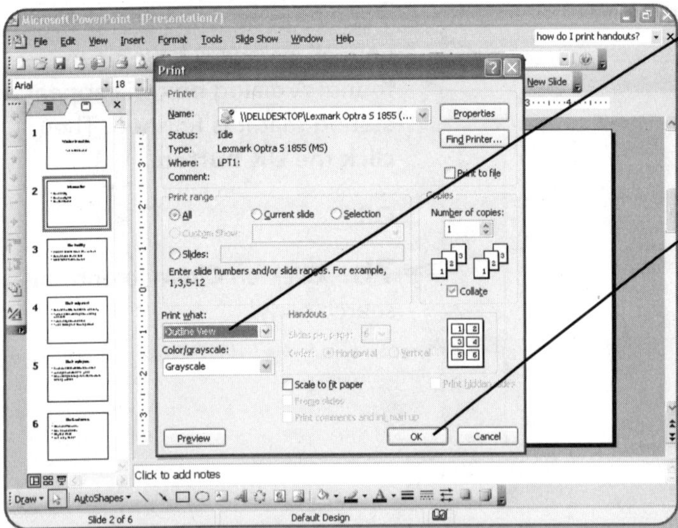

3. Click on the **Print what drop-down list arrow** and **select Outline View** from the list. The option will appear in the list box.

4. Click on **OK**. The outline will be sent to the printer.

5

Organizing and Improving the Presentation

Creating and editing the text is a good start, but for professional-quality materials, you must polish your work until it shines. This may include running a spelling check, using the thesaurus and other research tools in PowerPoint, and rearranging the order in which your slides appear. In this chapter, you will learn how to:

- Check a presentation for spelling errors
- Look up synonyms in the thesaurus
- Use the research tools for fact-finding
- Rearrange, copy, and delete slides in Slide Sorter view

Spell Checking the Presentation

Before your presentation makes its debut, run the spell checker. Not only will the spell checker help you spot misspelled words, but it will tell you when you repeat yourself.

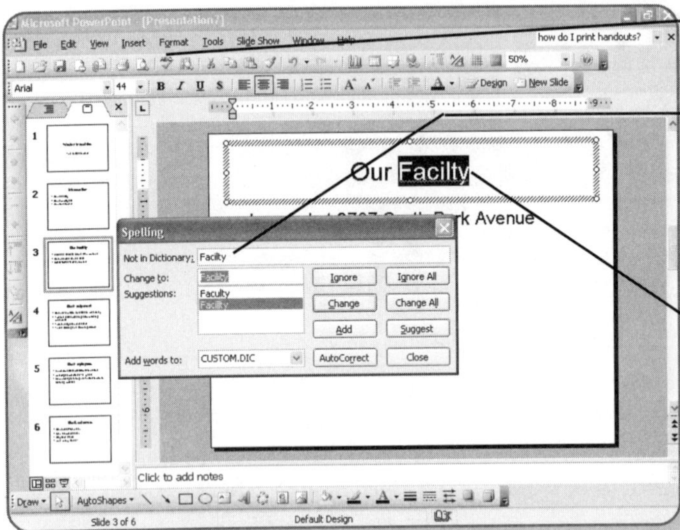

1. Click on the **Spelling button**.

The Spelling dialog box will open with the first misspelled word displayed in the Not in Dictionary text box.

> **TIP**
>
> Look for a red, wavy line while you are adding text to your presentation. Instead of running the full spell check, you can right-click on the word and select the correct spelling from the menu that appears.

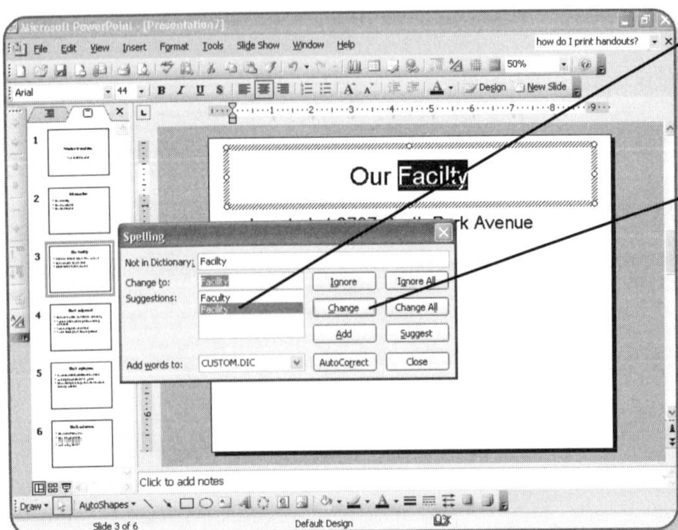

2. Click on the **correct spelling** in the Suggestions text box. The word will be selected and will appear in the Change to text box.

3a. Click on **Change**. The misspelled word will be corrected, and the next misspelled word will appear.

OR

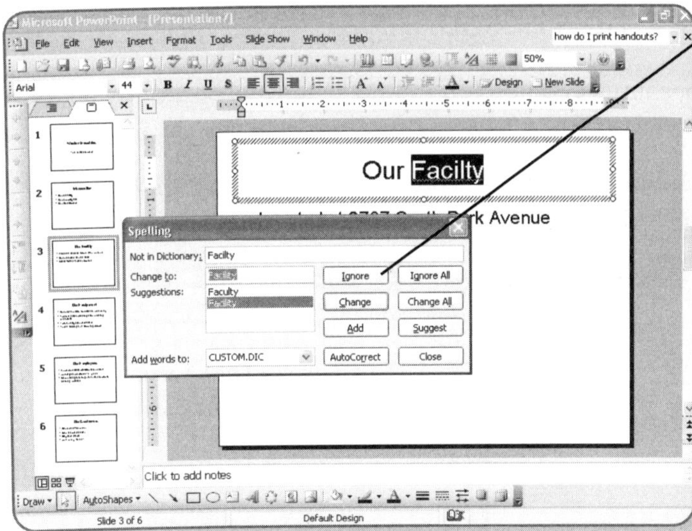

3b. Click on **Ignore**. The word will be left as is, and the next misspelled word will appear. When PowerPoint has checked the last word in the presentation, a confirmation dialog box will appear.

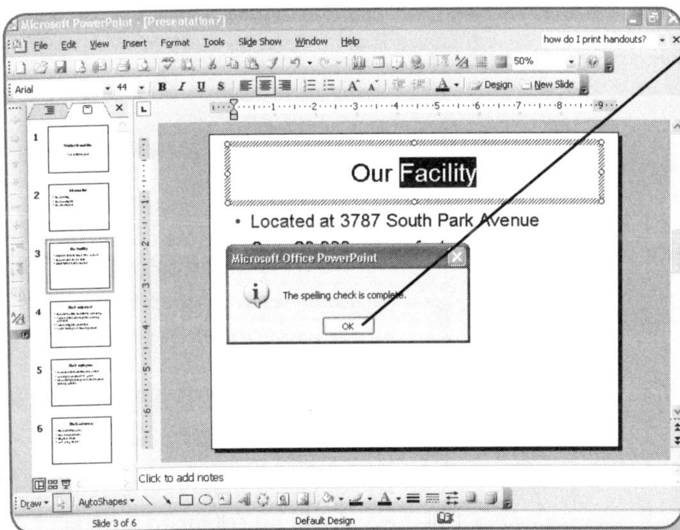

4. Click on **OK**. The presentation will be spell checked. You should save the file so that the corrections are preserved.

Using the Research Tools

The research tools, new in PowerPoint 2003, work best when you are connected to the Internet. They rely on Internet databases, such as encyclopedias and news services.

Using the Thesaurus

The thesaurus enables you to find synonyms or antonyms for a word.

1. Double-click on the **word** you want to look up. It will be selected.

2. Click on **Tools**. The menu will appear.

3. Click on **Thesaurus**. The Research task pane will open.

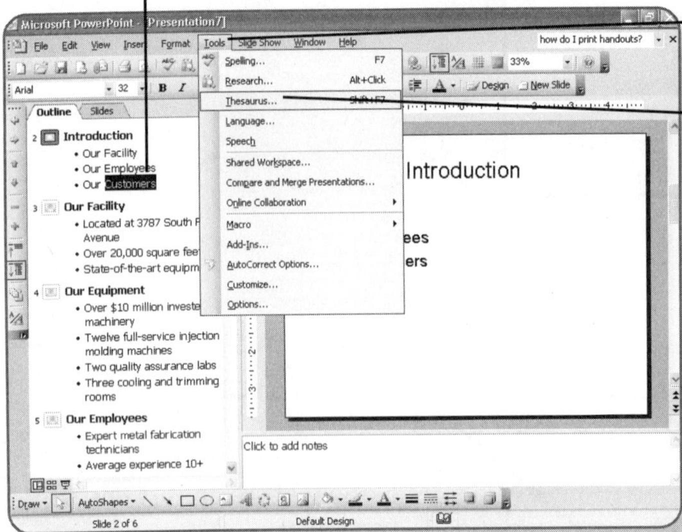

4. Point to the **desired replacement**. A drop-down arrow will appear beside it.

5. Click on the **down arrow**. A menu will appear.

6. Click on **Insert**. The selected word will be replaced by the new one.

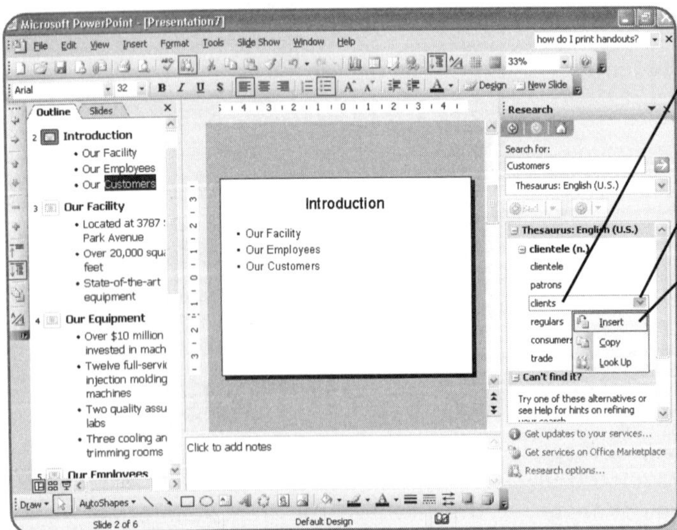

Using Other Research Tools

The thesaurus is only one of Office 2003's research tools. To find extended information about a topic, use the Research command.

1. Click on **Tools**. The menu will appear.

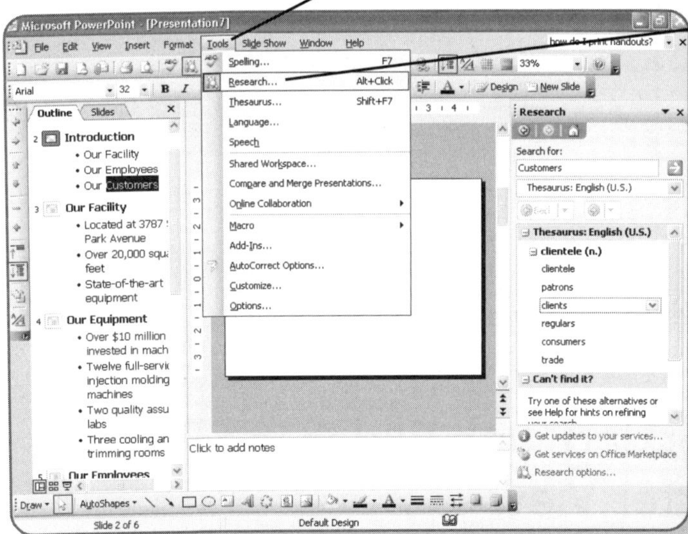

2. Click on **Research**. The Research pane will appear if it is not displayed already.

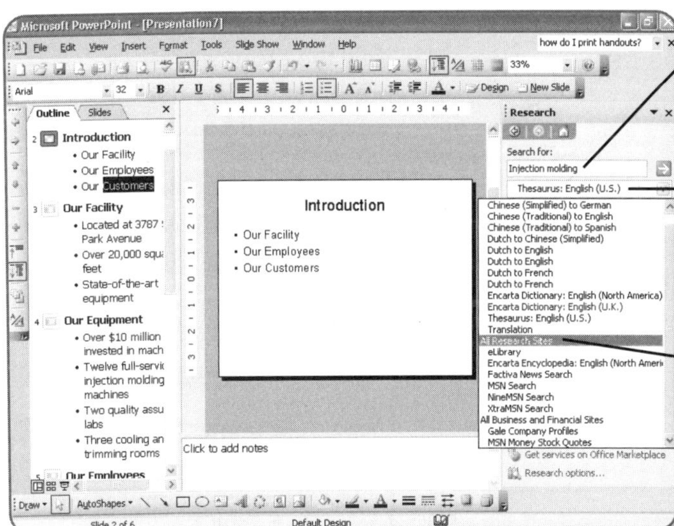

3. Type the **word or phrase** to research in the Search for box. The word or phrase will appear there.

4. Choose a source from the list of online reference sources.

> **TIP**
>
> **Choose All Research Sites** to search multiple sources.

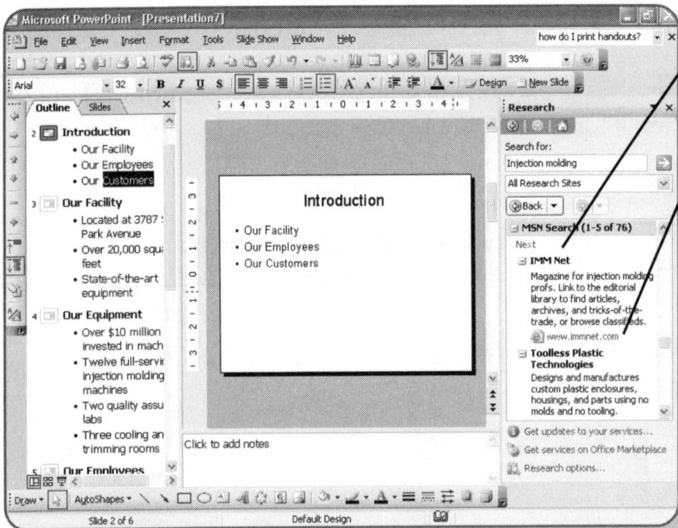

PowerPoint will look up the text in its online research libraries.

5. **Click** on the **article** you want to read. A Web browser window will display the article.

Working with Slides in Slide Sorter View

You don't have to work with just one slide at a time. The Slide Sorter view displays all the slides as miniatures in neat rows across the screen. This is a good way to see the big picture and view the progress of your presentation. Use this view to rearrange, add, and delete slides.

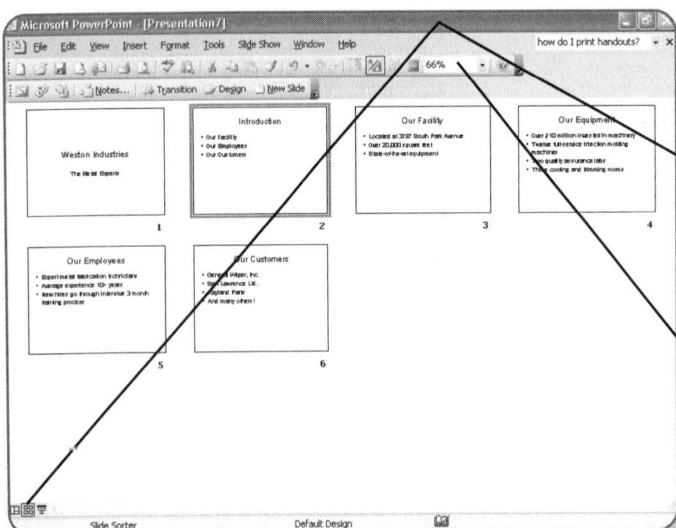

1. **Click** on the **Slide Sorter View button**. The presentation slides will appear in the Slide Sorter view.

> **TIP**
>
> To change the viewing size of the slides here, select a size from the Zoom list.

Selecting Slides

Before you can perform certain functions with slides (such as deleting or moving), you'll need to select the slides with which you want to work. You can select a single slide, a contiguous group of slides, or random slides.

Here are a few tips for selecting slides:

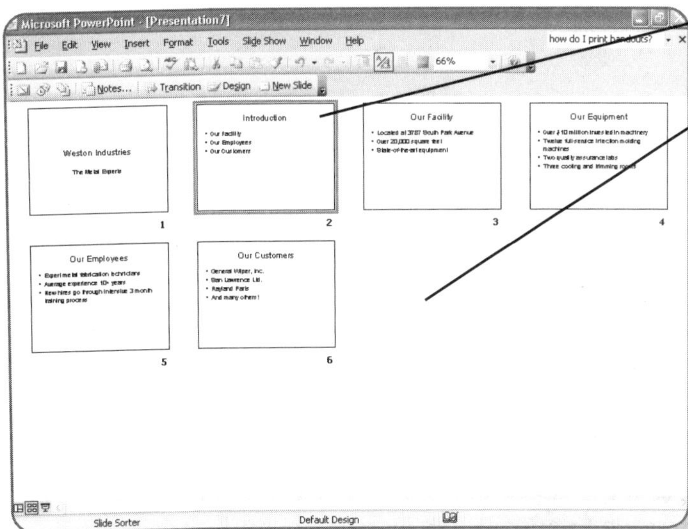

- To select a single slide, **click** on the **slide**.
- To deselect a slide, **click** on a **blank area** of the Slide Sorter view.

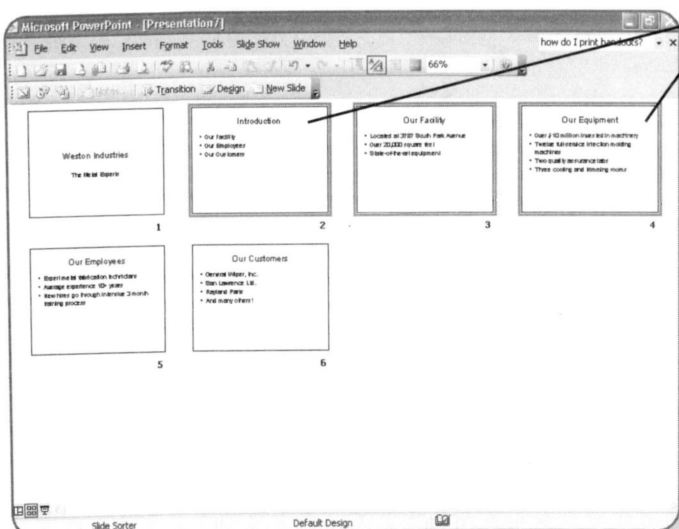

- To select a contiguous group of slides, **click** on the **first slide**, and then **press** and **hold** the **Shift key** while clicking on the last slide in the group.

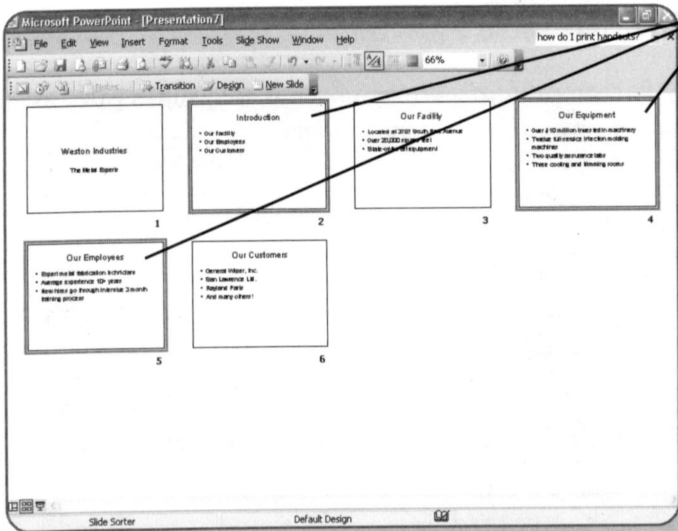

- To select random slides, **click** on the **first slide**, then **press** and **hold** the **Ctrl key** while clicking on the other slides you want to select.

Inserting a Slide

While browsing in the Slide Sorter view, you may find a place where an extra slide is needed. You can easily add a new slide.

1. **Click** in the **space** between the two slides where you want the new slide to appear. The insertion bar will appear between the two slides.

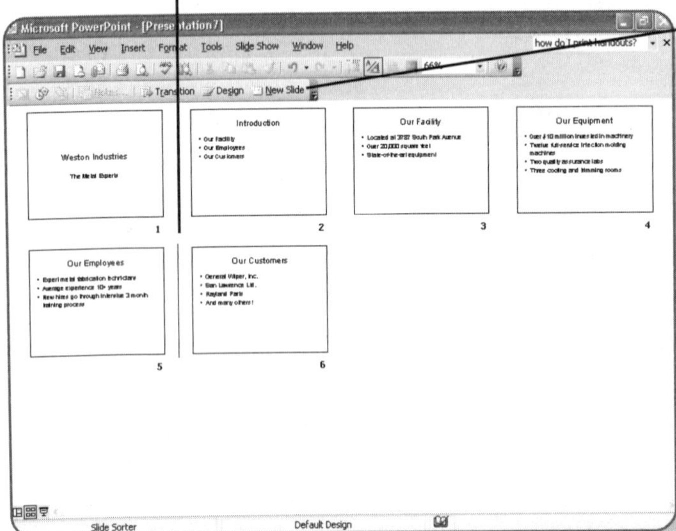

2. **Click** on **New Slide** on the Slide Sorter toolbar.

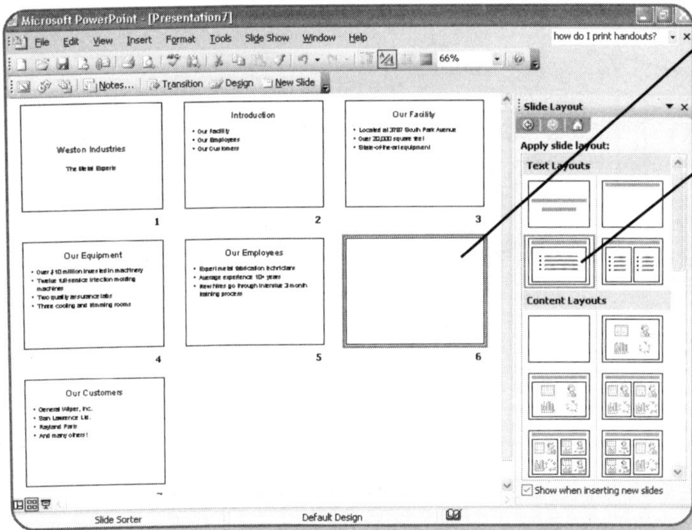

A new slide (using the default slide layout) will appear in the selected place.

The Slide Layout task pane will appear so you can select a layout. The default layout for new slides is Title and Text.

> **NOTE**
>
> To add text to the new slide, double-click on the slide to display it in Normal view.

Duplicating a Slide

When you want to make an exact copy of a slide, use the duplicate command.

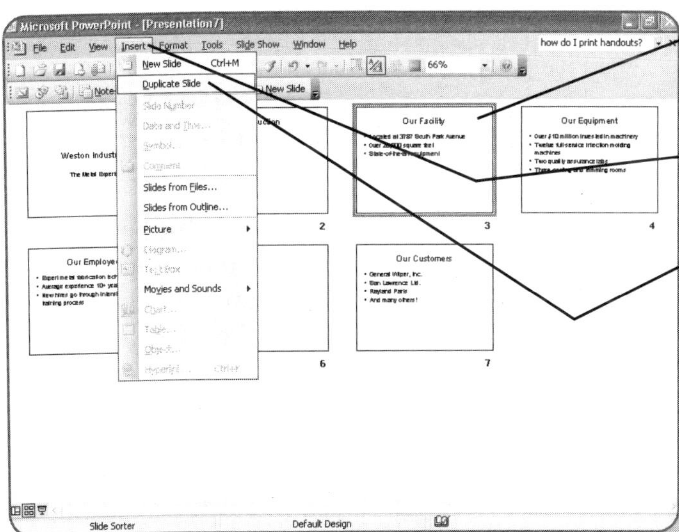

1. **Click** on the **slide** that you want to copy. The slide will be selected.
2. **Click** on **Insert**. The Insert menu will appear.
3. **Click** on **Duplicate Slide**. An identical slide will appear just after the original slide. The duplicate slide will be selected.

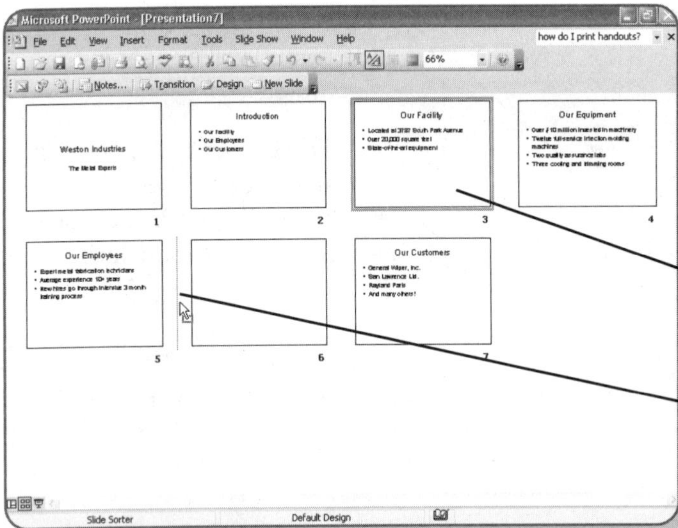

Moving a Slide

The Slide Sorter view can also be used to reorganize slides. Slides can be moved around to better present information with a simple drag and drop.

1. **Click** and **hold** on the **slide** that you want to move. The slide will be selected.

2. **Drag** the **mouse** to where you want to move the slide. The insertion bar will appear in the selected place.

3. **Release** the **mouse button**. The slide will appear in the new position.

Deleting Slides

You may find that you don't need a slide in a presentation. Here is how to delete slides that you do not want.

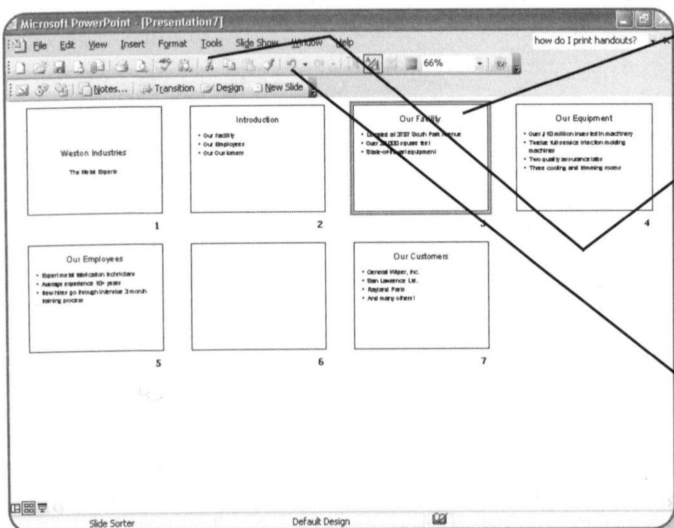

1. **Select** the **slide or slides** that you want to delete. The slide(s) will be selected.

2. **Click** on the **Cut button** on the Standard toolbar or **press** the **Delete key**. The slide(s) will be removed from the presentation.

> **NOTE**
>
> If you've deleted a slide in error, **click** on the **Undo button**. The slide will reappear.

6

Changing the Presentation's Look

In the last few chapters, we have been working with plain presentations—no design, no color. They've been pretty drab! But now it's time to change all that. In this chapter, you'll learn how to:

- Apply a design template
- Select an alternate color scheme
- Apply consistent formatting with slide masters

Changing the Design Template

A design template applies a preset font, color, background, and placeholder arrangement to every slide in the presentation. You learned how to start a new presentation using a design template in Chapter 3, "Learning About Presentations." You can change to a different design template at any time.

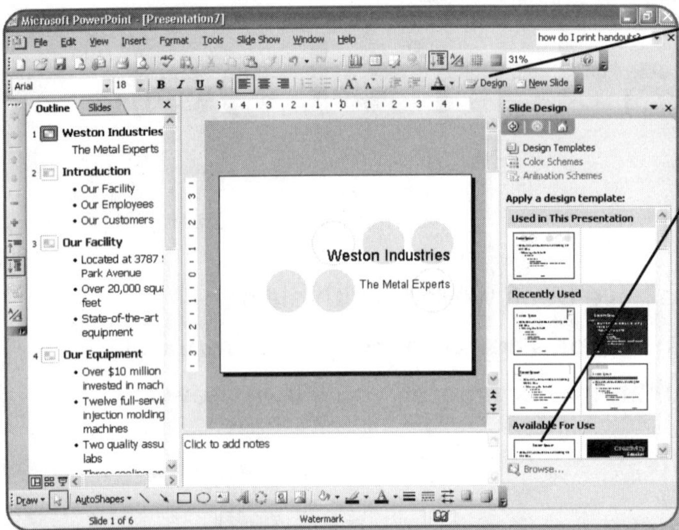

1. **Click** on the **Design button** on the toolbar. The Slide Design task pane will appear.
2. **Click** on the **design template** that you want to change to. The template will be applied.

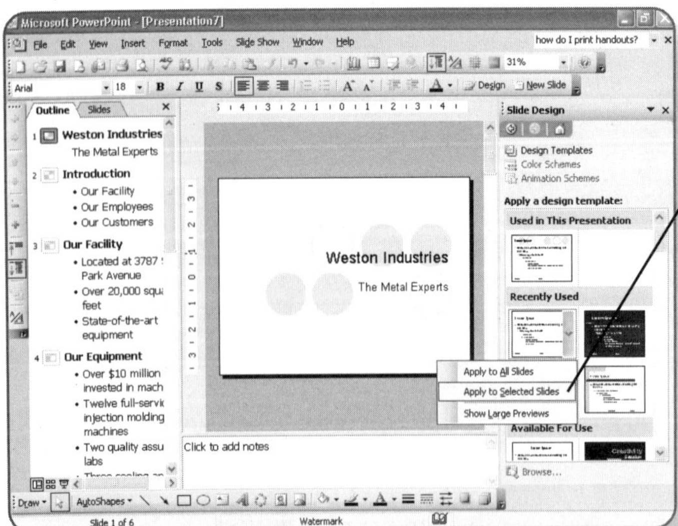

NOTE

You can also apply a template to only the selected slides. Point at the template, and a down arrow appears. Click the down arrow to bring up a menu, and then click on Apply to Selected Slides.

Changing the Color Scheme

Each design template comes with several different color schemes. You can switch to one of its alternate schemes, or you can start with one of those schemes and customize it to make your own color scheme.

Because the color schemes are associated with design templates, you should make your design template choice first, and then choose the color scheme.

Selecting an Alternate Color Scheme

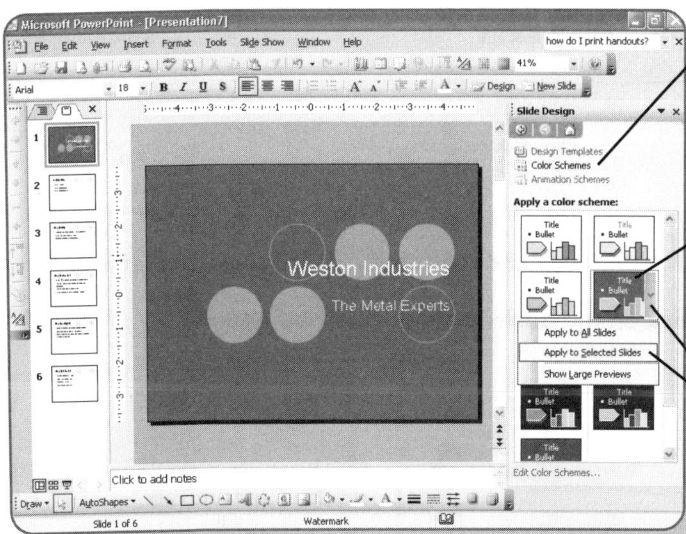

1. **Click** on the **Color Schemes hyperlink** in the Slide Design task pane. The color schemes will appear for the chosen design template.

2. **Click** on the **desired color scheme**. The presentation will change to that scheme.

> **NOTE**
>
> You can also apply a color scheme to the selected slides only, just like you did when applying the design template.

Customizing a Color Scheme

After selecting a color scheme, you may decide to change one or more of its colors.

1. **Click** on the **Edit Color Schemes hyperlink**. The Edit Color Scheme dialog box will open.

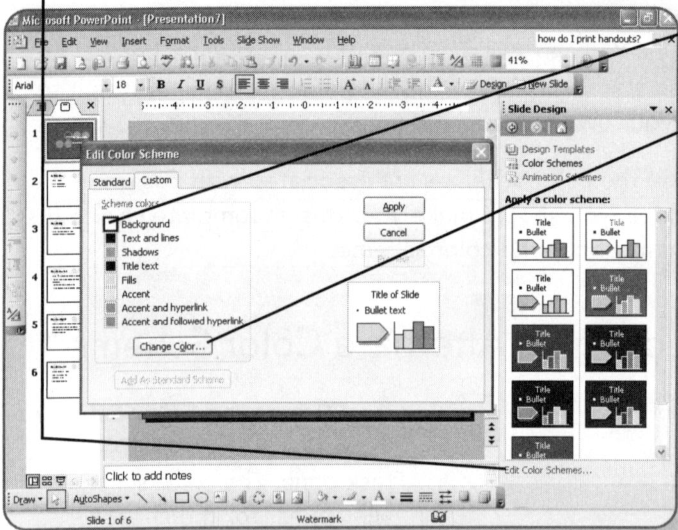

2. **Click** on the **color** you want to change. It will be selected.

3. **Click** on **Change Color**. A dialog box will appear for changing the selected item.

For example, if you chose the background color in step 2, the box will be called Background Color.

4. **Click** on the **Standard tab** if it is not already displayed.

5. **Click** on the **desired color**. It will be outlined.

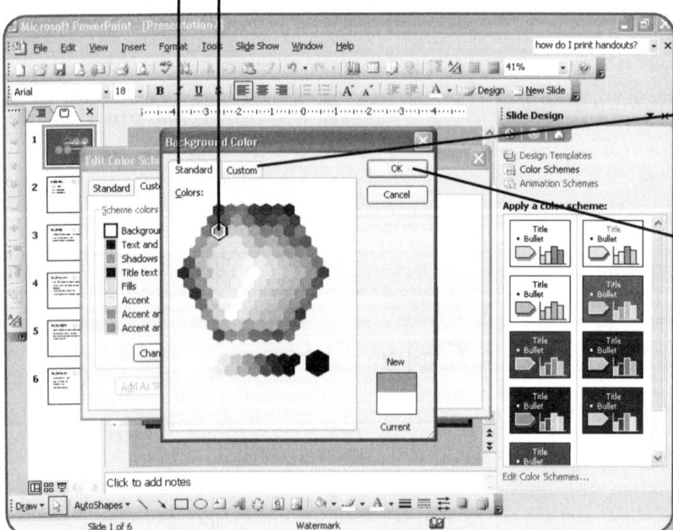

NOTE

More colors are available on the Custom tab.

6. **Click** on **OK**. The new color will appear in the Edit Color Scheme dialog box.

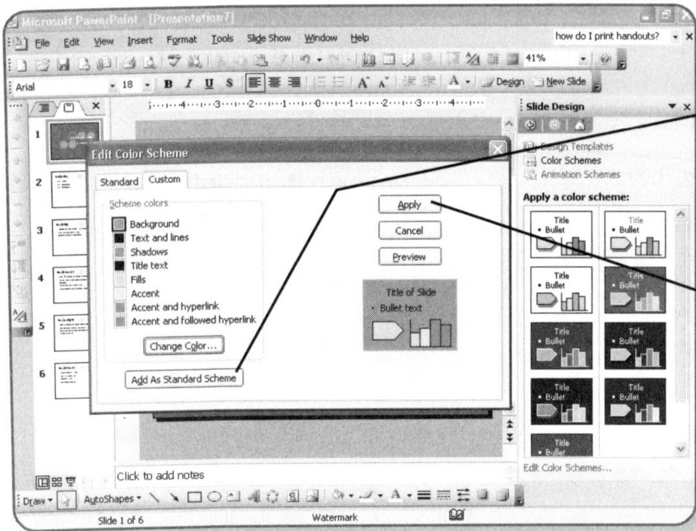

7. Repeat steps 2 through 6 for additional colors, if desired.

8. Click on **Add As Standard Scheme** if you want to save this color scheme. It will be added as a new color scheme on the Slide Design task pane.

9. Click on **Apply**. The dialog box will close and the new color scheme will be applied.

Working with Masters

The *Slide Master* is a template that applies to every slide in the presentation (except slides that use the Title Slide layout, because those take their design from the *Title Master* template).

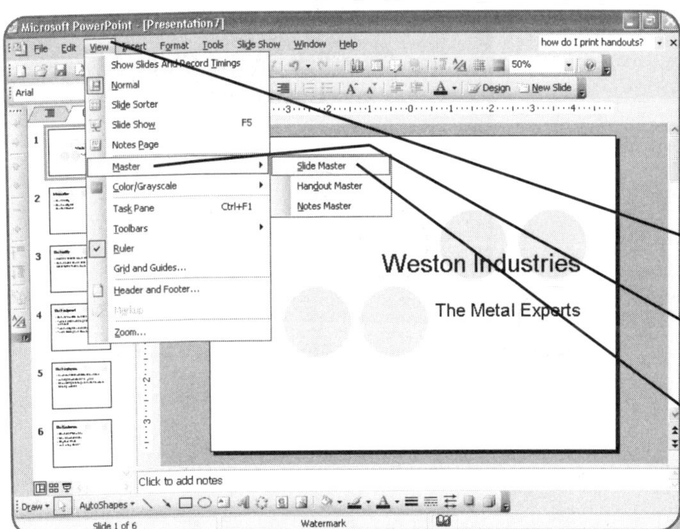

When you apply a design template, you are making changes to the Slide Master and Title Master. You can also change those Masters manually to customize the design.

1. Click on **View**. The View menu will appear.

2. Point to Master. The Master submenu will appear.

3. Click on **Slide Master**. The Slide Master view will appear.

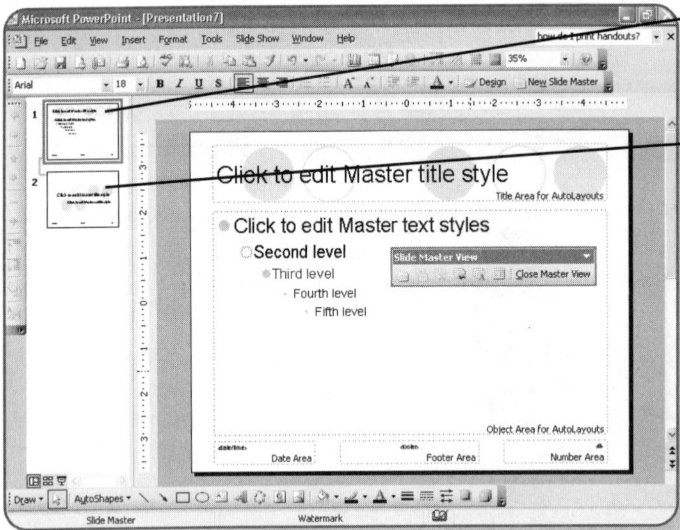

The Slide Master is the top template. It applies to all slides except title slides.

The Title Master is the one beneath it. It applies to title slides.

4. **Click** on the **Slide Master** or **Title Master** to select the one you want to edit.

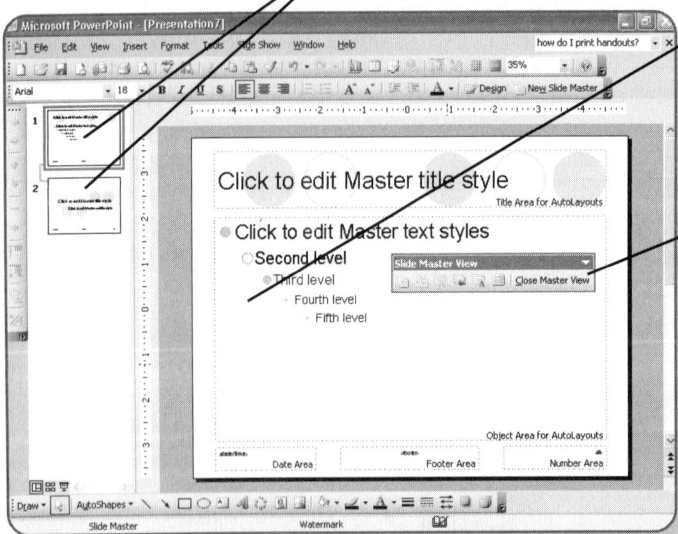

5. **Make changes** as desired. Keep reading to find out some of the changes you can make. You are limited only by how creative and artistic you want to be.

6. **Click** on the **Close Master View button** when you have finished.

Changing Text Formatting

In Chapter 7, "Formatting Slides," you will learn how to format slide text on a single slide, such as adding bold or italic, choosing a different font, or changing the size. You can do the same formatting to the text on the Slide Master or Title Master to change all the slides at once.

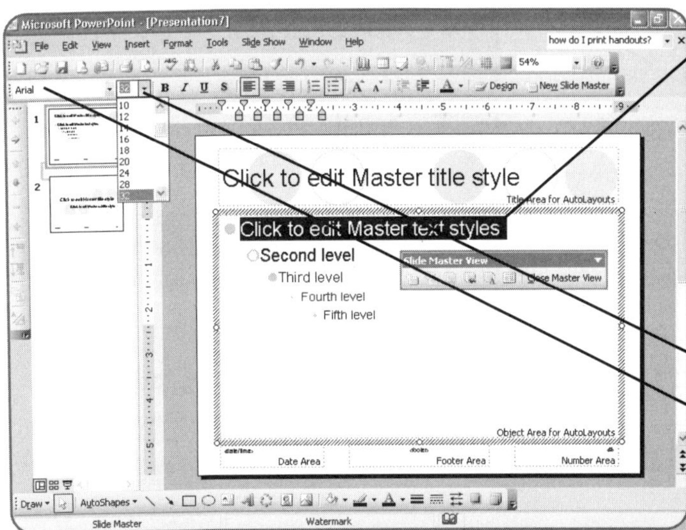

1. **Select** the **text** that you want to format. The text will be highlighted.

2. **Apply text formatting** to the text. See Chapter 7 for help, if needed.

Some of the formatting you can apply includes:

- Selecting a different font size
- Selecting a different font

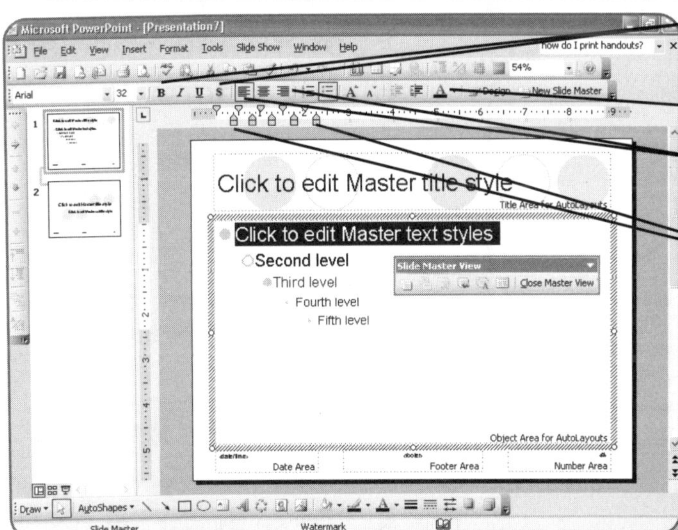

- Choosing bold, italic, underline, and/or shadow
- Selecting a different font color
- Choosing left, right, or center alignment
- Dragging the tab markers to change the indentation

Moving and Resizing Text Placeholders

You can change the size of the Title Area, Object Area, Footer Area, Date Area, and Number Area placeholders.

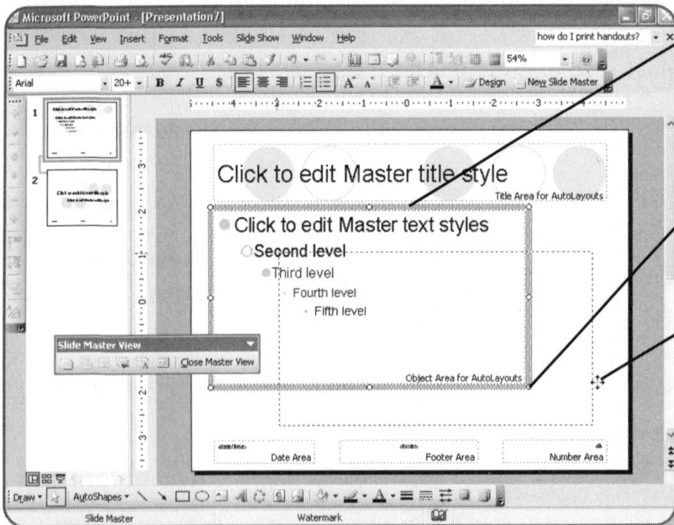

1. **Click** on a **placeholder**. A border will appear around the placeholder that contains resize handles.
2. **Click** and **drag** a **resize handle**. A dotted line will show the new size of the placeholder.
3. **Position** the **mouse pointer** over the placeholder. The mouse pointer will become a four-headed arrow.
4. **Click** and **drag** the **placeholder** to a new location.

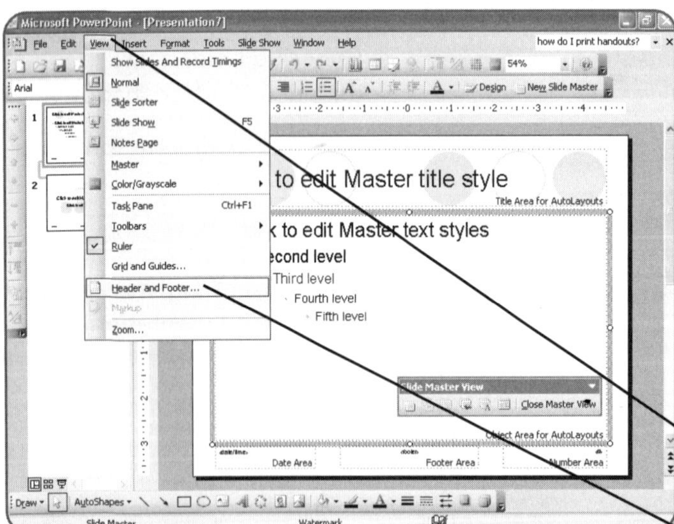

Working with Footers and Special Placeholders

The Slide Master contains placeholder boxes for date/time, slide number, and footer. These can be moved around or resized (see the preceding steps). You can also turn them on or off.

1. **Click** on **View**. The View menu will appear.
2. **Click** on **Header and Footer**. The Header and Footer dialog box will open.

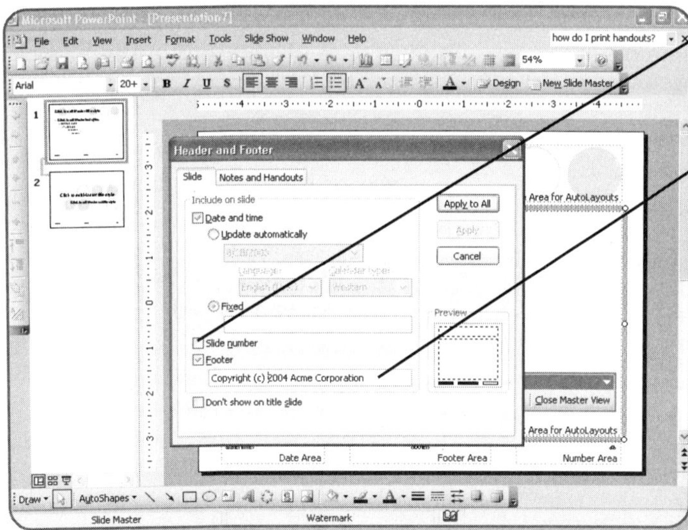

3. Click in the **Slide number check box** if you want the slides to be numbered.

4. Type text in the **Footer box** if you want footer text on each slide.

> **NOTE**
>
> You can deselect the Footer check box to turn off the footer temporarily, without deleting the footer text that you entered in step 4.

5. Click in the **Don't show on title slide check box** if you want to omit all placeholders from title slides.

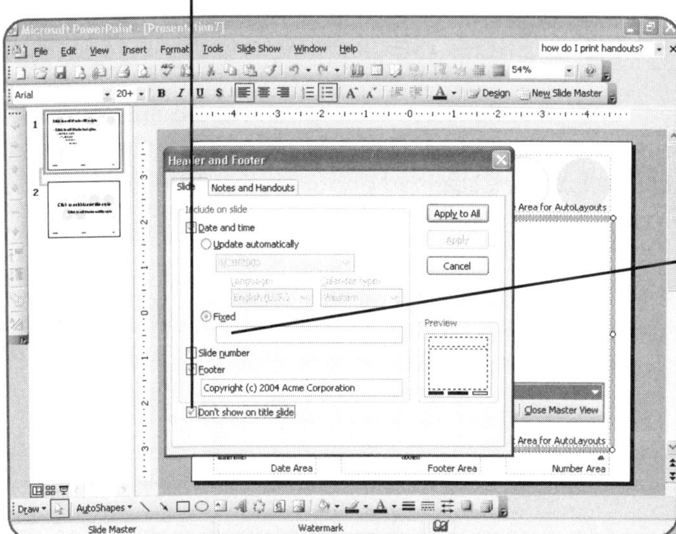

By default, the date/time does not appear, even though the placeholder is turned on. That's because Fixed is the default setting, and the Fixed box is blank.

6a. Type today's date in the Fixed box to make it appear on each slide. Then skip to step 9.

OR

6b. Click on **Update automatically** to set up an automatic date/time on each slide. Today's date will appear in the box beneath it.

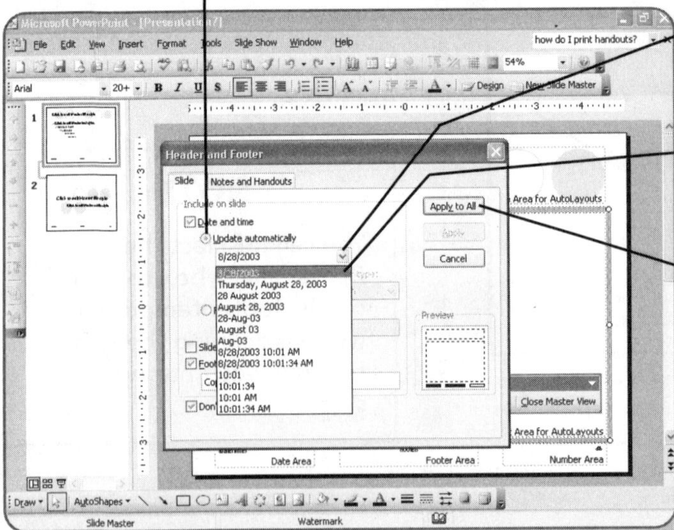

7. Click on the **down arrow** next to the date. A menu will appear.

8. Click on the **date format** that you want. It will appear in the box.

9. Click on the **Apply to All button**. The footer information on the slide master will be updated.

Applying a Slide Background

You have hundreds of choices for a slide background. You can use clip art from the Microsoft Clip Organizer or that you've found on the Internet, scanned photographs, or images you've created in a graphics program, such as Microsoft Photo Editor. Explore your options.

1. **Click** on **Format.** The Format menu will appear.

2. **Click** on **Background.** The Background dialog box will open.

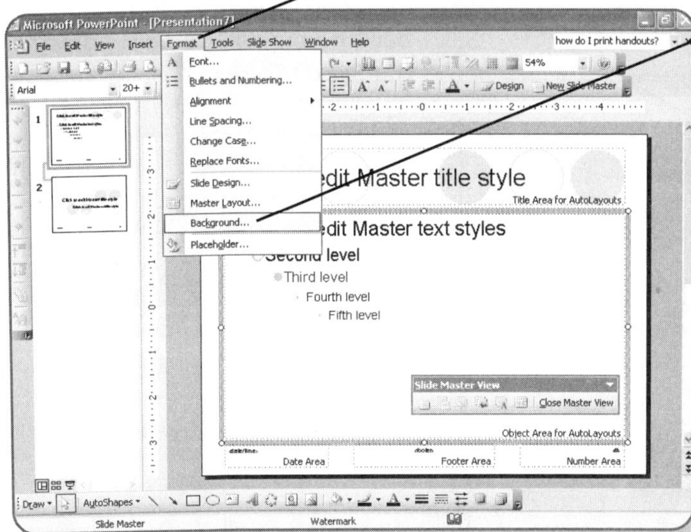

3. **Click** on the **down arrow next to Background fill**. A list of color options will appear.

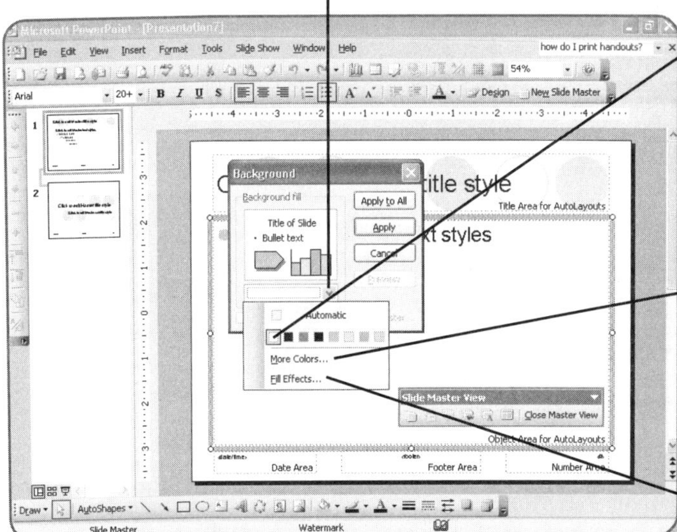

4a. **Click** on a **placeholder color**. A color will be used from the current color scheme. If you change color schemes, the background color will change.

OR

4b. **Click** on **More Colors** and then select a color from the Background Color box. A specific solid color will be used.

OR

4c. **Click** on **Fill Effects** and then select a gradient, texture, pattern, or picture as the background.

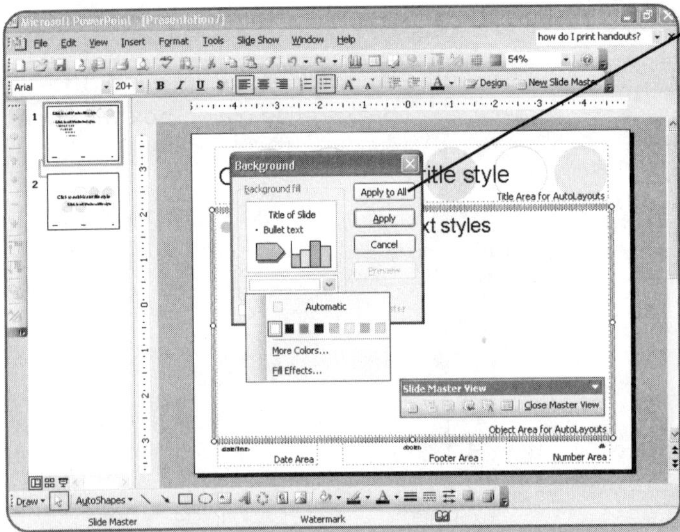

5. Click on **Apply to All** after selecting a background. The background will be applied to the Slide Master.

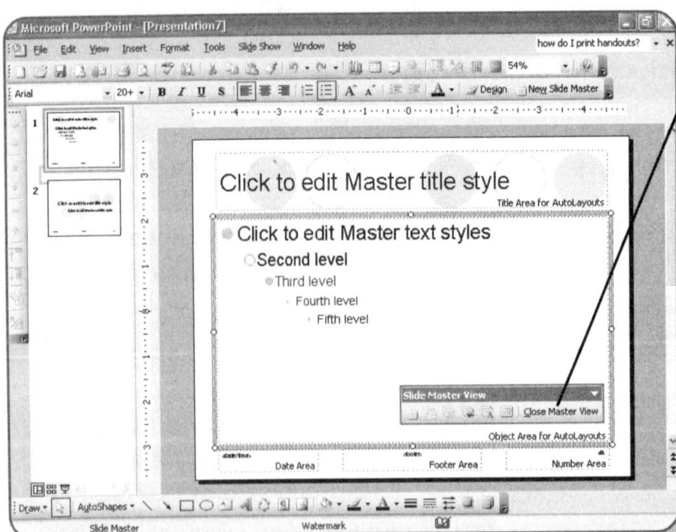

When you are finished working with the Slide Master, you can return to Normal view by clicking Close Master View.

7

Formatting Slides

So far in this book, you have been working mostly with the presentation as a whole. In this chapter, you'll learn how to change the appearance of individual slides by modifying various layout and appearance characteristics. In this chapter, you'll learn how to:

- Apply text formatting
- Change the look of bullets
- Choose different slide layouts
- Insert non-text content with layout placeholders

Formatting Slide Text

Generally speaking, it's a good idea to maintain formatting consistency on all slides. However, sometimes you may want to emphasize a word or group of words by using boldface, italics, color, a larger or smaller size, or a different font.

Working with the Formatting Toolbar

1. **Select** the **text** that you want to format. The text will be highlighted.

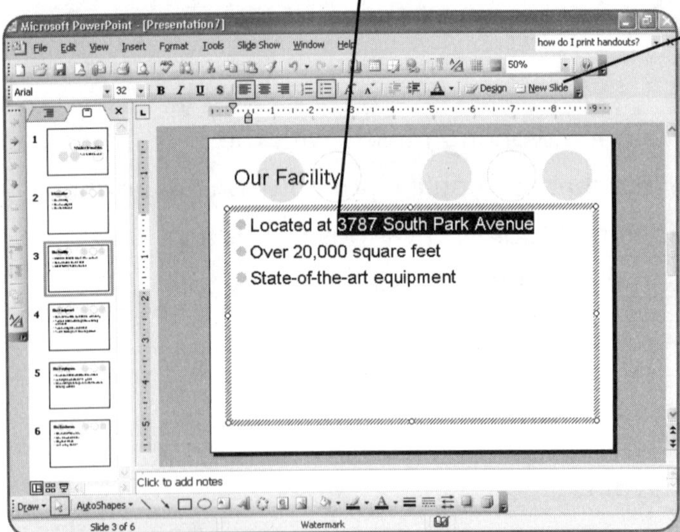

2. **Click** on a **Formatting toolbar button**. The text will be formatted in the style you've selected.

Here are a few formatting styles that you may want to apply to text:

- The **Font list** changes the typeface used for the text.

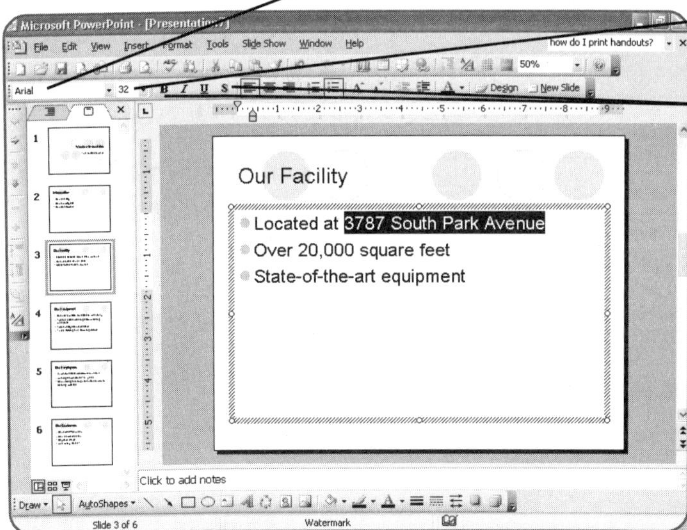

- The **Font Size list** makes the text larger or smaller.
- Emphasize text so that it stands out from other text by using the **Bold**, **Italic**, **Underline**, and **Shadow buttons**.

- By default, all placeholder text is left-aligned. To change the way paragraphs appear on a slide, use the **Align Left**, **Center**, and **Align Right** buttons.

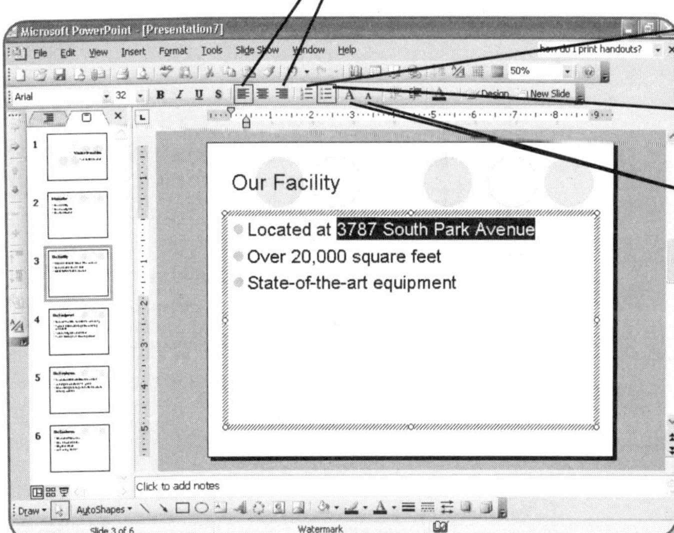

- To make a numbered list, use the **Numbering button.**
- You can turn the bullets on or off with the **Bullets button.**
- The **Grow Text button** increases the font size, and the **Shrink Text button** decreases it.

Copying Text Formatting

You can also copy the formatting of text and apply it to other text in a presentation slide:

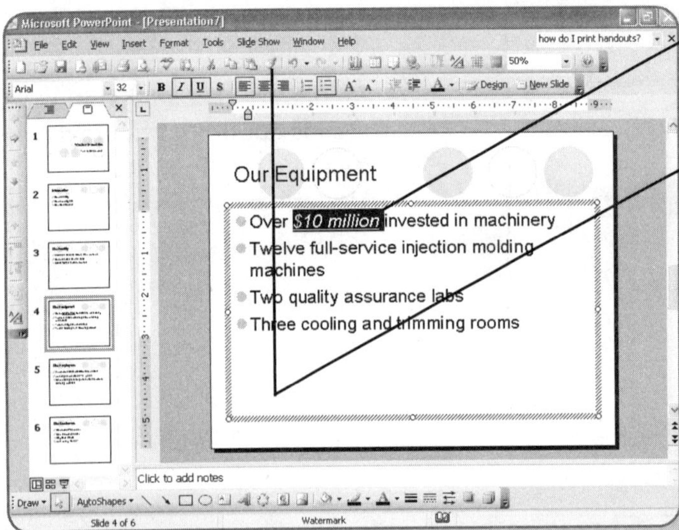

1. Select the **text** that is formatted in the style you want to apply to the other text.

2. Click on the **Format Painter button** on the Standard toolbar. The mouse pointer will turn into a paintbrush.

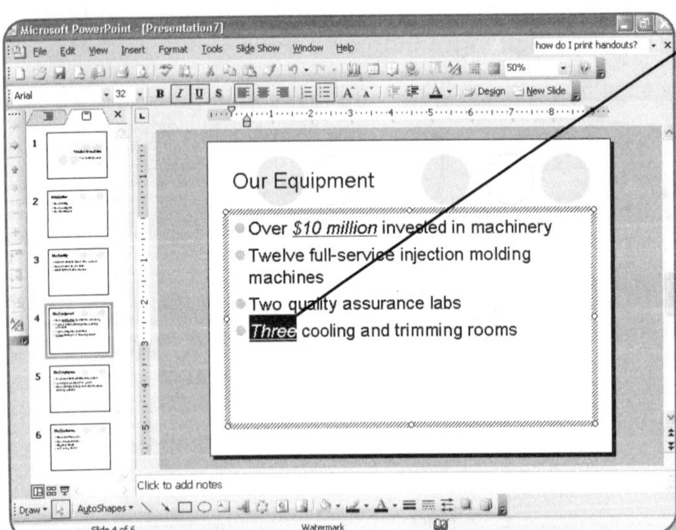

3. Select the **text** to which you want to apply the formatting. The formatting will be copied.

> **TIP**
>
> To apply the copied formatting to more than one text element, double-click in step 2. Then press Esc after step 3 to return to normal mode.

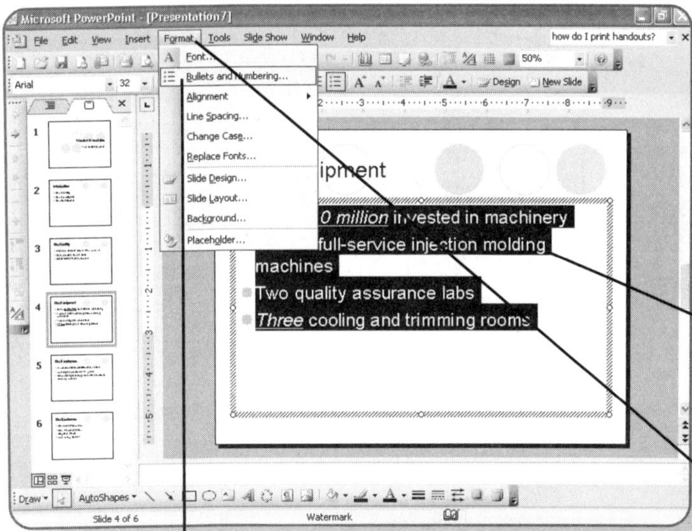

Selecting a Different Bullet Character

The default bullet character depends on the design template you've chosen. You can select a different bullet character without changing the design template.

1. **Select** the **paragraphs** to which you want to apply a different bullet character. The paragraphs will be selected.
2. **Click** on **Format**. The Format menu will appear.
3. **Click** on **Bullets and Numbering**. The Bullets and Numbering dialog box will open.

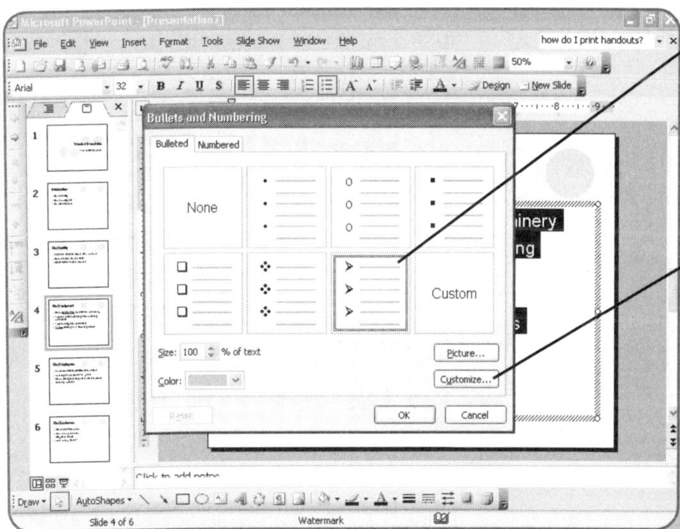

4a. Click on the **bullet character** that you want to use for the bullet list. The bullet will be selected. Then skip to step 10.

OR

4b. Click on **Customize**. The Symbol dialog box will open.

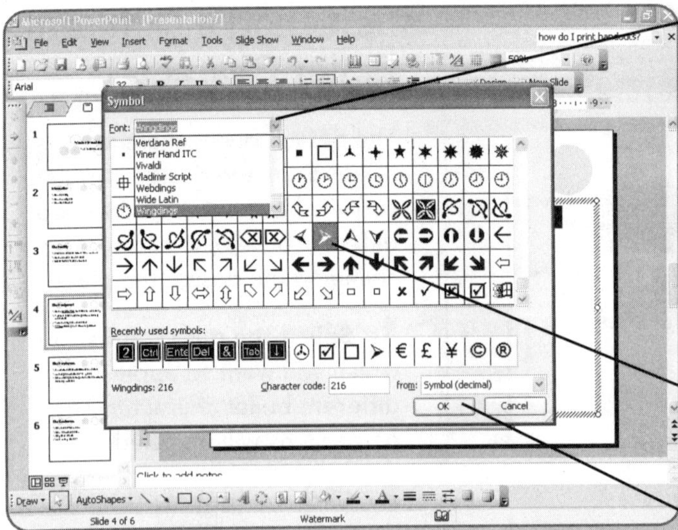

5. Click on the **Font box's down arrow** and choose a different font if desired. The characters in the font will appear.

> **TIP**
>
> Wingdings is a good font for selecting bullet characters.

6. Click on the **character you want** for the bullets. It will be selected.

7. Click on **OK**. The Symbol dialog box will close.

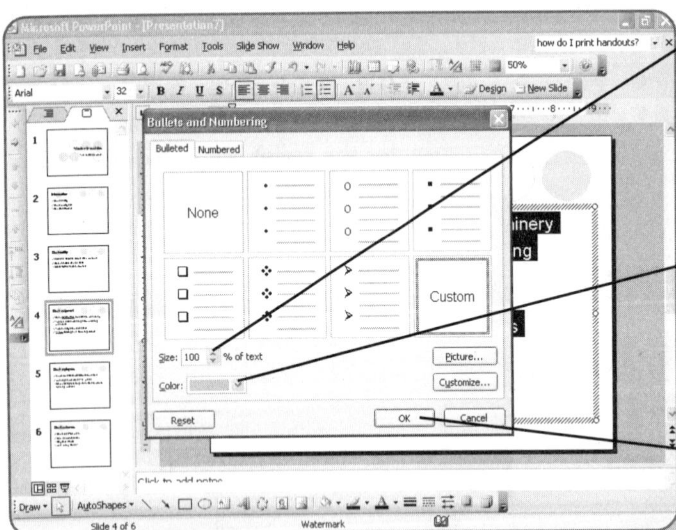

8. Click the **Size up and down arrows** to select how large or small the bullet will be, compared to the text. The percentage you choose will appear in the list box.

9. Click the **Color down arrow** and **select** a color from the list. The color that appears in the list box will be applied to the bullet character.

10. Click on **OK**. The bullet character and color will be applied to all the bullet points in the placeholder.

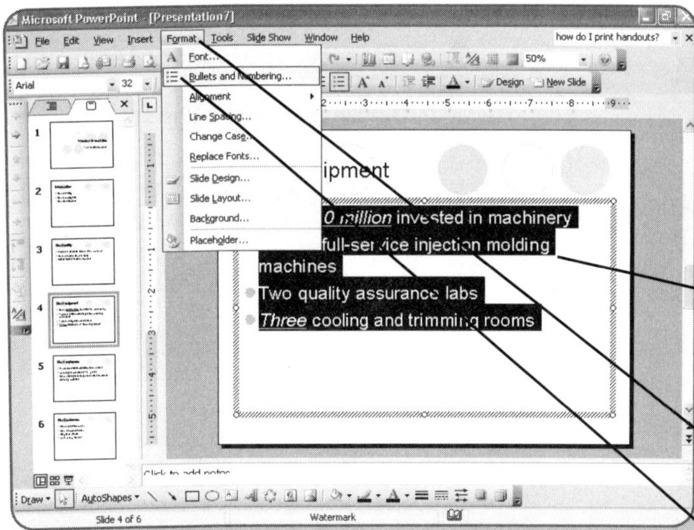

Selecting a Picture Bullet

In addition to the standard bullet types in the preceding steps, you can choose from a variety of pictures for bullets.

1. **Select** the **paragraphs** to which you want to apply a different bullet character. The paragraphs will be selected.
2. **Click** on **Format**. The Format menu will appear.
3. **Click** on **Bullets and Numbering**. The Bullets and Numbering dialog box will open.

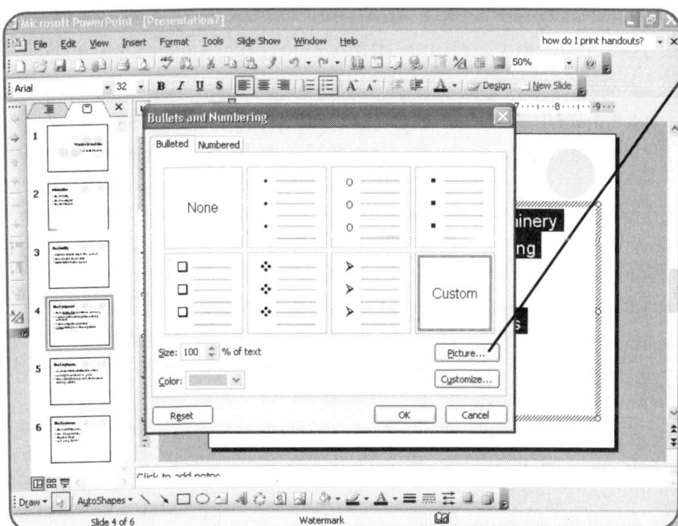

4. **Click** on **Picture**. The Picture Bullet dialog box will open.

> **NOTE**
>
> You will have many more bullet choices if you are connected to the Internet.

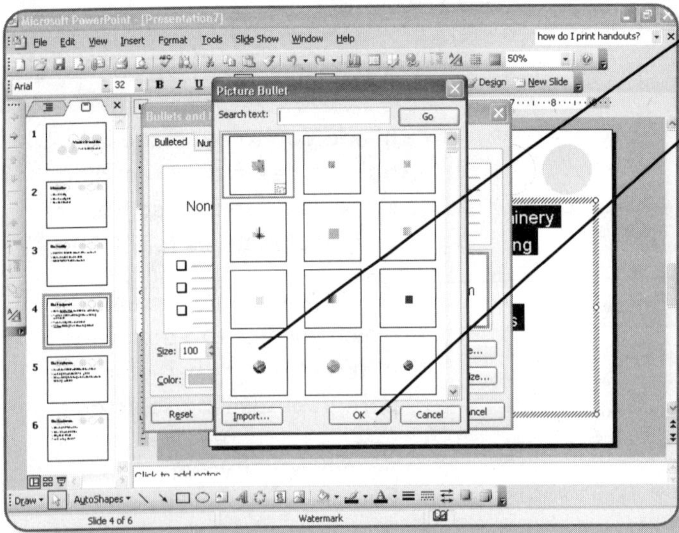

5. Click on the **bullet character** you want to use.

6. Click on **OK**. The new bullet will be applied.

Selecting a Slide Layout

The first slide in the presentation has a Title layout by default, and other slides have a Title and Text layout. Other layouts may be useful when you have other content besides text to display, such as pictures, graphs, or diagrams. You can add such items to a slide manually, but it is easier to do so by changing the layout and then using the layout placeholders.

1. **Click** on the **slide** that you want to change. The slide will be selected.

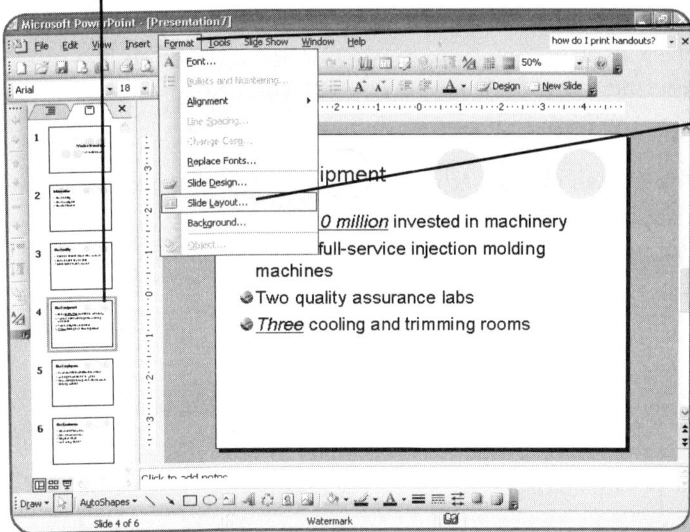

2. **Click** on **Format**. The Format menu will appear.

3. **Click** on **Slide Layout**. The Slide Layout task pane will open and the list of available slide layouts will be displayed.

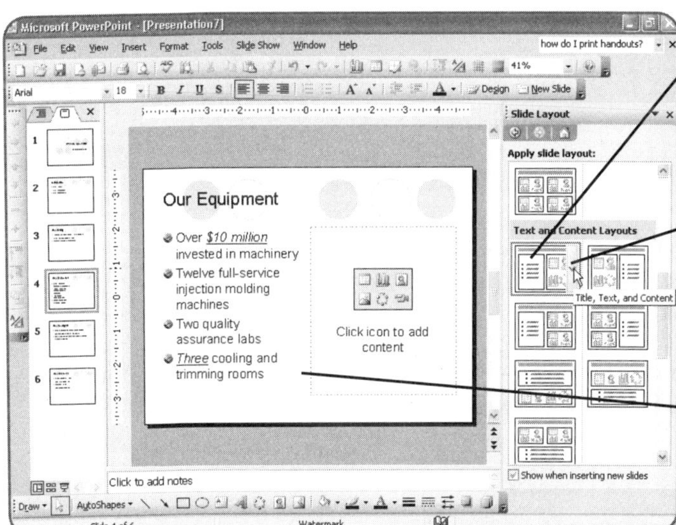

4. **Click** on the **layout** you want to apply to the slide.

> **NOTE**
>
> **Hold** the **mouse pointer** over a **slide layout** in the Task Pane to see a description of the layout.

The slide will change to the new layout format.

Inserting a New Slide Based on a Layout

When you insert a new slide in Normal view, the Slide Layout pane appears automatically so you can select the desired layout for the new slide.

1. **Click** on the **slide** that the new slide should follow. It will be displayed and selected.

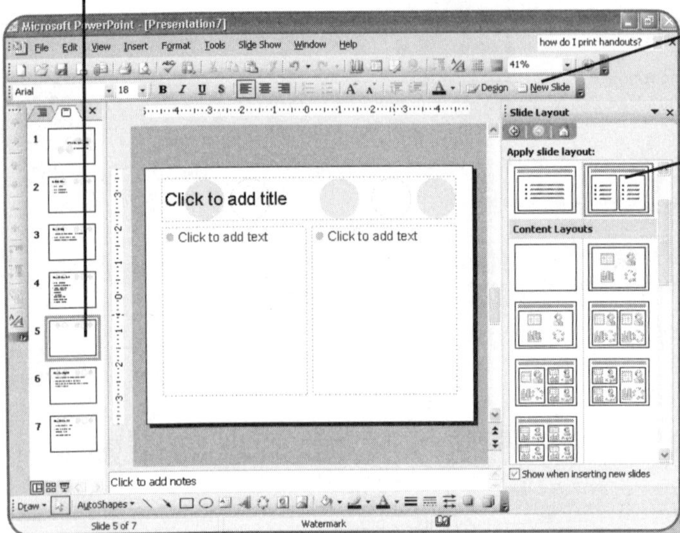

2. **Click** on the **New Slide button**. A new slide and the Slide Layout pane will appear.

3. **Click** on the **desired layout.** The layout will be applied to the new slide.

Inserting Content with Layout Placeholders

You have already seen how to use text placeholders: Simply click in the box and type. Now you will learn about other content placeholders.

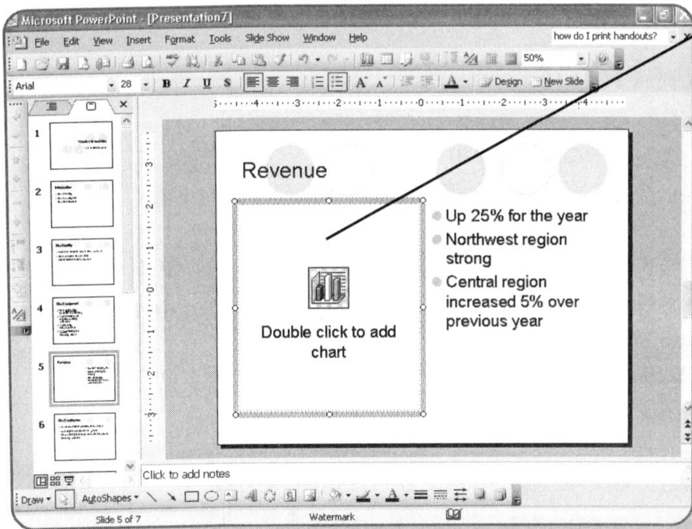

Some slide layouts have a placeholder for a single type of non-text content. Double-click the placeholder to insert that content.

Other slide layouts have a multipurpose placeholder with icons for six types of content. Double-click on the appropriate icon for the content type you want. Future chapters will address these content types in more detail.

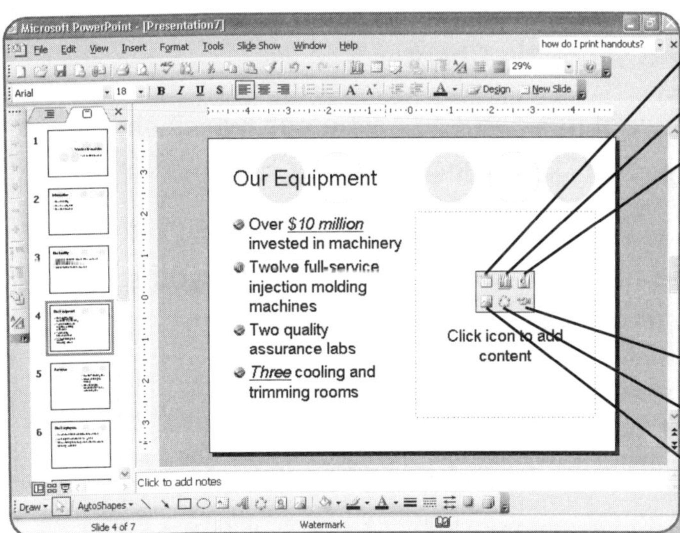

Table

Graph

Clip art

Sound or video clip

Diagram

Picture from file

Part II Review Questions

1. If the Outlining toolbar does not appear, how can you make it display? See "Displaying the Outlining Toolbar" in Chapter 4.
2. What are the keyboard shortcuts for promoting and demoting outline text? See "Promoting and Demoting Lines" in Chapter 4.
3. What command imports an outline from Word into PowerPoint? See "Importing an Outline" in Chapter 4.
4. What color is the wavy underline beneath a spelling error? See "Spell Checking the Presentation" in Chapter 5.
5. What kinds of resources are available through the Research Tools feature? See "Using the Research Tools" in Chapter 5.
6. If you want to select more than one non-contiguous slide in Slide Sorter view, what key do you hold down as you click on each one you want? See "Selecting Slides" in Chapter 5.
7. When applying design templates and color schemes, which should you apply first, and why? See "Changing the Color Scheme" in Chapter 6.
8. The Slide Master applies to slides that use all different layouts except one. Which one does not use the Slide Master? See "Working with Masters" in Chapter 6.
9. How would you create a bullet character out of a symbol such as $ or #? See "Selecting a Different Bullet Character" in Chapter 7.
10. What is the significance of the placeholder in some slide layouts with six different small icons in it? See "Inserting Content with Layout Placeholders" in Chapter 7.

PART III

Jazzing Up the Presentation

8

Inserting Graphics

You don't need to be a great illustrator to create slides with good-looking pictures. You just need to know how to work with the tools provided by PowerPoint. Myriad clip art images are at your disposal so that you can vary the design of your presentation. Change the color and size of clip art images to fit on the slide. Delete parts of an image if you want. Let your imagination have fun. You'll also find an arsenal of ready-made shapes and text effects that you can fill, color, and position anywhere. In this chapter, you'll learn how to:

- Select clip art from the Clip Organizer
- Use WordArt to enhance text on a slide
- Create line art images with AutoShapes

Working with Clip Art

The Microsoft Office programs use the clip art in the Clip Organizer. You can find a clip by entering a topic keyword.

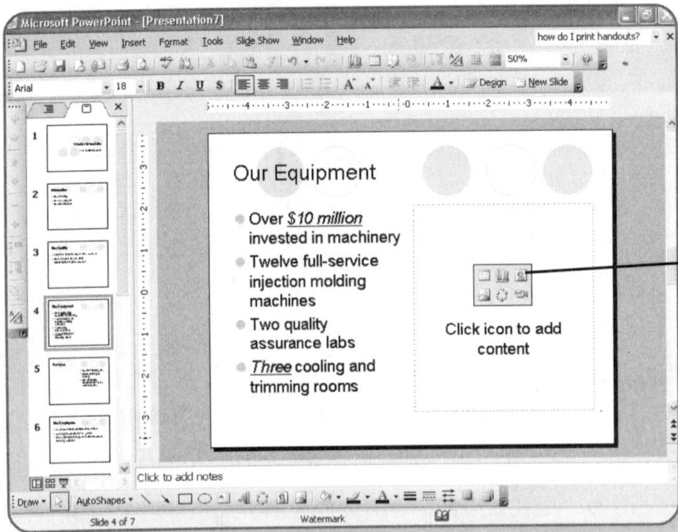

Using a Clip Art Placeholder

One way to open the Clip Organizer is with a Clip Art placeholder on a slide layout.

1. **Click** on the **Clip Art icon** on a slide layout. The Select Picture dialog box will appear.

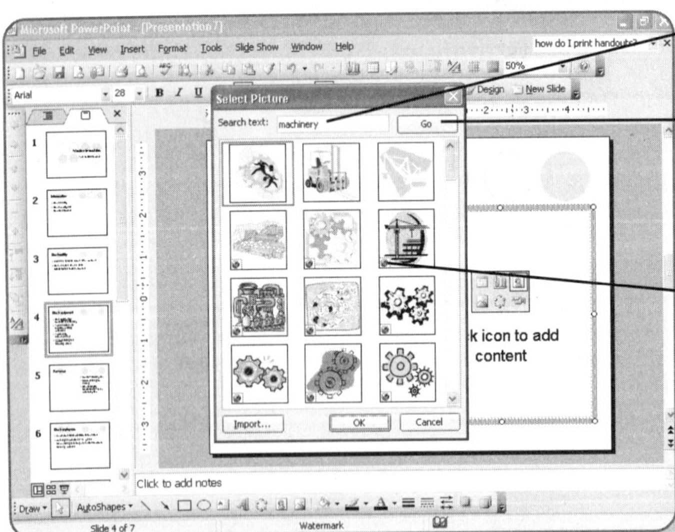

2. **Type** a **word** in the Search text box.

3. **Click** on **Go**. Clips matching that keyword will appear.

> **NOTE**
>
> A clip with a globe icon in the corner is from the Internet. If you choose it, it will be downloaded.

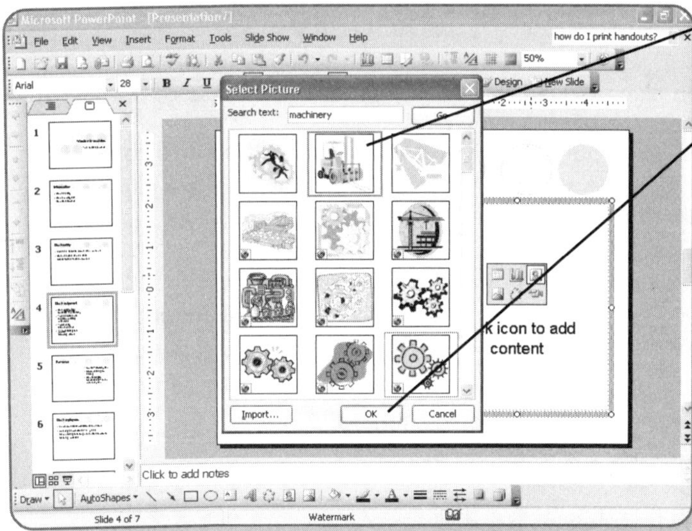

4. Click on the **desired clip**. The clip will be selected.

5. Click on **OK**.

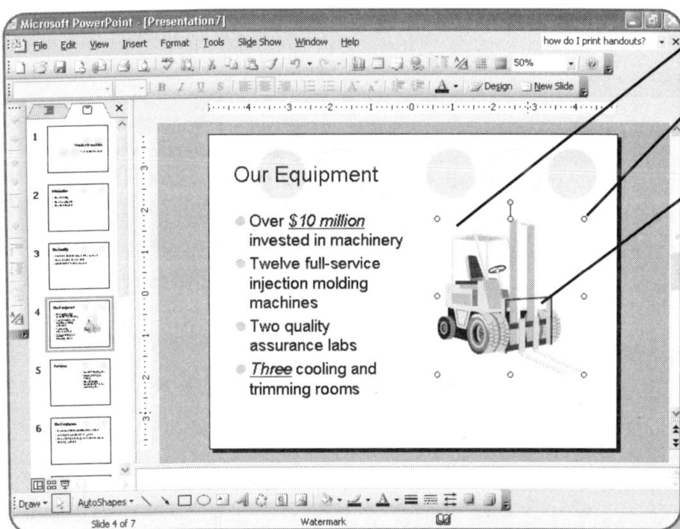

The clip will appear on the slide.

Drag one of the selection handles to resize it.

Drag it by its center to move it.

Adding Clip Art Manually

You can also add clip art to any slide, regardless of its layout.

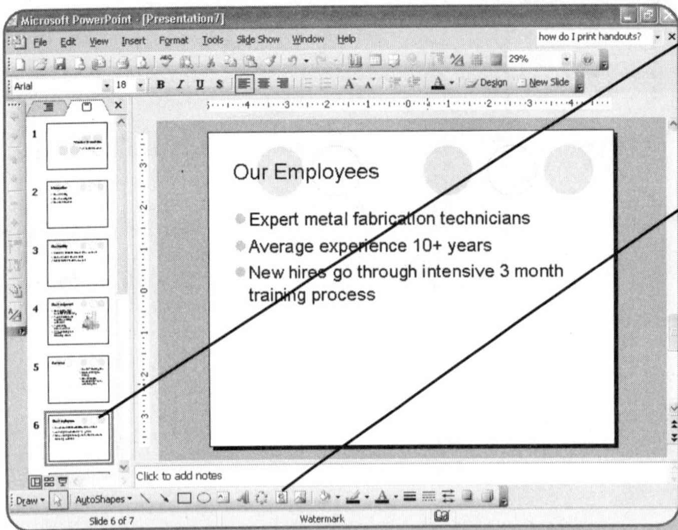

1. **Display** the **slide** to which you want to add the clip art image. The slide will appear in Normal view.

2. **Click** on the **Insert Clip Art button** on the Drawing toolbar. The Clip Art task pane will appear.

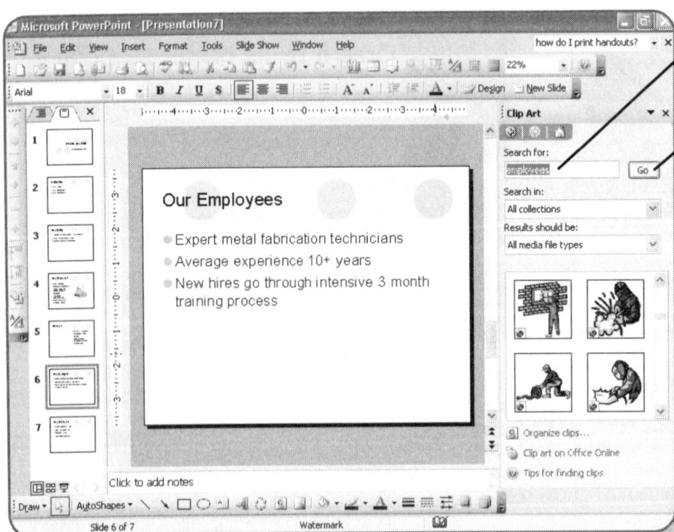

3. **Type** a **keyword** in the Search for box.

4. **Click** on **Go** or **press Enter**. Clips matching that keyword will appear in the task pane.

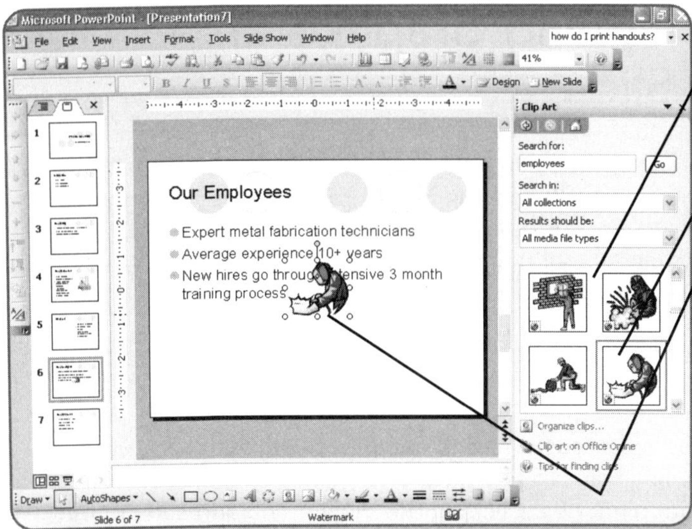

5. **Browse** through the **images** until you find one that fits your needs.

6. **Click** on the **clip**.

It will appear on the slide.

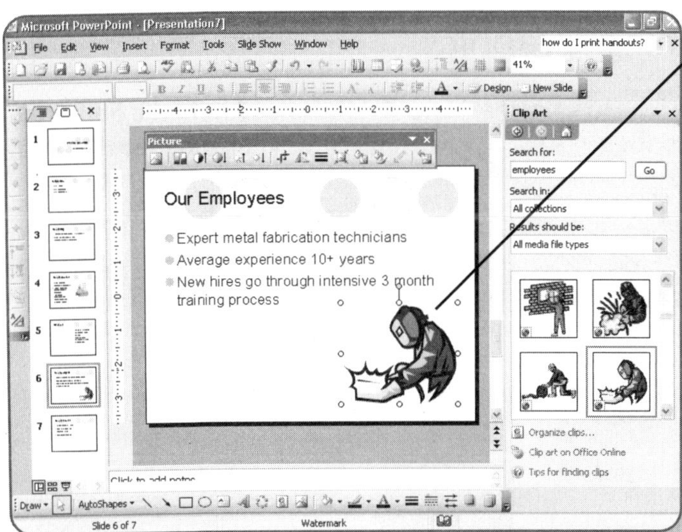

7. **Move** and **resize the clip** as needed.

Positioning Graphics on the Slide

It's not always easy to look at something (such as a picture hanging on a wall) and line it up straight. That's when you need to break out the tools, such as a T-square, a level, or a ruler. You'll find all the tools you need to do the job in the PowerPoint toolbox.

> **TIP**
>
> If you are accustomed to using page layout programs, you may want to use grids and guides to help you position images. Click on the View menu and select Grid and Guides to get started.

Aligning Graphics

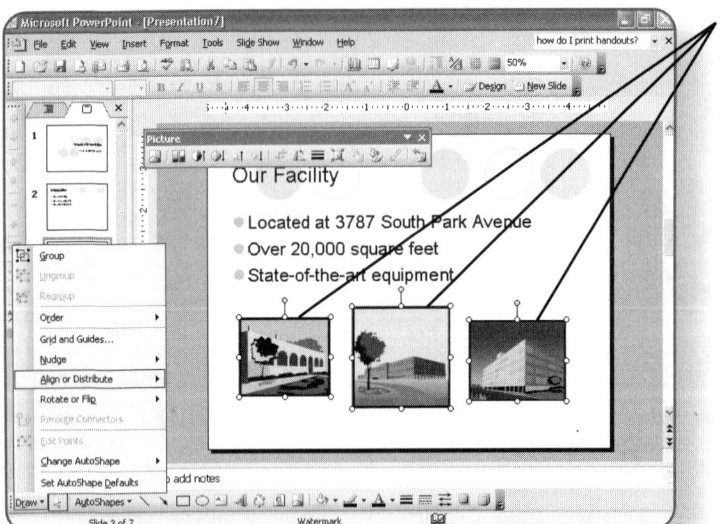

1. **Press and hold** the **Shift key**, and **click** on the **images** that you want to align with each other. The images will be selected.

2. Click on the **Draw button** on the **Drawing toolbar.** A menu will appear.

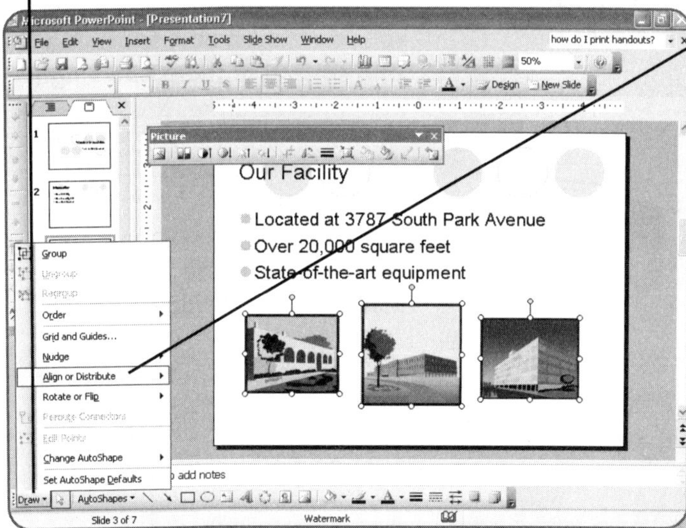

3. Move the mouse pointer to **Align or Distribute.** A second menu will appear.

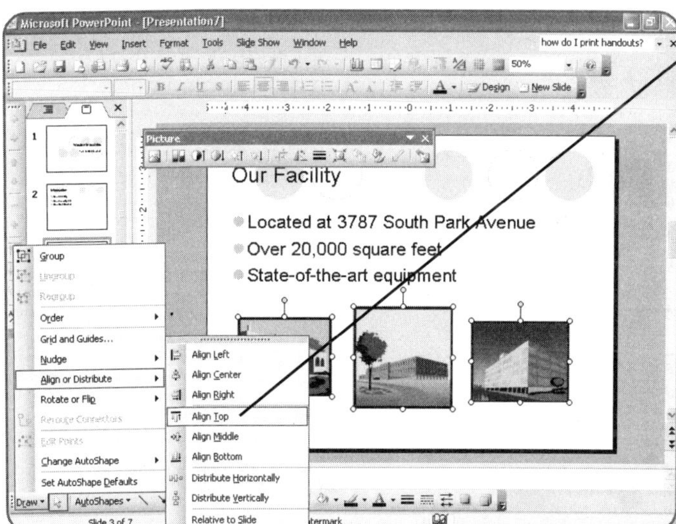

4. Click on the **method** that you want to use to align the objects. The icon to the left of each menu command illustrates the type of alignment. The objects will be aligned relative to each other using the method you've specified.

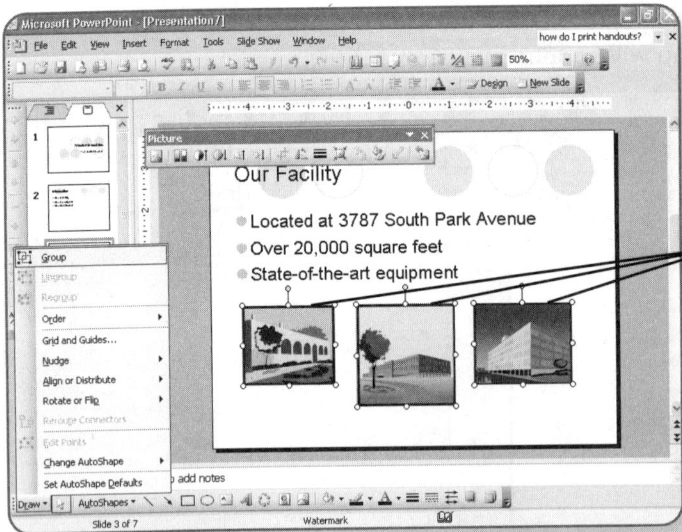

Grouping Graphics

Grouping items is useful when you want to be able to work with several of them as a single item (move, resize, etc.).

1. **Press and hold** the **Shift key**, and **click** on the **images** that you want to combine to create a single image. The images will be selected.

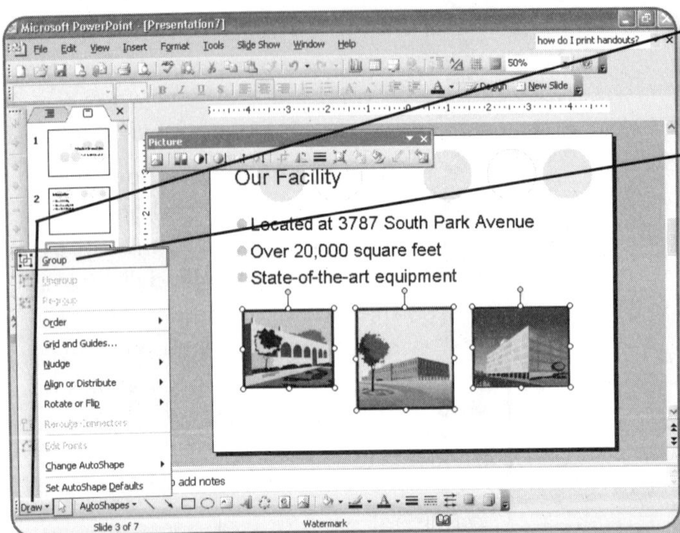

2. **Click** on the **Draw button** on the Drawing toolbar. A menu will appear.

3. **Click** on **Group**. The grouped images can now be treated as a single image.

To ungroup, select the grouped object, click on the Draw button, and select Ungroup.

Designing with WordArt

WordArt is another tool that you'll find in all Microsoft Office applications. It's an easy way to create wavy and 3-D text effects. Here's another chance for you to play, but don't get too carried away. Overdone text effects can be a distraction, and you don't want to lose a good audience.

Creating the WordArt Object

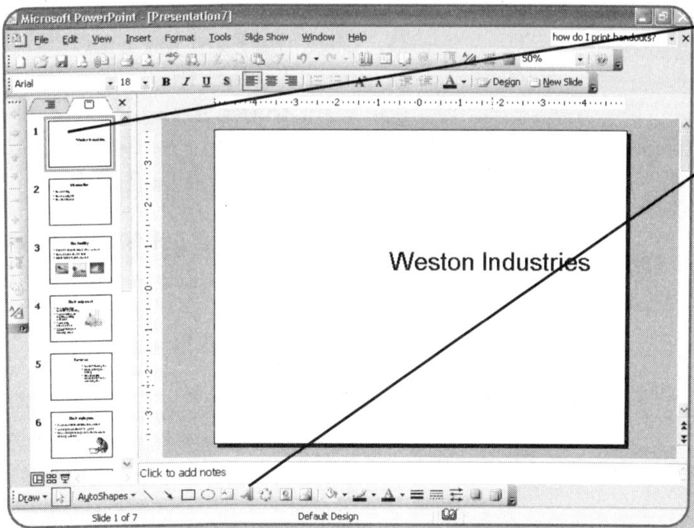

1. **Display** the **slide** that will contain the WordArt object. The slide will appear in Normal view.

2. **Click** on the **Insert WordArt button** on the Drawing toolbar. The WordArt Gallery dialog box will open.

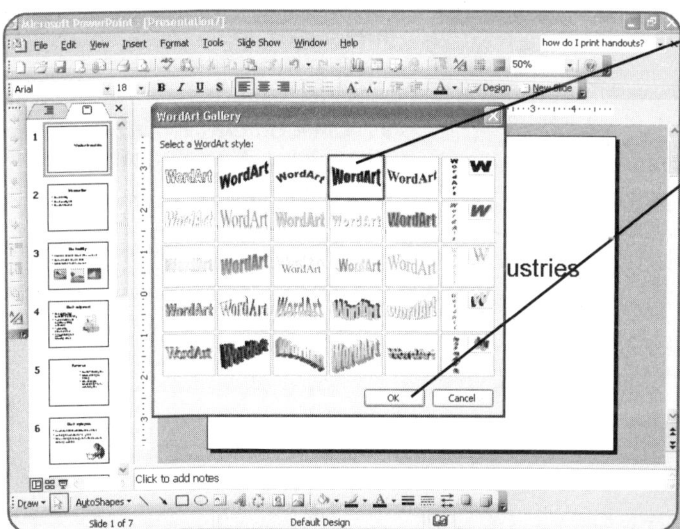

3. **Click** on the **WordArt style** that you want to use. The style will be selected.

4. **Click** on **OK**. The Edit WordArt Text dialog box will open.

5. **Select** the **text** in the Text list box, if necessary, and **type** the **text** you want to appear in the WordArt object.

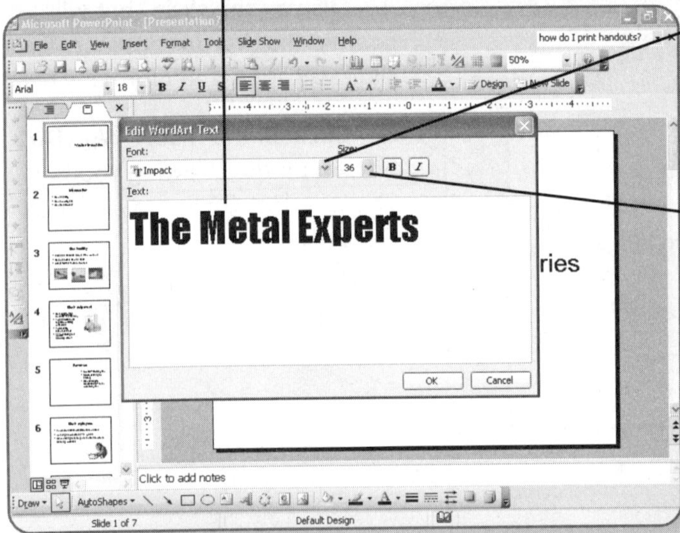

6. **Click** the **Font list box arrow** and select the font that you want to use in the WordArt object. The font name will appear in the Font list box.

7. **Click** the **Size list box arrow** and select the font size for the WordArt object. The font size will appear in the Size list box.

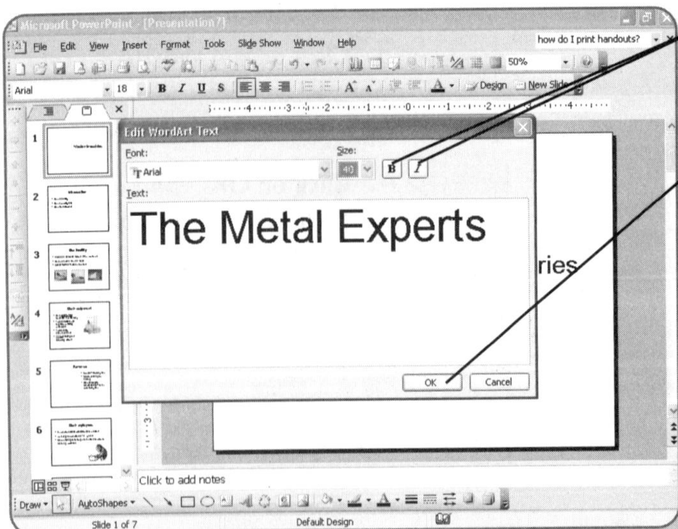

8. **Click** on the **Bold** or **Italic buttons** to apply these styles to the text.

9. **Click** on **OK**. The dialog box will close and the WordArt object will appear on the slide.

Formatting WordArt

After the WordArt has been placed, you can format it in several ways:

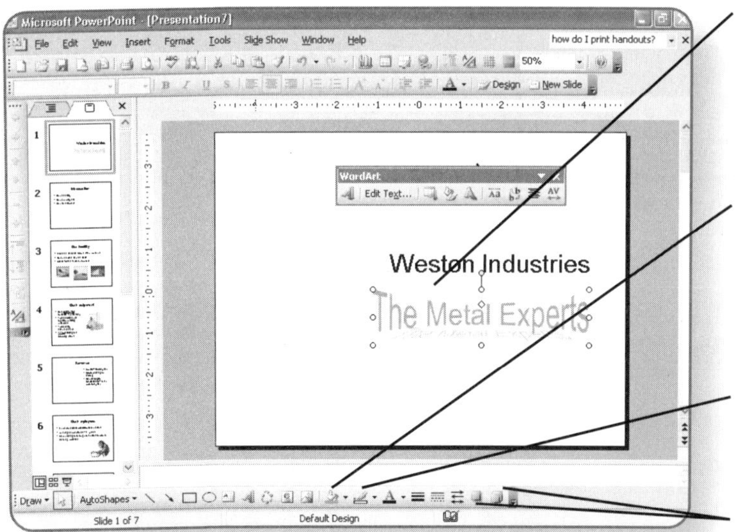

- Double-click the WordArt to reopen the Edit WordArt Text dialog box at any time. Edit the text as needed and click OK to close it when done.
- Change the color of the WordArt with the Fill Color button. You can also apply fill effects such as gradients and textures.
- Change the line color outlining each letter with the Line Color button.
- Apply a shadow or 3-D effect with the Shadow or 3D button. See "Adding a Shadow or 3-D Effect" later in this chapter.

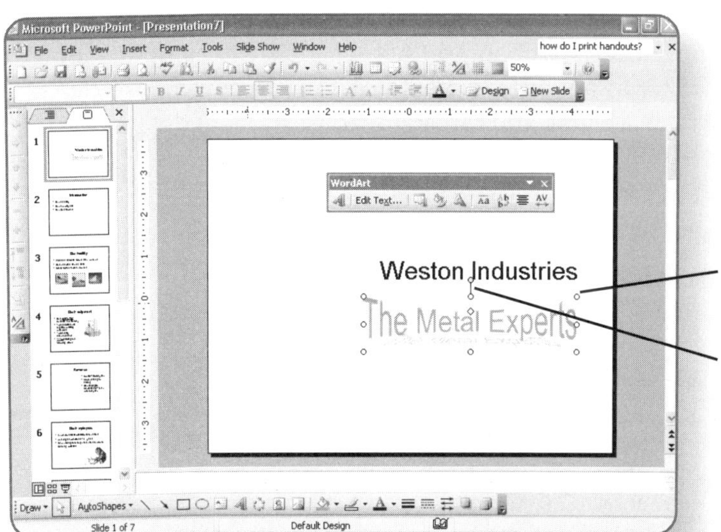

Resizing and Rotating WordArt

In addition to changing the WordArt's color, you can also resize and rotate it.

- Click and drag a handle to resize it.
- Click and drag the Rotate handle to rotate it.

Changing the WordArt's Shape

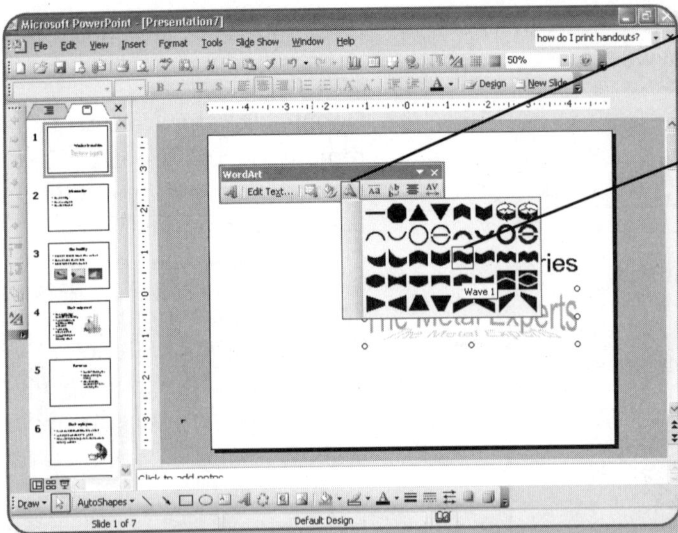

1. **Click** on the **WordArt Shape button** on the WordArt toolbar. A list of shapes will appear.
2. **Click** on a **shape**. The shape of the WordArt object will change.

Adding Line Art

When you need a box, a circle, arrows, or callouts, you'll find a variety of ready-made styles from which to choose. When you're looking for banners and stars, or some irregular shapes, there's probably an AutoShape that can do the job. AutoShapes are easy to create. With just a few mouse clicks, you have a shape you can adjust to fit your needs.

Drawing a Line

1. **Click** on the **Line button**. The mouse pointer will turn into a crosshair.

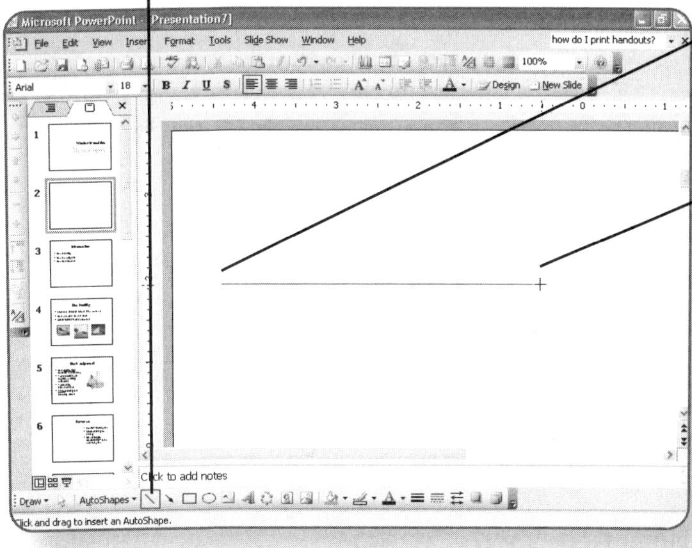

2. **Position** the **mouse pointer** where the line should begin, and **press and hold** the **left mouse button**.

3. **Drag** to where the line should end and **release** the **mouse button**. The line will appear.

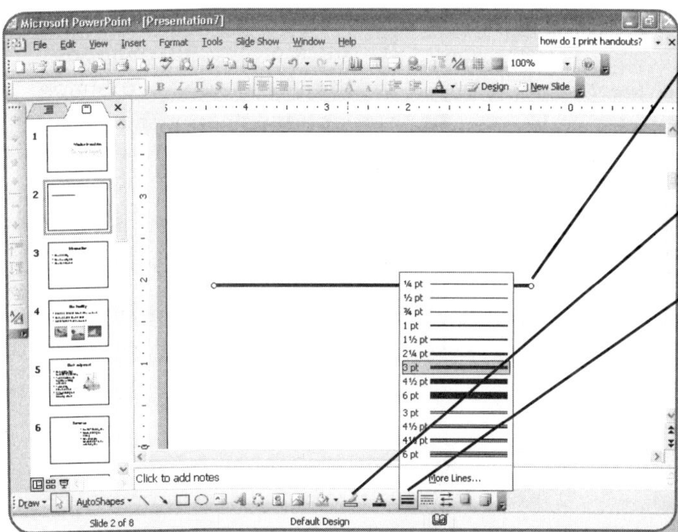

After drawing a line, you can move it by dragging it, or you can resize it by dragging one of its handles.

You can also change its color with the Line Color button

You can adjust its thickness with the Line Style button.

Drawing a Rectangle or Oval

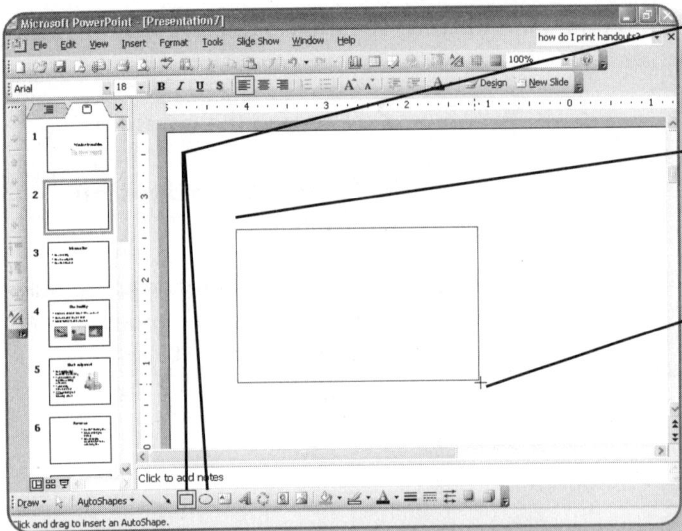

1. **Click** on the **Rectangle** or **Oval button**. The mouse pointer will turn into a crosshair.
2. **Position** the **mouse pointer** where the shape should begin, and **press and hold** the **left mouse button**.
3. **Drag** to where the shape should end and **release** the **mouse button**. The shape will appear.

Drawing an AutoShape

AutoShapes offer a wider variety of drawing options than just ovals, rectangles, and lines.

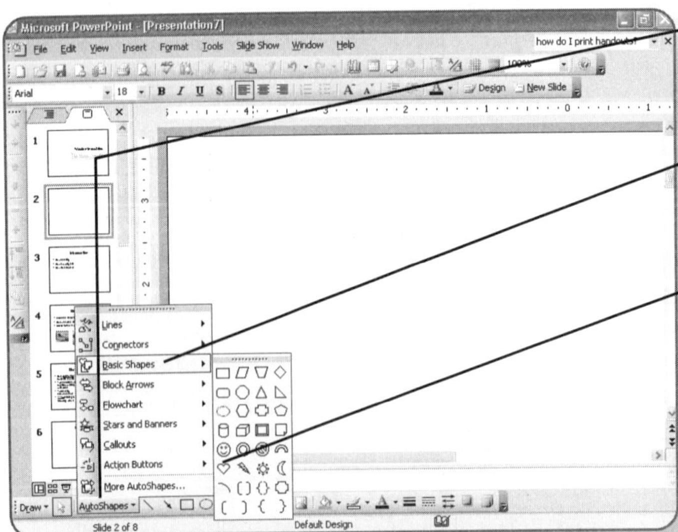

1. **Click** on the **AutoShapes button**. A menu of AutoShape categories will appear.
2. **Move** the mouse pointer to a **category**. A list of shapes will appear.
3. **Click** on a **shape.** The mouse pointer will turn into a crosshair.

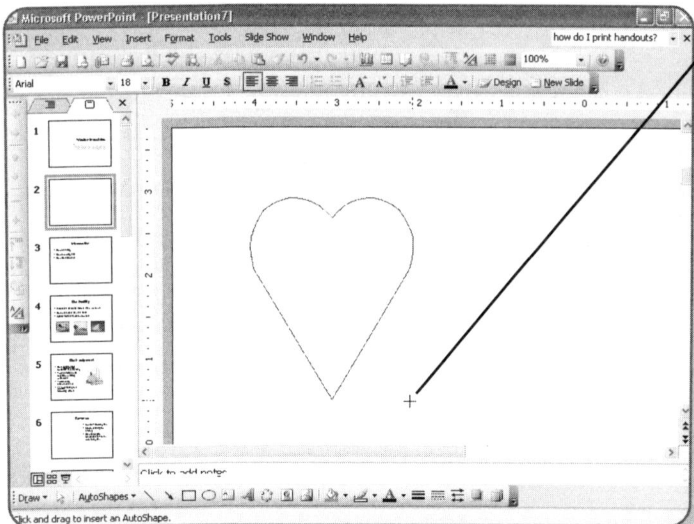

4. Click and drag the **mouse pointer** across the area on the slide where you want the **AutoShape** to appear. An outline will appear on the slide.

5. Release the **mouse button** when the shape is the desired size. The shape will appear on the slide, filled in with the default fill color.

Recoloring the AutoShape

You can change the color with which an AutoShape is filled and/or the color of its border.

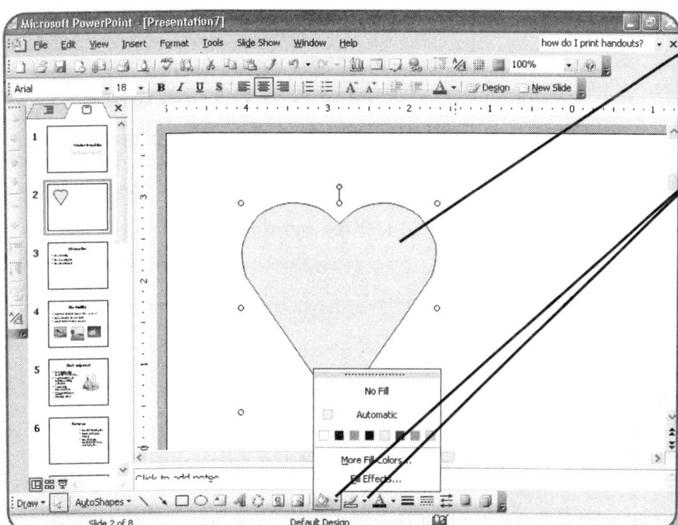

1. Click on the **AutoShape** that you want to change. The AutoShape will be selected.

2. Click on the **down arrow** next to the Fill Color or Line Color buttons. A menu of colors will appear.

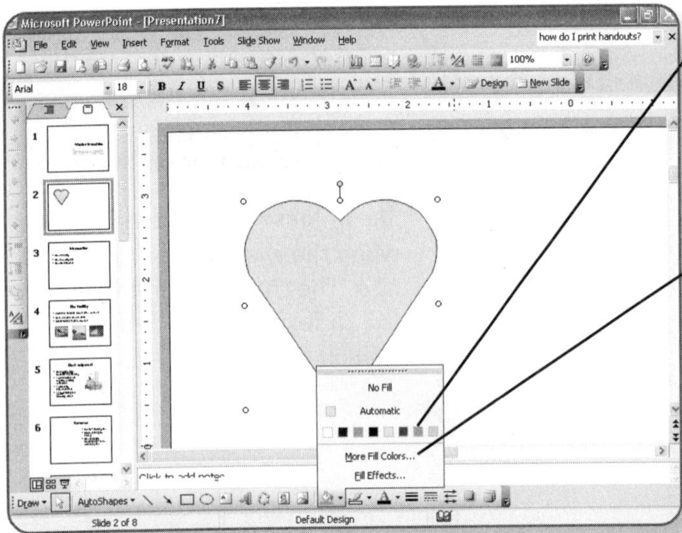

3. Select a **color** from the menu. The color will be applied to the shape.

> **NOTE**
>
> As with other objects, you can choose a placeholder color, you can choose More Fill Colors for a specific solid color, or you can choose Fill Effects for gradients, textures, etc.

Adding a Shadow or 3-D Effect

Sometimes, adding a shadow or 3-D effect to a shape makes it appear to stand out from the slide. This is an easy way to make subtle enhancements that will attract the audience's eye.

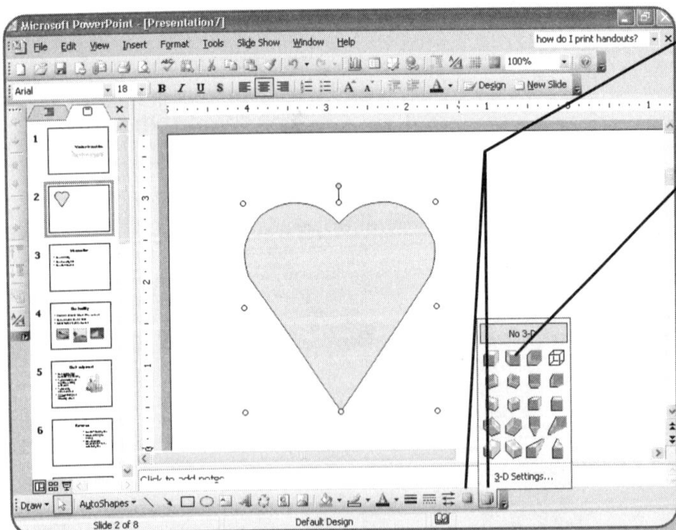

1. Click on the **Shadow Style button** or **3-D Style button**. A list of styles will appear.

2. Click on a **style**. The effect will be applied to the shape.

9

Using Digital Photographs

If you enjoy taking pictures and have a scanner attached to your computer, consider using your own photographs in your presentation. Before you begin scanning photos, set up the scanner and install all the software and drivers necessary to operate it. The scanner software may also come with photo-editing software. Since each scanner comes with its own software, read the user manual carefully so that you can operate the scanner efficiently. Once this is accomplished, it's time to sort through the photo album and select a few pictures to scan. In this chapter, you'll learn how to:

- Scan photographs and place the images directly on a presentation slide
- Resize and crop images after they are inserted on a slide
- Do minor photo touch-ups, such as adjusting the brightness and contrast

Scanning Photographs

Windows XP has built-in support for a number of scanners. If you have a supported scanner and Windows XP, you can scan directly into PowerPoint using the Windows-based scanner interface. You can do it with other Windows versions too, but the interface may vary from the one shown here.

1. **Position** the **photograph** in the scanner.
2. **Display** the **slide** on which you want to insert the scanned photograph.
3. **Click** on **Insert**. The Insert menu will appear.

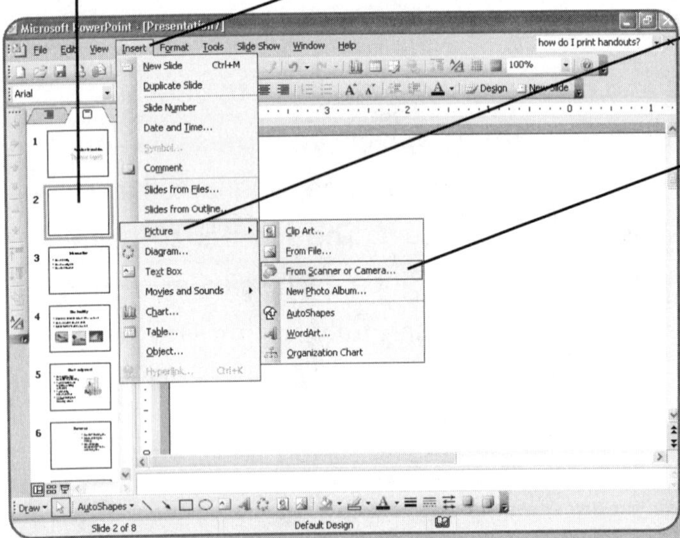

4. **Move** the mouse pointer to **Picture**. The Picture menu will appear.
5. **Click** on **From Scanner or Camera**. The Insert Picture from Scanner or Camera dialog box will open.

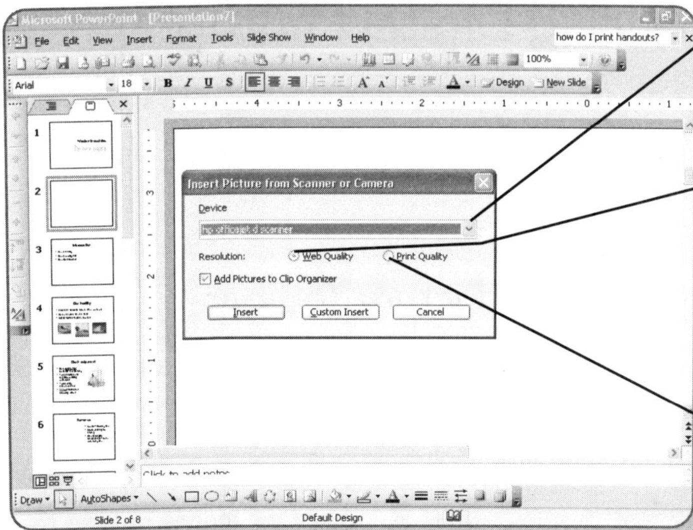

6. Click on the **Device drop-down list** and select the scanner from the list. The scanner name will appear in the list box.

7a. Click on the **Web Quality option button** if the presentation will be viewed over the Internet or on a computer screen. The option will be selected.

OR

7b. Click on the **Print Quality option button** if the presentation will be printed. The option will be selected.

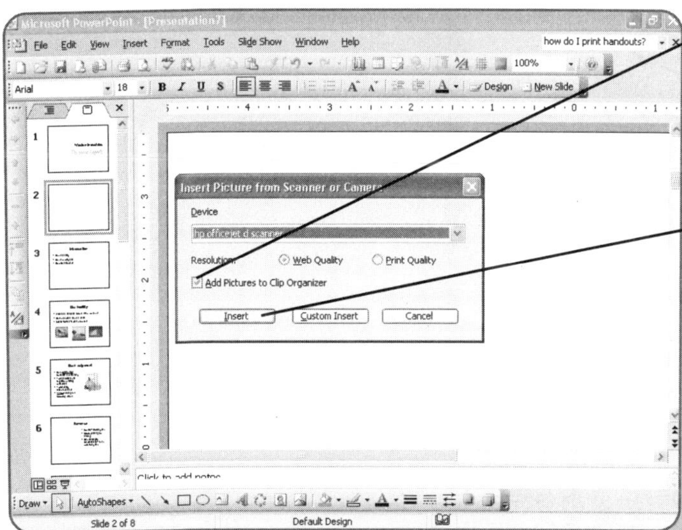

8. Click the **Add Pictures to Clip Organizer check box** if you want to keep a copy of the photo in the Clip Organizer. A check will appear in the check box.

9. Click on the **Insert button.** The scanner will scan the picture, and it will appear on the slide.

Enhancing Digital Photographs

After you've inserted a picture into a presentation slide, you may want the picture to look different. If you have simple image enhancements to make, you'll find a number of tools on the Picture toolbar.

Displaying the Picture Toolbar

The Picture toolbar should be displayed automatically when a picture is selected. If it doesn't, you can force it to appear.

1. **Click** on **View**. The View menu will appear.

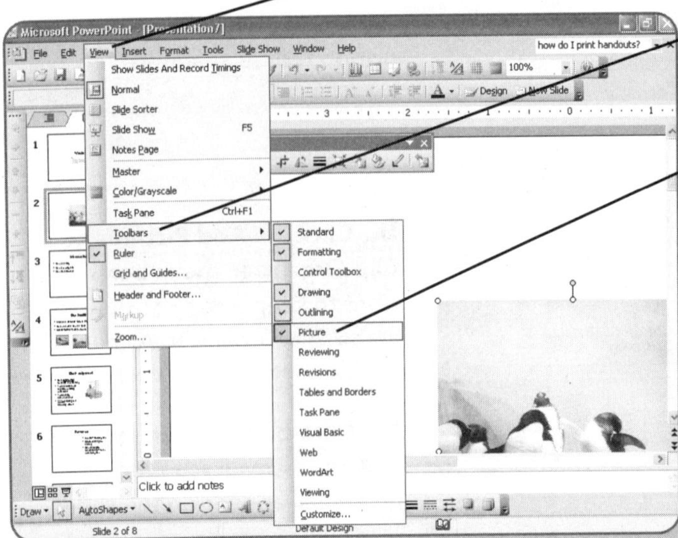

2. **Move** the mouse pointer to **Toolbars**. The Toolbars menu will appear.

3. **Click** on **Picture**. The Picture toolbar will appear.

Cropping Pictures

You can remove unwanted parts of an image easily with the Crop button.

1. **Click** on the **Crop button** to display the crop marks.
2. **Click** and **drag** the **crop handles** until the part of the picture that you want to keep is inside the crop marks.

The crop handles are the black lines in the corners and sides of the image.

> **TIP**
>
> To reset cropping, drag the crop handles back out again.

3. **Click** on the **Crop button** again or **press Esc** to apply the changes to the image.

Rotating the Picture

There are several ways to rotate a picture.

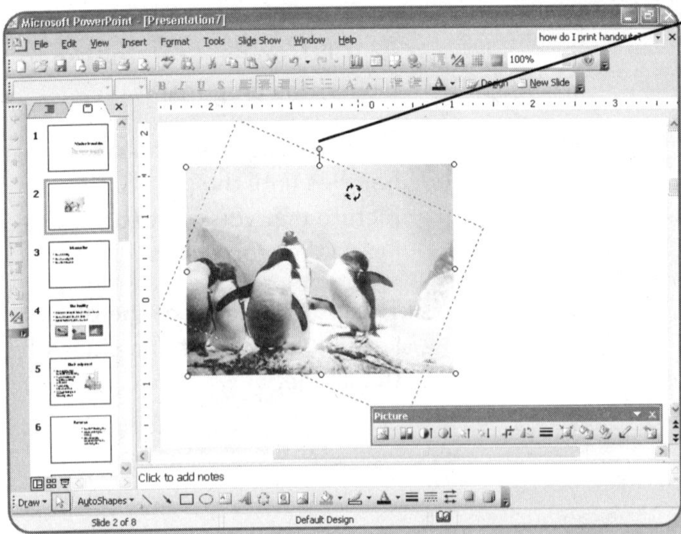

- **Click** and **drag** the **rotate handle** to the right or left. The picture will turn as you move the mouse.

- **Click** on the **Rotate Left button**. The picture will turn counterclockwise by 90 degrees.
- **Click** on **Draw**, **click** on **Rotate or Flip**, and then **click** on a **rotation**.

Adjusting Brightness and Contrast

Sometimes all you need to make a picture look better is a little image enhancement. When an adjustment to the brightness or contrast is in order:

- **Click** on the **More Contrast button** to add definition between the light and dark colors in the image.
- **Click** on the **Less Contrast button** to soften images that are too harsh.
- **Click** on the **Less Brightness button** to make an image appear darker.
- **Click** on the **More Brightness button** to lighten the colors in an image.

Changing the Image Mode

The default mode for an image is Automatic. It shows in color. To convert the image to grayscale, black-and-white, or a watermark, select one of those modes instead.

1. Click on the **Color button** on the Picture toolbar. A menu will appear.

2. Click on the **desired mode**.

- To give images an elegant, old-fashioned look, use the Grayscale command.
- Give images a faded look by selecting Washout. This command creates a light-colored, almost transparent version of the image. The washout effect works well when you don't want an image to stand out on a page, or if you want to place text over the image.

10

Incorporating Tables

You've probably seen tables used in spreadsheets and word processing documents. Tables are a great way to organize information into neat rows and columns. They can be simple, or you can make them fashionable with designer lines and colors. In this chapter, you'll learn how to:

- Insert a table on a slide and add text to the table cells
- Change the size of the table and the size of rows and columns within the table
- Create borders around the table and around individual cells in the table

Creating a Table

Before you begin building a table, you should have an approximate idea of the size you want. If you aren't exactly sure, you can always add and delete rows and columns later.

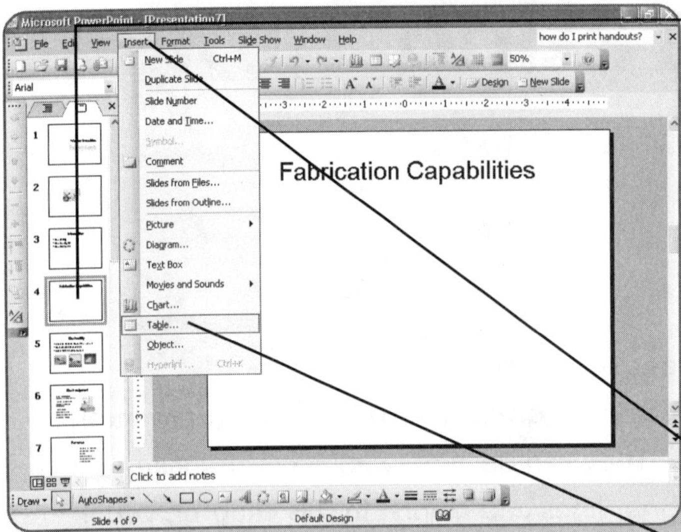

1. **Open** the **slide** on which you want to insert a table. The slide will appear in Normal view.

> **TIP**
>
> Place the table on a slide that has plenty of room for it. You might want to switch to a different slide layout first.

2. **Click** on **Insert**. The Insert menu will appear.
3. **Click** on **Table**. The Insert Table dialog box will appear.

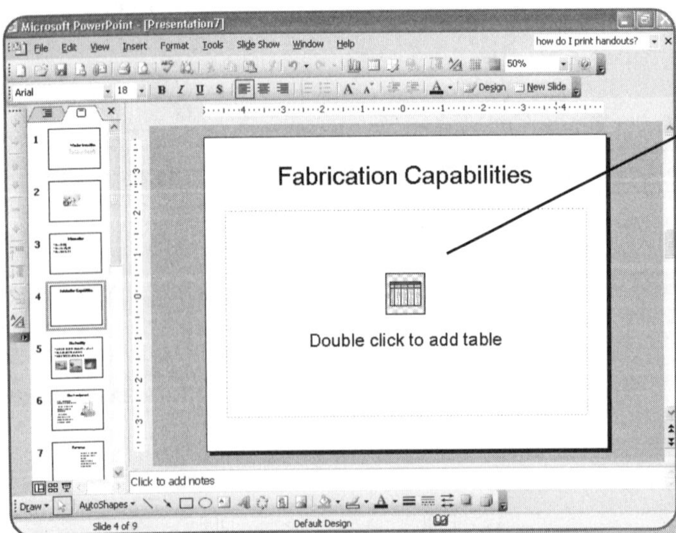

> **NOTE**
>
> Instead of steps 1-3, you can display a slide that has a Table placeholder layout, and then double-click the placeholder icon.

4. **Click** in the **Number of columns text box** and **type** the **number of columns** that should be contained in the table.

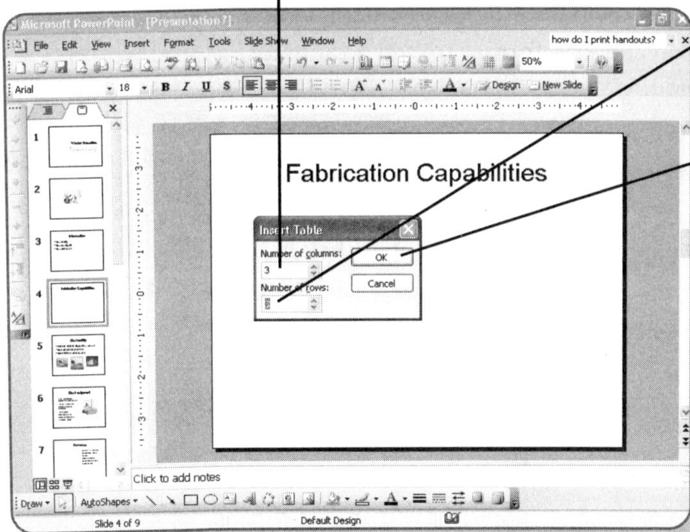

5. **Click** in the **Number of rows text box** and **type** the **number of rows** in the table.

6. **Click** on **OK**.

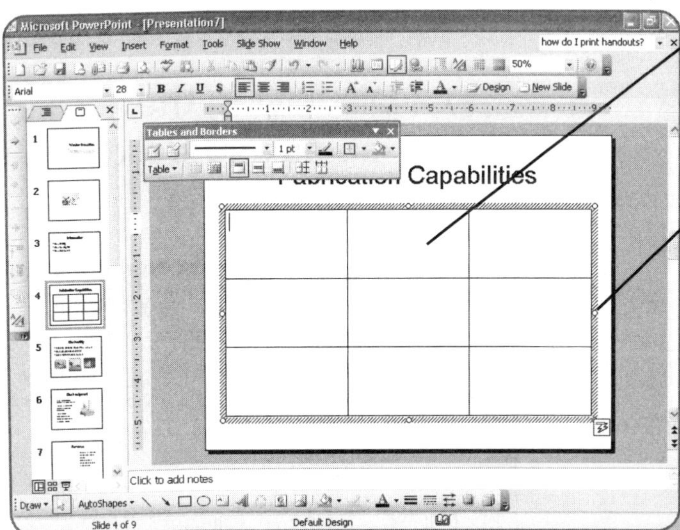

The table will appear on the slide.

> **TIP**
>
> Click and drag the resize handles to change the width and height of the table.

Inserting Text into the Table

After creating the table, you can add words to the different cells. You can also format text in a table just as you would on a slide.

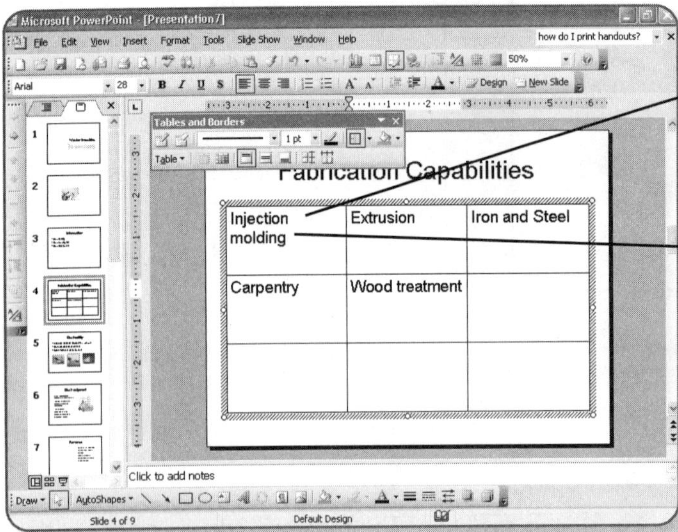

Adding Text

1. **Click** in the **cell** where you want to place the text. The insertion bar will appear in the cell.
2. **Type** the **text**. Several lines of text can appear in a single cell.
3. **Press** the **Tab key**. The insertion point will move to the next cell.
4. **Repeat steps 2 and 3** as needed to enter more text.

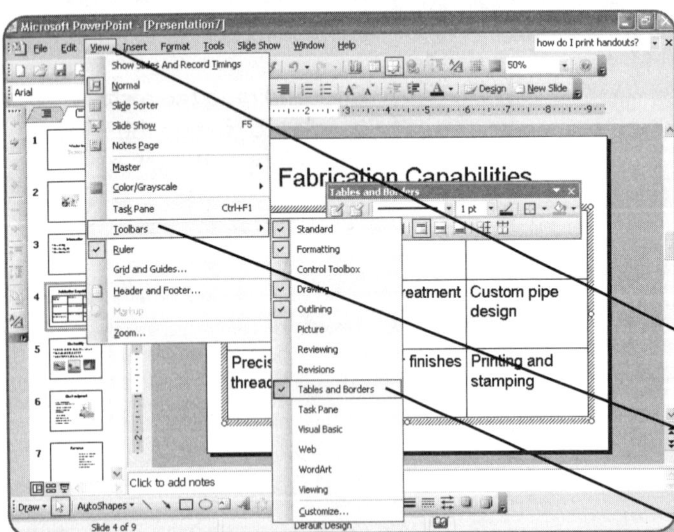

Displaying the Tables and Borders Toolbar

If the Tables and Borders toolbar does not automatically appear when you are working with a table, you can display it manually.

1. **Click** on **View**. The View menu will open.
2. **Point** to **Toolbars**. The submenu will open.
3. **Click** on **Tables and Borders**. The Tables and Borders toolbar will appear.

Aligning Text in a Cell

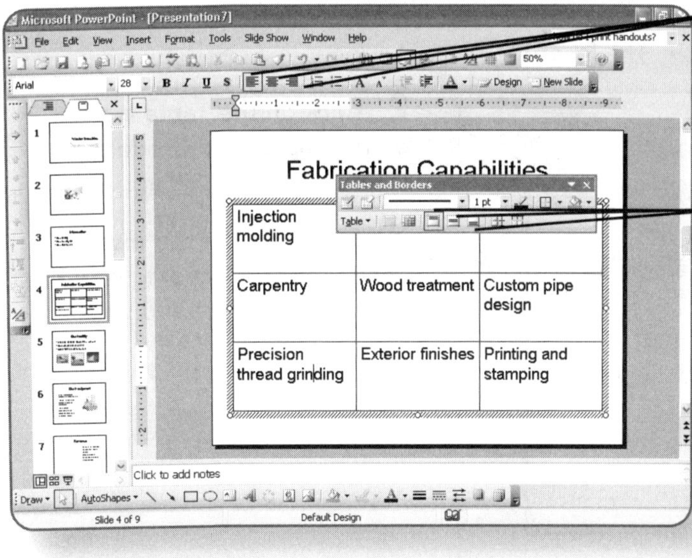

Use the **Align Left**, **Center**, and **Align Right** alignment buttons on the Formatting toolbar for horizontal alignment within cells.

Use the **Align Top**, **Center Vertically**, and **Align Bottom** alignment buttons on the Tables and Borders toolbar for vertical alignment within cells.

Modifying the Table

If you find that a table doesn't contain enough cells, you may need to add a few rows or columns. Or, if you got carried away and have more table space than you need, start deleting extra cells.

Adding Rows and Columns

1. **Click** in the **row or column** that will be adjacent to the new row. The insertion bar will appear in a cell.

2. **Click** on the **Table button** on the Tables and Borders toolbar. A menu will appear.

3. **Select** one of the **Insert commands**, depending on what you want to insert and where.

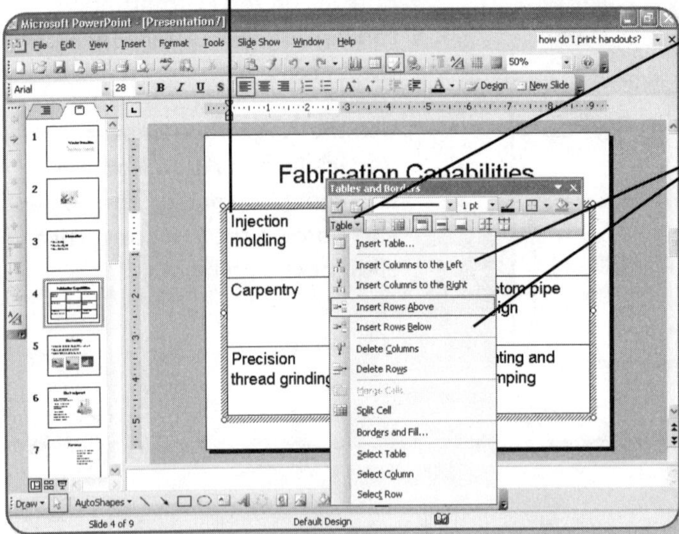

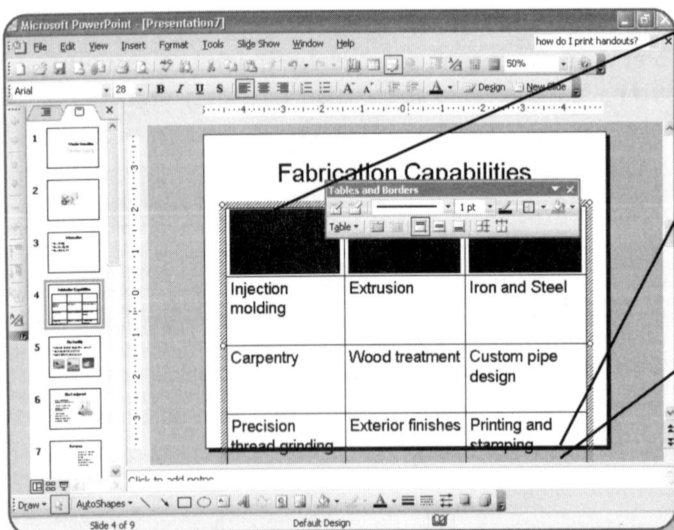

The new row or column will appear in your table. It will be highlighted.

The table might hang over the edge of the slide after the insertion. If it does, drag a handle to resize it. See "Resizing the Table" later in this chapter.

To add a new row at the bottom, click in the last cell and press Tab.

Deleting Rows and Columns

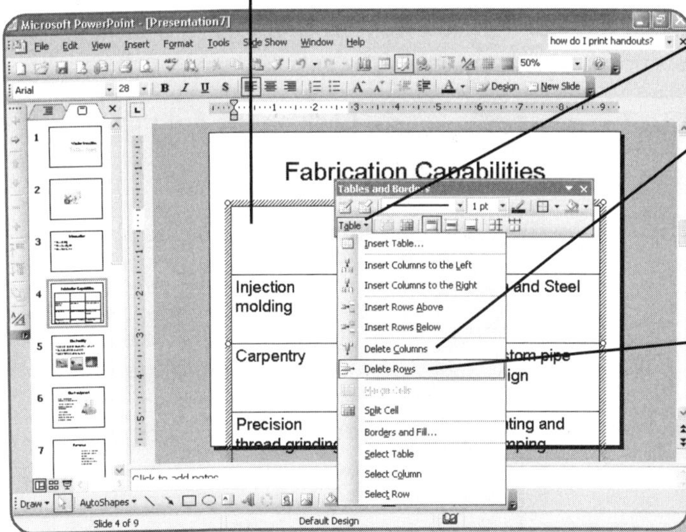

1. **Click** in a **cell** that is contained in the row or column that you want to delete. The cursor will appear in the cell.

2. **Click** on the **Table button**. A menu will appear.

3a. **Click** on **Delete Columns**. The column in which the insertion point was positioned will be deleted.

OR

3b. **Click** on **Delete Rows**. The row in which the insertion point was positioned will be deleted.

Merging Cells

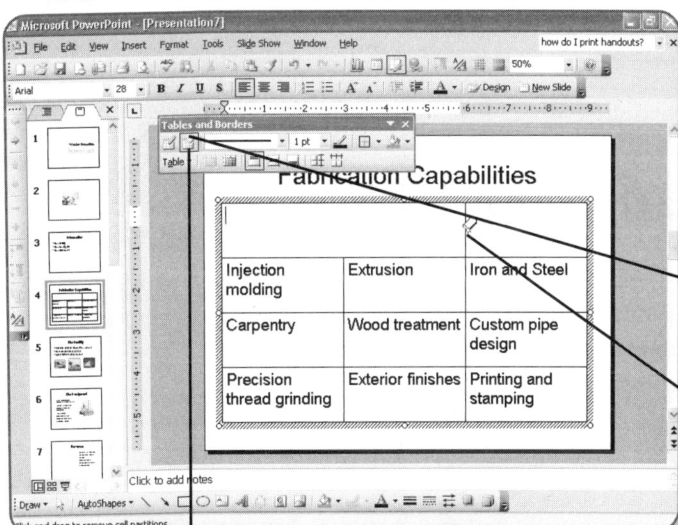

If you want to create a row across the top of the table in which to make a heading, you can combine several cells into a single cell.

1. **Click** on the **Eraser button**. The mouse pointer will turn into an eraser.

2. **Click** on the **cell border** between the two cells that you want to merge. The border between the two cells will be deleted.

3. **Click** on the **Eraser button** again when you are finished merging cells.

Splitting Cells

You can also split a cell into several cells to make space for additional information.

1. Click in the **cell** that you want to split into two cells. The insertion bar will appear in the cell.

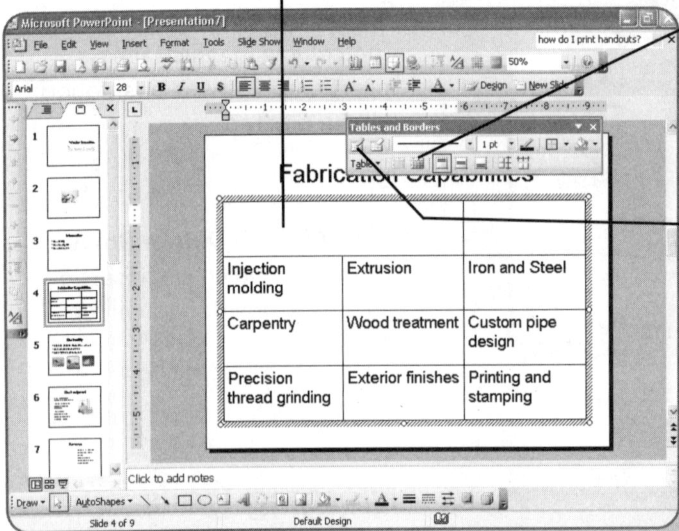

2. Click on the **Split Cell button**. A new cell will be added to the table.

> **TIP**
>
> You can also click the Draw Table button and then drag the cursor where you want additional cell borders.

Resizing the Table

Sometimes tables need to be resized to fit on a slide or to display information in a neat and tidy format. Not only can you change the outer dimensions of a table, but you can make rows wider and cells taller.

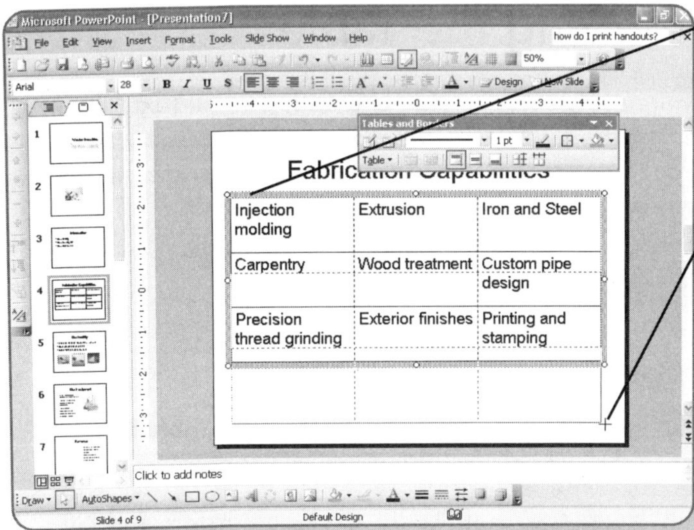

1. **Click** on the **table**. The table placeholder and the resize handles will appear around the outside border of the table.
2. **Click** and **drag** a **resize handle**. An outline will show the new size of the table.
3. **Release** the **mouse button**. The table and all of the cells will be resized proportionately.

You can also resize individual rows and columns. To resize rows:

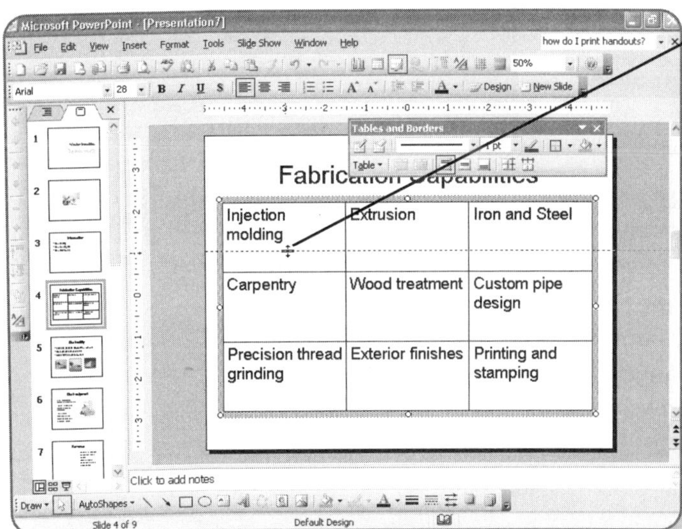

4. **Click** and **drag** on the **border** between two rows. The border will turn to an outline to show how the two rows will be resized.
5. **Release** the **mouse button**. The two rows will be different heights.

Columns work the same way, except you drag the vertical lines between them.

Formatting the Table

After you have created a table and added some text, you may decide that the table lacks color. Spruce up tables by adding background colors and by changing the color and style of the border lines.

Designing a Border

1. **Click** on the **table border**. The table will be selected.

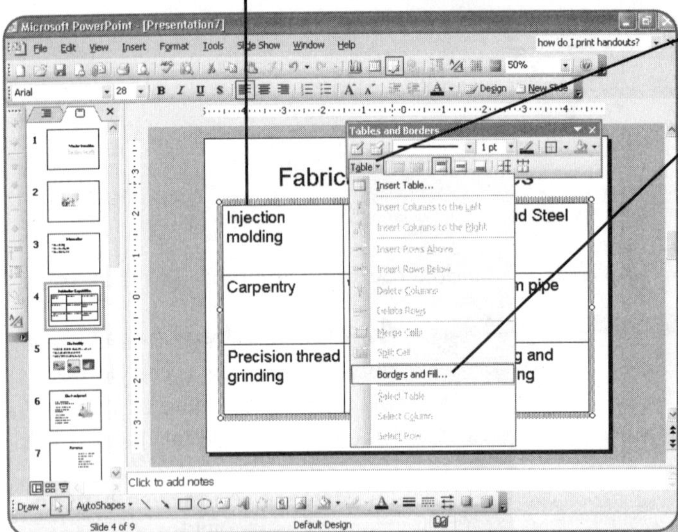

2. **Click** on the **Table button**. A menu will appear.

3. **Click** on **Borders and Fill.** The Format Table dialog box will open, and the Borders tab will be displayed.

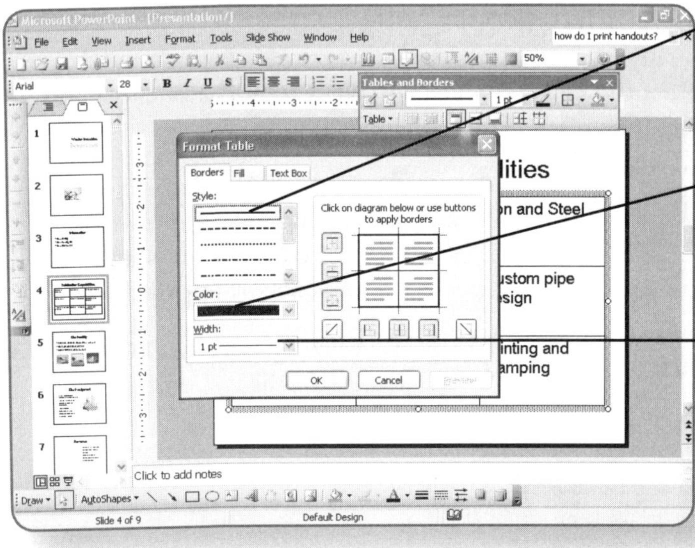

4. **Click** on the **line** in the Style list box that you want to apply to a border. The line style will be selected.

5. **Select** a **color** from the Color list box to apply to the line style. The color will appear in the list box.

6. **Select** a **line width** from the Width list box. The width will appear in the list box.

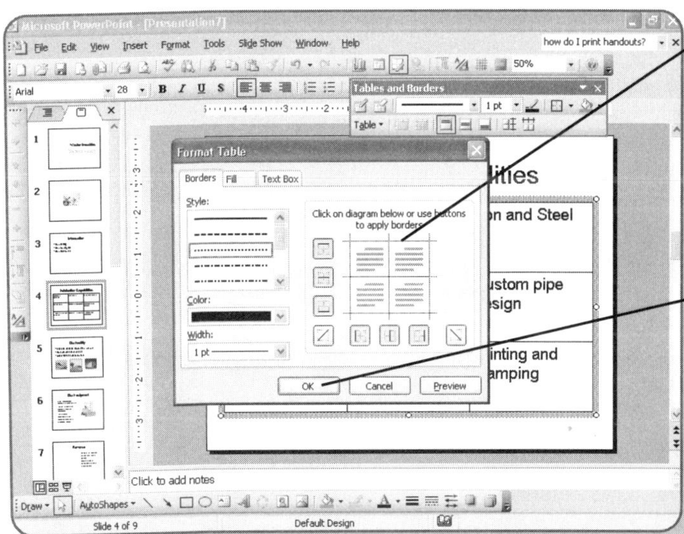

7. **Click** on the **border** in the diagram to which you want to apply the line style. The diagram will be updated with the new border line style. You will need to click once for each border you want to affect.

8. **Click** on **OK** when you are done. The table border will be updated with the new line style format.

Adding Color to Cells

1. Select the **cells** to which you want to add a background fill color. The cells will be highlighted.

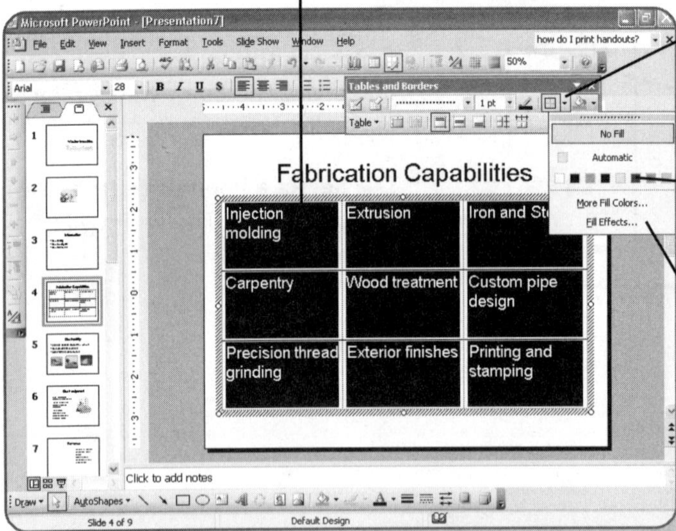

2. Click on the **down arrow** next to the Fill Color button. A list of colors from which you can choose will appear.

3. Click on a **Color**. The selected cells will be filled with the new color.

> **TIP**
>
> Use Fill Effects for gradient and pattern fills.

11

Producing Charts and Graphs

Charts and graphs are the visual representation of a relationship between two or more items. They can show a trend over a period of time or an item's size in relation to the total. All these relationships can be displayed with bars, pies, lines, and scattered dots. Your charts can be flat or 3-D. PowerPoint can create some complex charts, but keep your audience in mind. Ease of understanding should be your major goal. In this chapter, you'll learn how to:

- Use a datasheet to enter information for a graph
- Display datasheet information using different chart and graph formats
- Create a graphical representation of the hierarchy within a group

Entering Data for the Chart

Before building a chart, organize the data you'll be depicting. Most charts compare two types of data, such as a budget where the amount spent on certain items is listed for a range of dates. PowerPoint provides a small example to get you started. Just replace the sample data with your own information.

1. **Display** the **slide** on which you want to insert the chart. The slide will appear in Normal view.

2. **Click** on **Insert**. The Insert menu will appear.

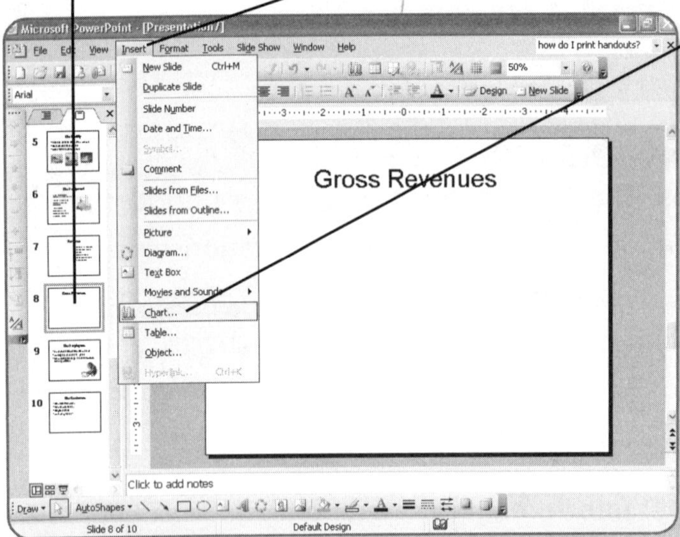

3. **Click** on **Chart**. The sample chart and chart datasheet will appear on the slide.

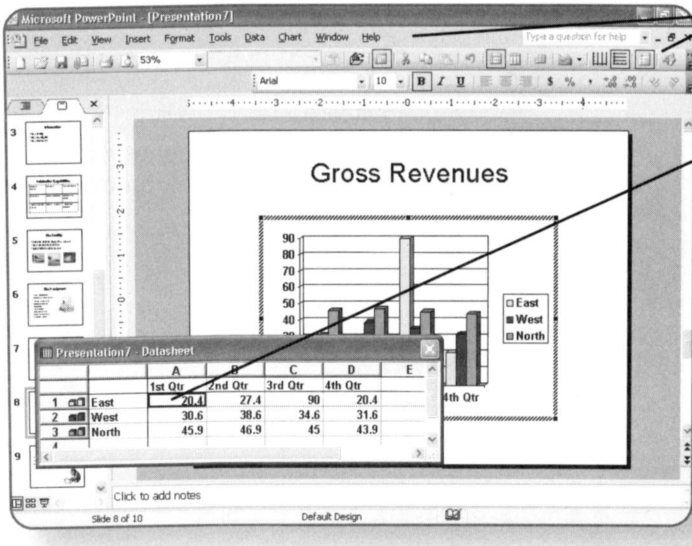

Notice that the toolbars and menus are different while you're working with a chart.

4. Click in a **cell** on the datasheet. The cell's contents will be selected.

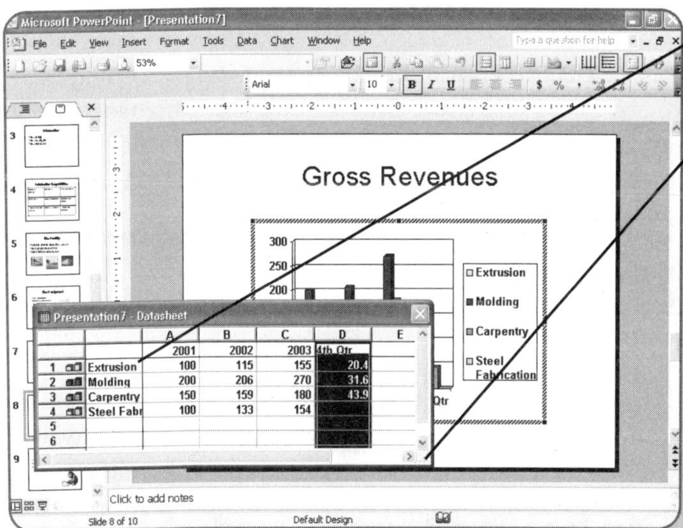

5. Type the **data** that you want to appear in the chart.

You can resize the datasheet to display more rows and columns.

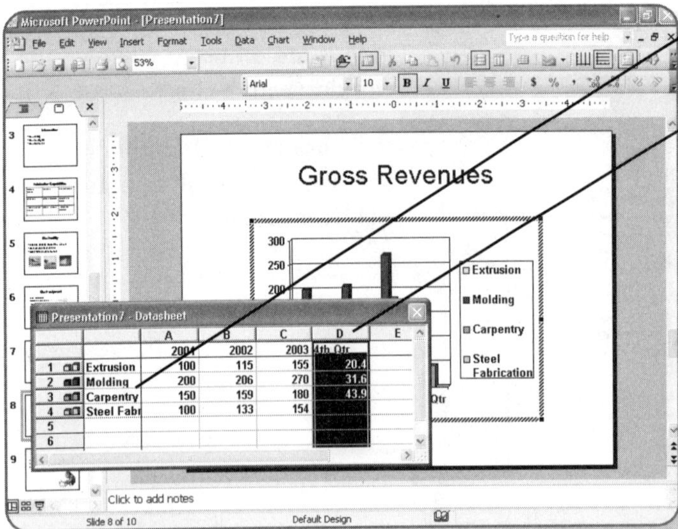

Type in additional rows and columns as needed.

To clear unused rows or columns, click on the row or column heading and press the Delete key.

Exiting and Entering Microsoft Graph

The tools you use to create the chart, as in the preceding section, are called *Microsoft Graph*. You enter Microsoft Graph by starting a new chart or double-clicking an existing one. You exit it by clicking on the slide area outside the chart.

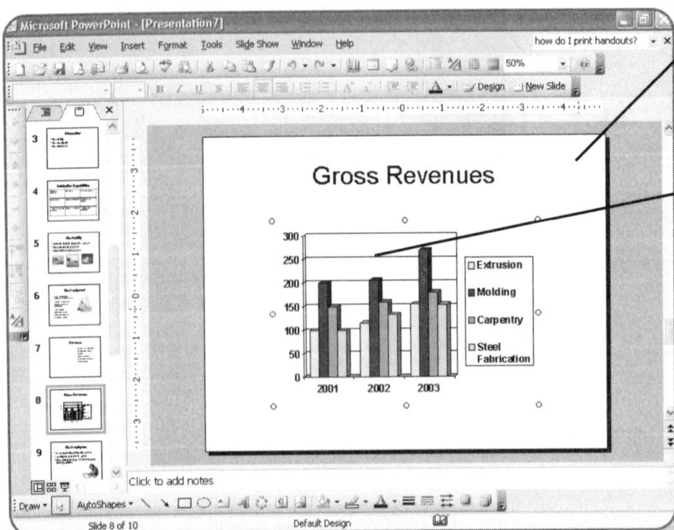

1. **Click** on a **blank area** of the slide. The datasheet will close and your information will appear in the chart.
2. **Double-click** on the **chart**. The Microsoft Graph tools will reopen, including the different menus and toolbar buttons.

Changing How the Data Is Plotted

You can change the meaning of a chart by changing how the data is plotted in the worksheet grid—either by rows or by columns.

1. Double-click on the **chart**. The chart will be selected and the charting tools will appear in the toolbar.

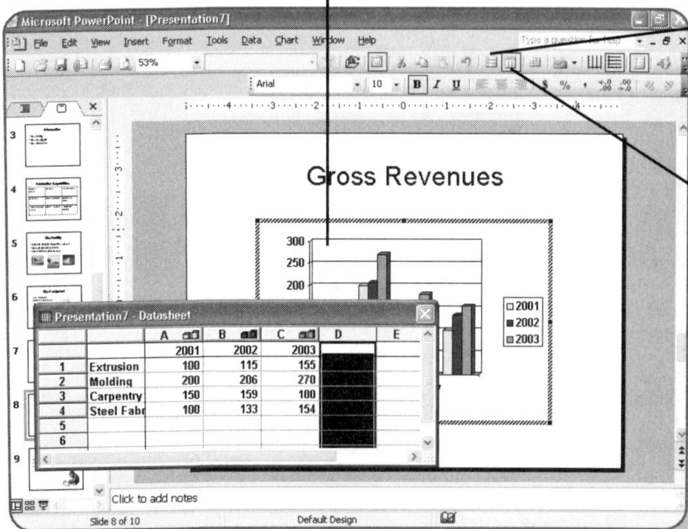

2a. Click on the **By Rows button**. The data will be plotted by rows.

OR

2b. Click on the **By Columns button**. The data will be plotted by columns.

Formatting the Chart

After you have entered all the data into the datasheet, it's time to create charts that will most effectively display the relationship between the two types of data you are comparing.

Selecting a Chart Type

The default chart type is the column chart. You'll also find an assortment of bar charts, pie charts, line charts, scatter charts, and many more. After you select a chart type, customize the chart to make it look the way you want.

1. **Double-click** on the **chart**. The datasheet will open and the Microsoft Graph tools will appear.

2. **Click** on **Chart**. The Chart menu will appear.

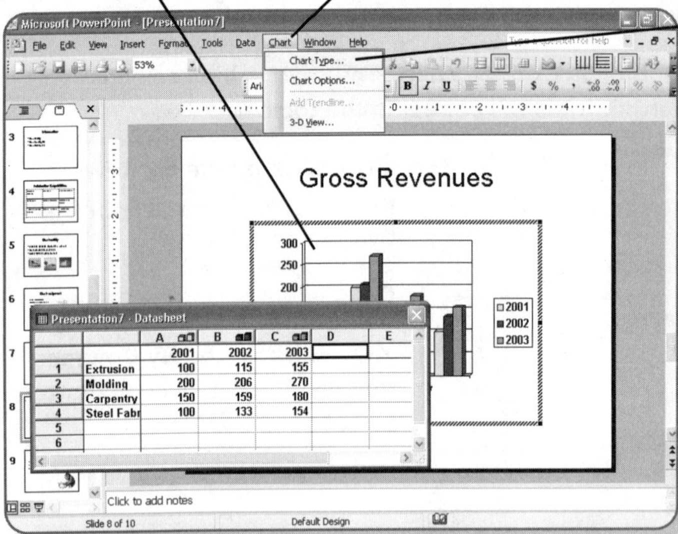

3. **Click** on **Chart Type**. The Chart Type dialog box will open, and the list of standard charts will appear.

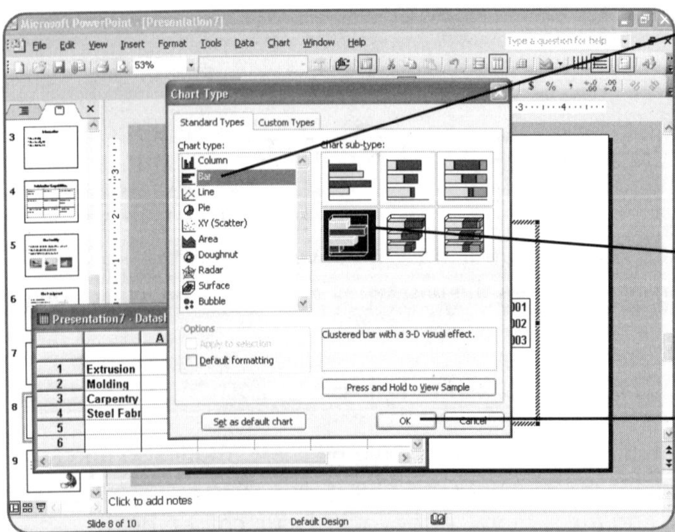

4. **Click** on the **category** of chart in the Chart type list. The category will be selected, and the variations of the chart type will appear in the Chart sub-type area.

5. **Click** on a **style** of chart in the Chart sub-type area. The chart will be selected, and you can read a description of it.

6. **Click** on **OK** when you have selected a chart type. The chart will be updated to display the selected chart type.

Including Text Labels

If the chart appears on a slide that already has a title, you might not need a title on the chart itself. It is available if you want it. Labels for the vertical and horizontal axes are also available.

1. **Double-click** on the **chart**. The chart will be selected.

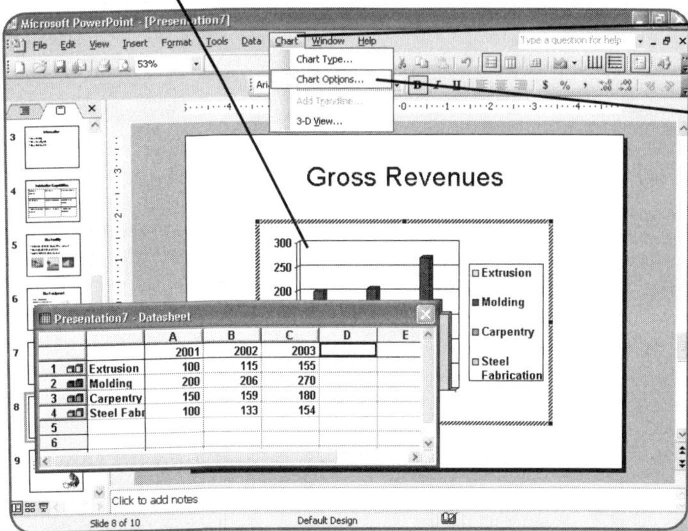

2. **Click** on **Chart**. The Chart menu will appear.

3. **Click** on **Chart Options**. The Chart Options dialog box will open, and the Titles tab will be displayed. If the Titles tab is not selected, click on it.

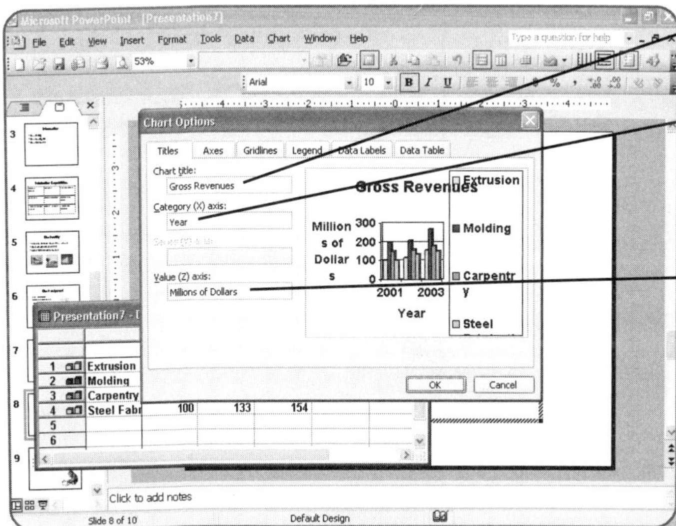

4. **Click** in the **Chart title text box** and **type** a **title** for the chart.

5. **Click** in the **Category (X) axis text box** and **type** a **label** for the information displayed on the X (horizontal) axis.

6. **Click** in the **Value (Z) axis text box** and **type** a **label** for the information displayed on the Z (vertical) axis. This box is available only for 3-D charts.

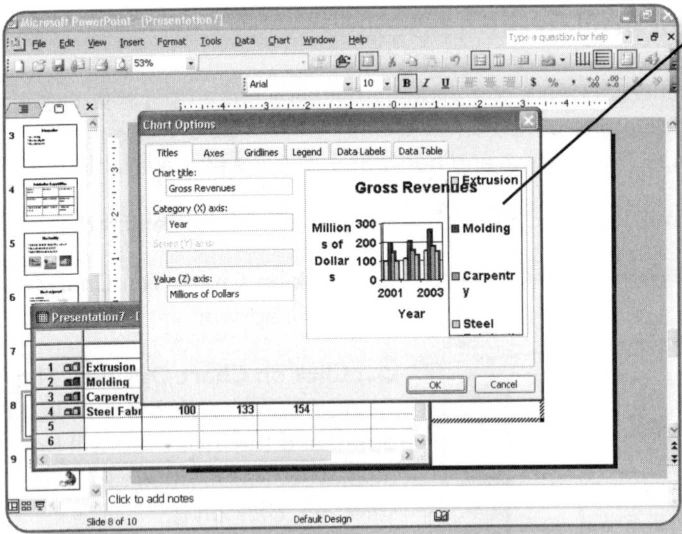

Don't worry if the sample doesn't look right. The fonts and sizing may be off, but it will appear correctly on the actual slide.

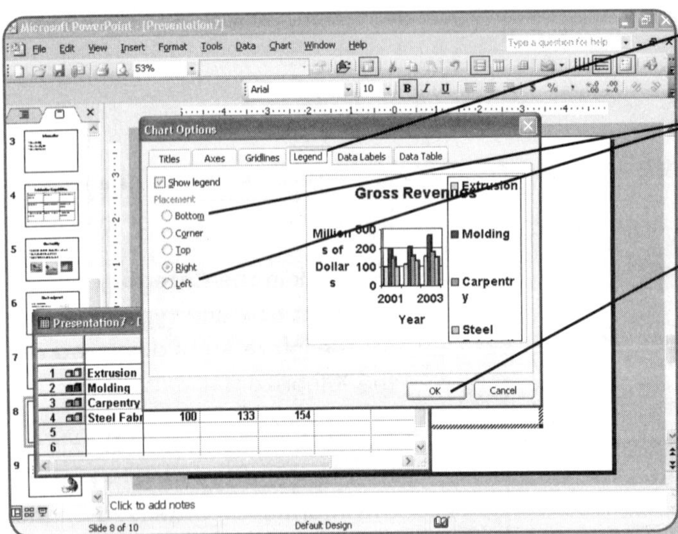

7. **Click** on the **Legend tab**. The legend options will appear.

8. **Click** on a **Placement option button** to move the legend to a different place on the slide.

9. **Click** on **OK**. Your changes will be applied to the chart.

Changing a Font

You can change the fonts and font sizes used in various elements of the chart.

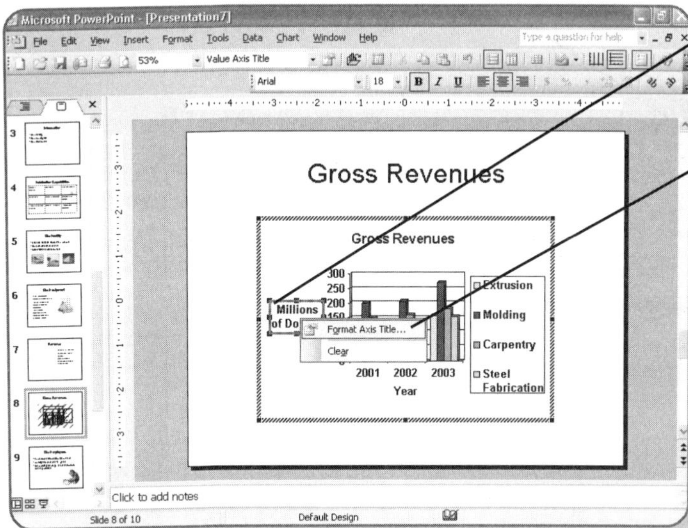

1. **Click** on some **text** on the chart that you want to change. It will be selected.
2. **Right-click** the **text** and choose **Format [*the type of text you've chosen*]**. A Format dialog box will appear.
3. **Click** on the **font** you want on the Font tab. If the Font tab does not appear automatically, click it.

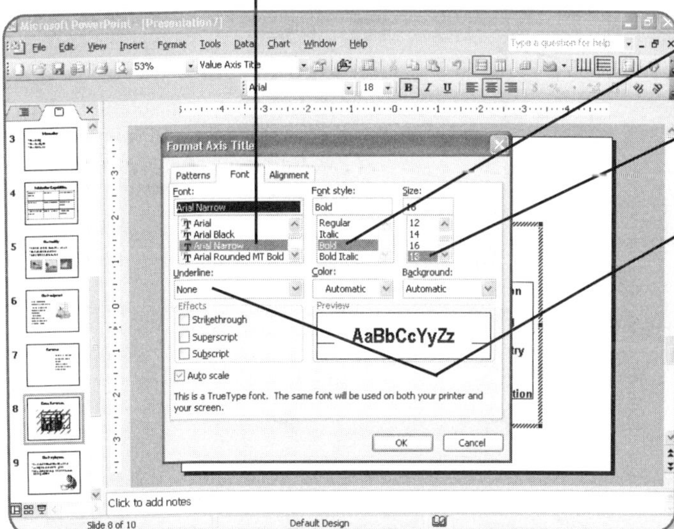

4. **Click** on the desired **text attributes**, such as bold or italic.
5. **Click** on the **font size** you want.
6. **Select** an **underline style**, if desired.

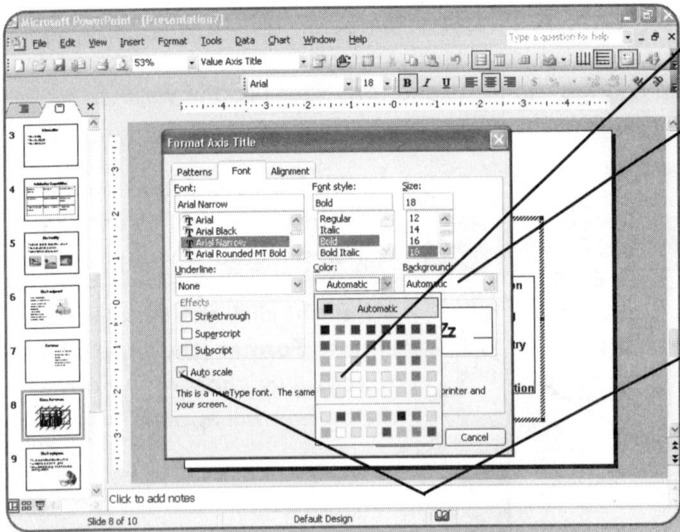

7. Select a **specific text color**, if desired.

8. Select a **background style** for the text, if desired. The default is Automatic.

NOTE

Auto scale allows PowerPoint to resize the text if you resize the chart later. Leave it on in most cases.

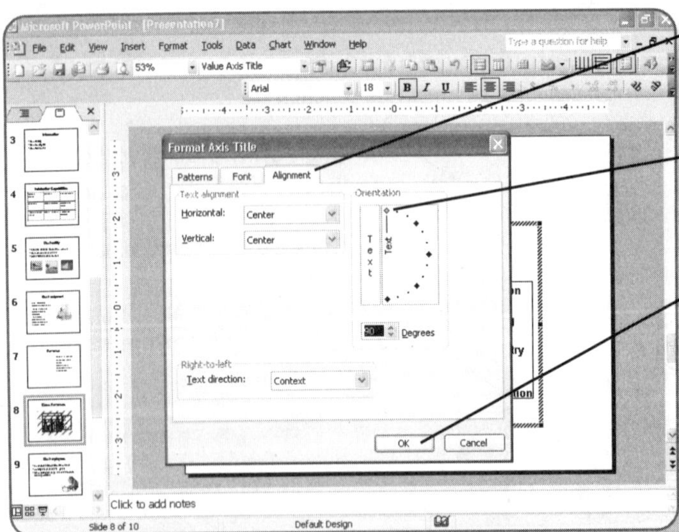

9. Click on the **Alignment tab**. The Alignment controls will appear.

10. If desired, **drag** the **red diamond** to rotate the text. This is useful for vertical axis labels.

11. Click on **OK**. Your changes will be applied.

12

Creating Diagrams

The Diagrams feature in PowerPoint offers several graphical ways of presenting information to an audience. One of the most common is an organization chart, a type of diagram that shows the people in an organization and their relationships to one another. Other types of graphics include pyramids and circle diagrams. In this chapter, you'll learn how to:

- Insert a diagram
- Add text to a diagram
- Add and remove boxes from an organization chart
- Format a diagram

Inserting a Diagram

PowerPoint contains several types of diagrams, and they all can be customized to fit your needs. They're all inserted the same way.

1. Select the **slide** on which you want to place the diagram. The slide will appear.

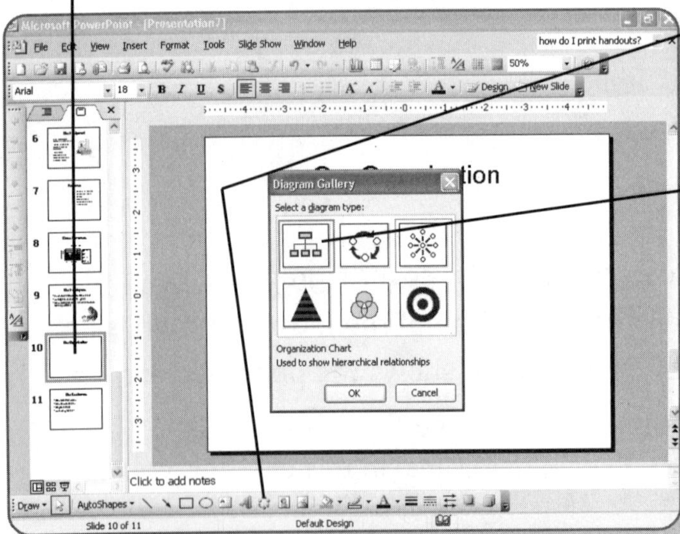

2. Click on the **Insert Diagram or Organization Chart** button. The Diagram Gallery dialog box will open.

3. Double-click on a **diagram type**. The diagram will appear on the selected slide.

Adding Text to a Diagram

After placing the diagram, you can click inside any part of it and type text.

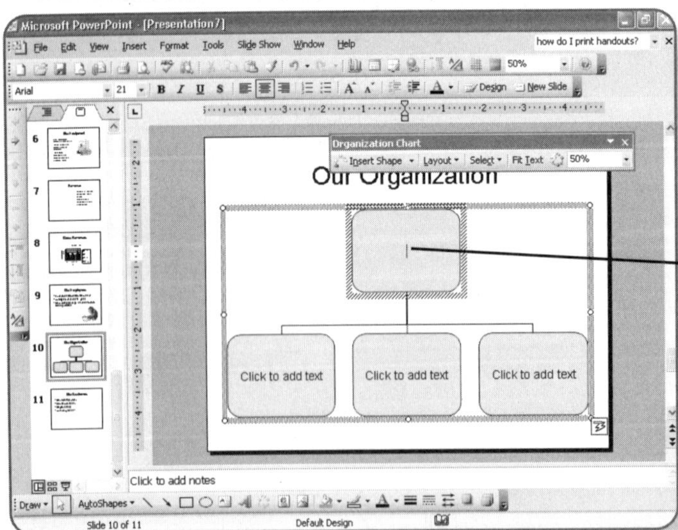

1. Click on the text placeholder for the **shape** to which you want to add a text caption. The text placeholder will disappear, and the cursor will appear in the middle of the shape.

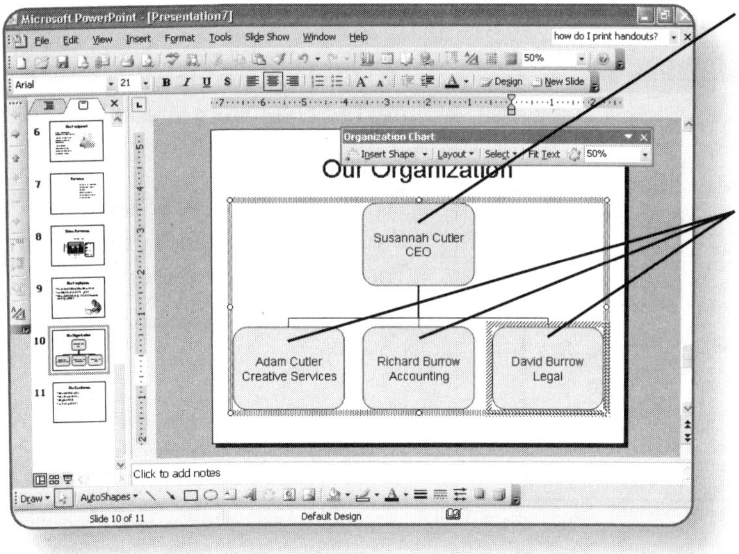

2. **Type** the **text**. To add multiple lines of text to a shape, press Enter at the end of each line. The text will appear inside the shape.
3. **Add text** to the other shapes in the diagram.

Changing the Diagram Structure

In many respects, all of the diagram types are the same. However, when it comes to changing the structure (that is, adding and removing text boxes), the organization chart is somewhat different from the others. Let's address it separately.

Adding Organization Chart Boxes

In an organization chart, each box has a relationship to another box. It is either subordinate to it or a peer (at the same level).

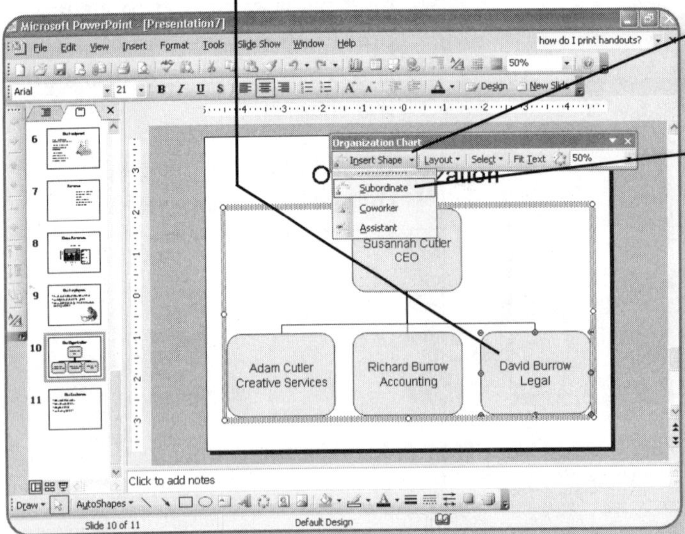

1. **Click** on an **existing box** that the new box will be related to.
2. **Click** on the **down arrow** next to the Insert Shape button. A menu will open.
3. **Click** on the **relationship** of the new box to the existing one. The new box will appear.

> **TIP**
>
> Subordinate is the default. If you want Subordinate, you can click the Insert Shape button instead of opening its menu.

Adding Boxes on Other Diagrams

To add a box:

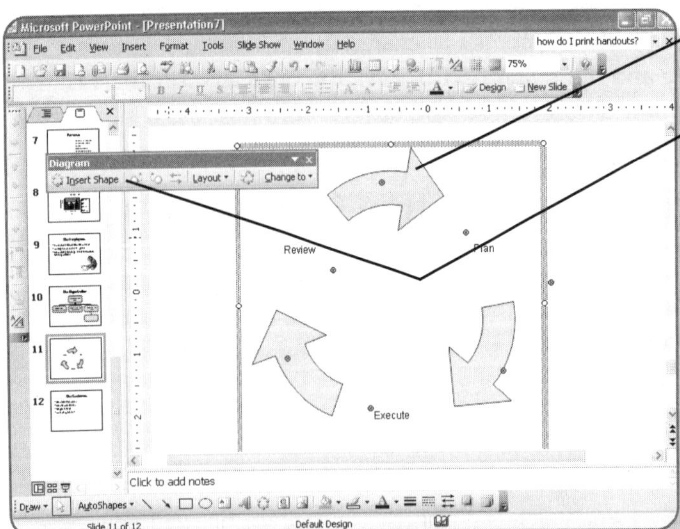

1. **Click** on the **diagram**. The Diagram toolbar will appear.
2. **Click** on the **Insert Shape button**. A new shape and accompanying text box will appear.

Deleting Boxes

This works for any diagram type.

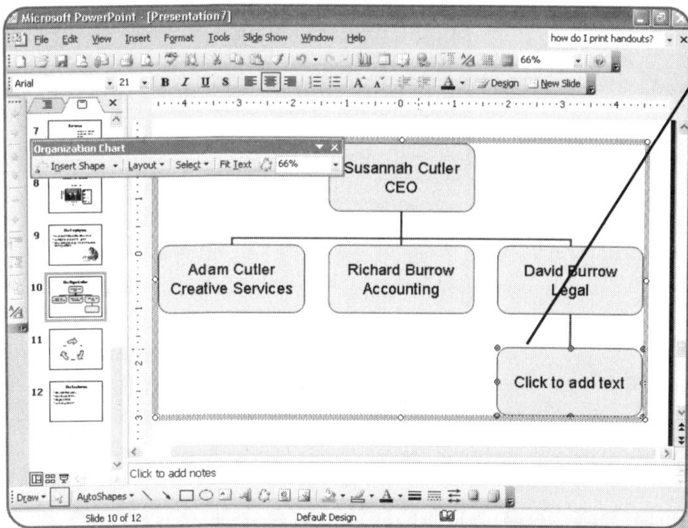

1. Click on the **border around the box** you want to delete. Gray circles will appear as its selection handles, with Xs inside the circles.

> **TIP**
>
> Don't click inside the box, or you'll just be deleting the text.

2. Press the **Delete** key. The box will be deleted.

Changing Reporting on an Organization Chart

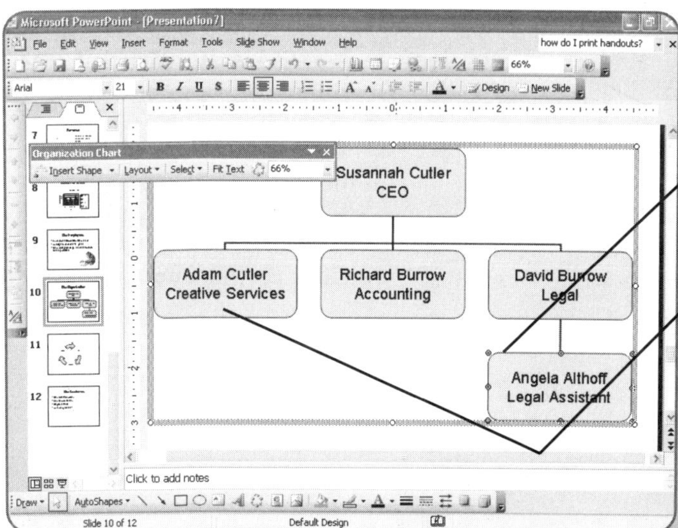

You can move a subordinate box so that the person it represents reports to some other supervisor.

1. Click on the **border of the box** to be moved. Gray circles will appear as its selection handles.

2. Drag and **drop** it on top of a **different supervisor**.

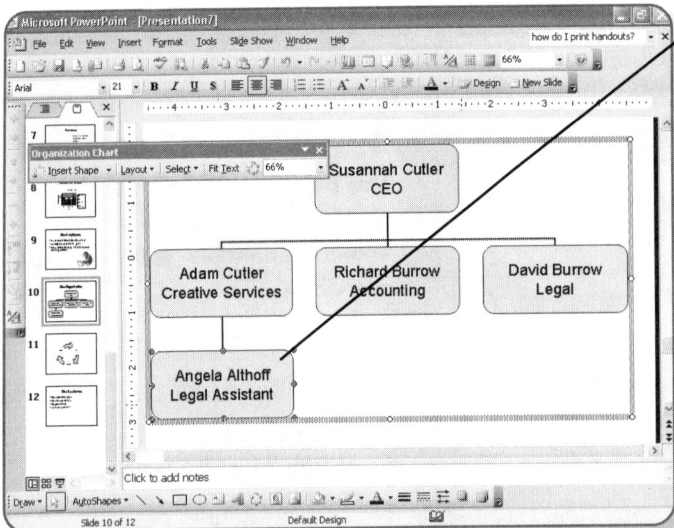

It will be moved so that it is subordinate to the new supervisor.

You must drag it *on top of* the other box. Dragging it below the box, where it will appear after it's connected, will not work.

Changing the Subordinate Layout on an Organization Chart

When there are multiple subordinates, it may be useful to change the way the subordinates' boxes hang off their supervisor's box.

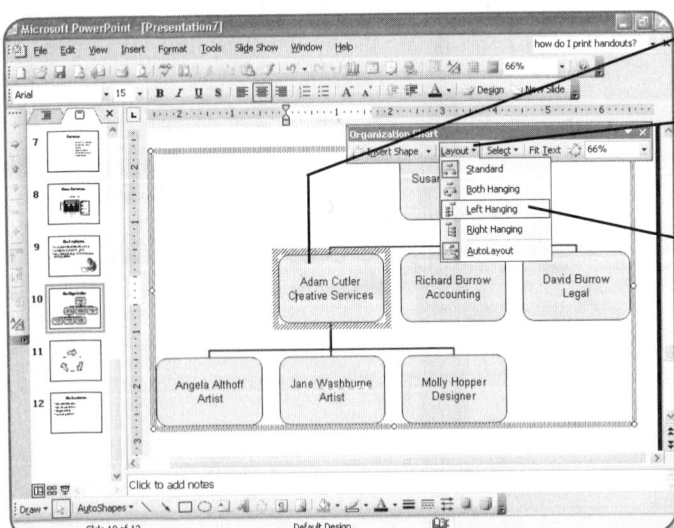

1. **Select** the **supervisor's box**. An outline will appear around it.
2. **Click** on the **Layout button** on the Organization Chart toolbar. A menu will appear.
3. **Click** on the **layout** you want.

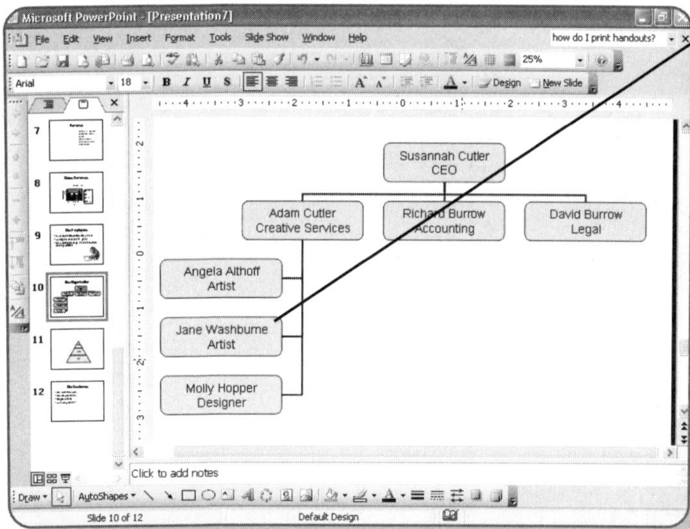

The subordinate boxes will change to that layout.

Reversing the Order on Diagrams

Some diagram types can be reversed. For example, the text on a pyramid that goes from top to bottom can be reversed so that the label that was previously on the bottom of the pyramid is now on the top. Or for diagrams that go in a circle, the labels can be changed from clockwise to counterclockwise.

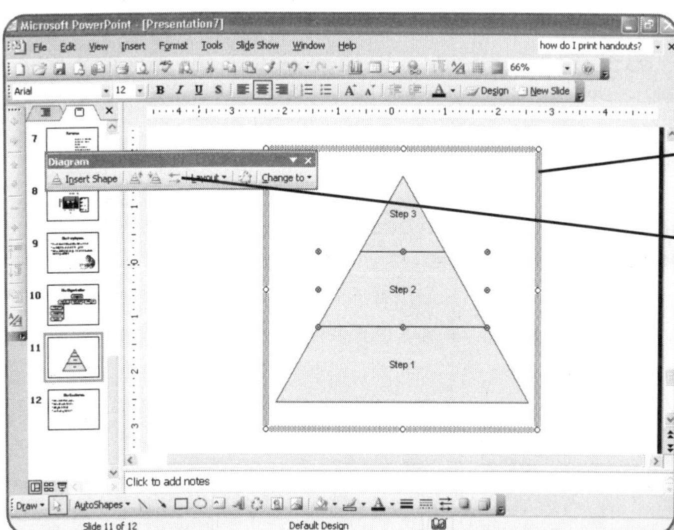

1. **Select** the **diagram**. Its outer border will be selected.
2. **Click** on the **Reverse button**.

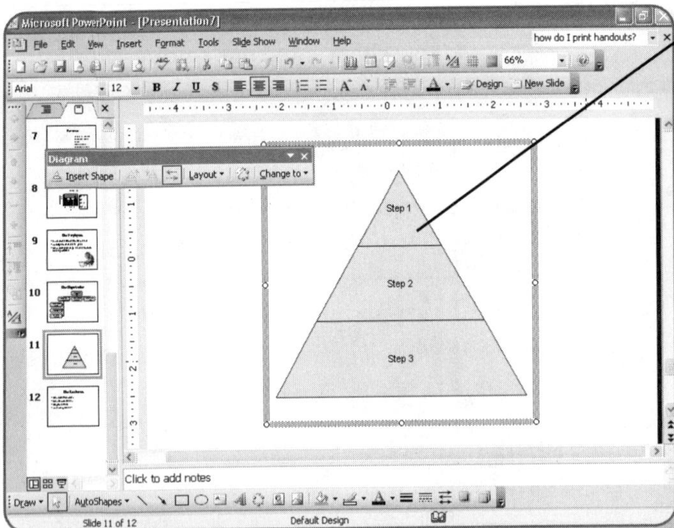

The order of the text will be reversed.

Applying Formatting to the Diagram

There are several ways to give the diagram a different look. If you'd like a quick and easy way to stylize a diagram, use one of the AutoFormats. You can also apply a unique color and line style to each shape and add a background to the diagram area.

Using AutoFormats

This works on all diagram types, although the choices of style are different for each type.

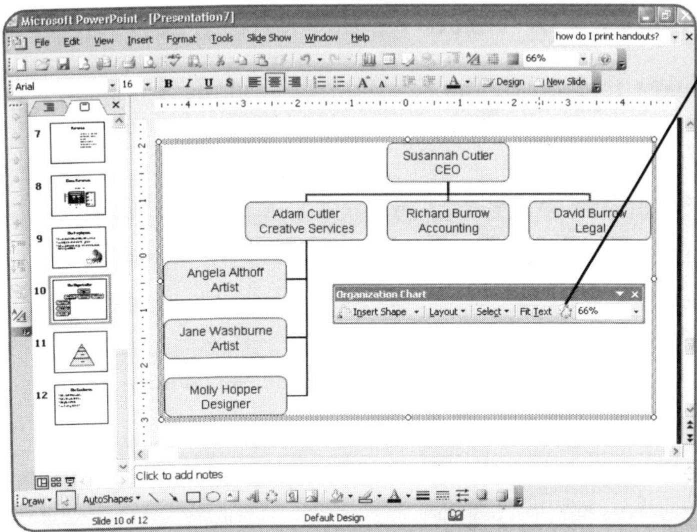

1. Click on the **AutoFormat button**. The Style Gallery dialog box for the diagram will open.

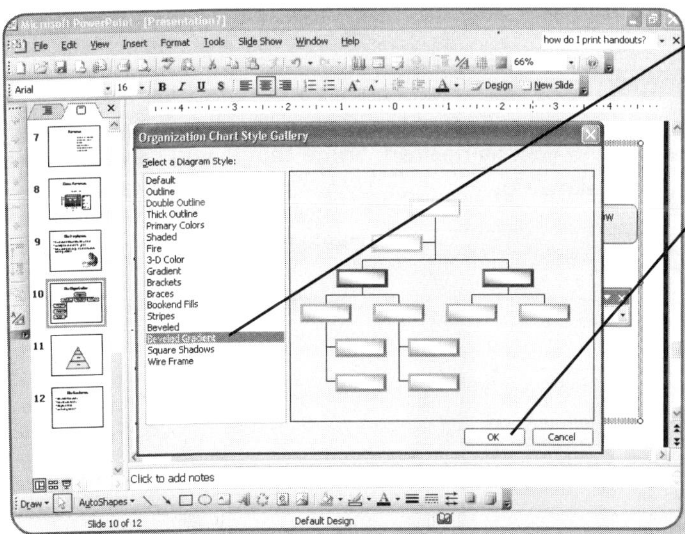

2. Click on a **style** from the Select a Diagram Style list. A preview of the selected style will appear in the Preview pane.

3. Click on **OK** when you have made your selection. The diagram style will be updated.

Manually Formatting the Diagram

If you want to override the AutoFormat settings, you must turn AutoFormat off. Then you can apply different colors, lines, fonts, and so on.

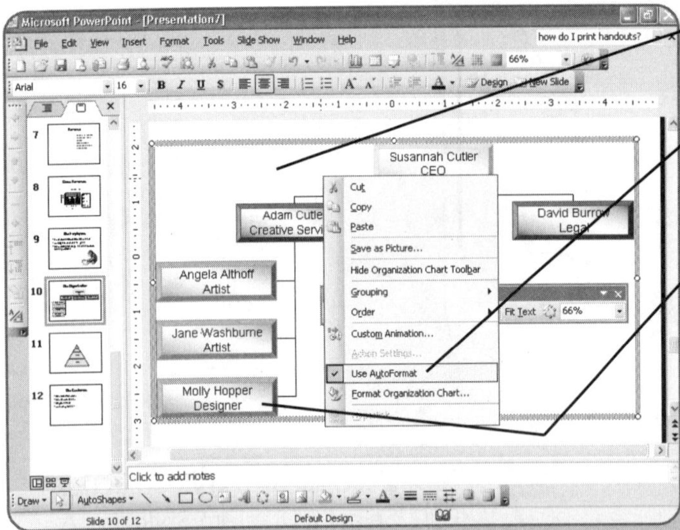

1. **Right-click** on any part of the diagram. A menu will appear.
2. **Click** on **Use AutoFormat**. The menu will close, and AutoFormat will be turned off.
3. **Click** on a **box** of the diagram. That box will be selected.
4. **Format** the **box** as desired. Some things you can do include the following:

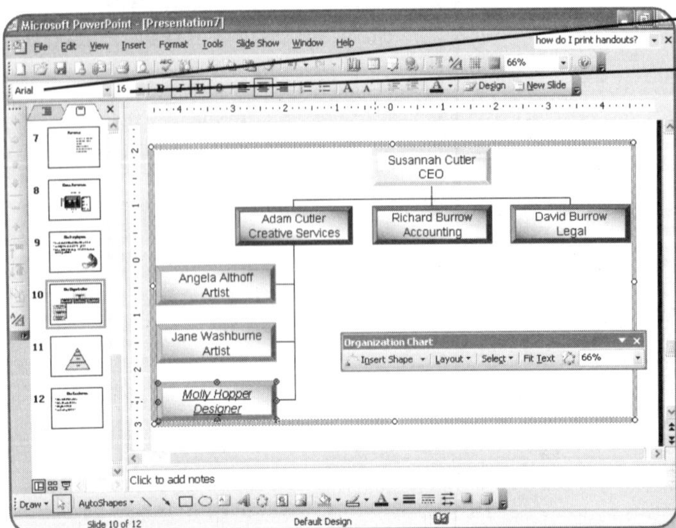

- Change the font
- Change the font size

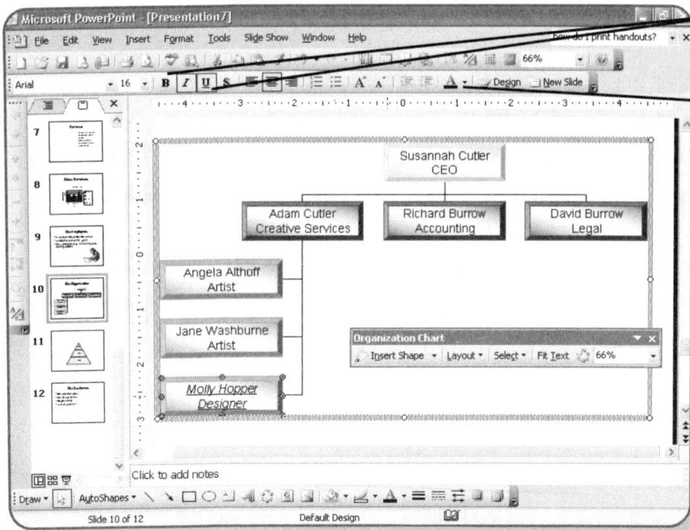

- Apply font attributes such as bold, italic, and underline
- Change the font color

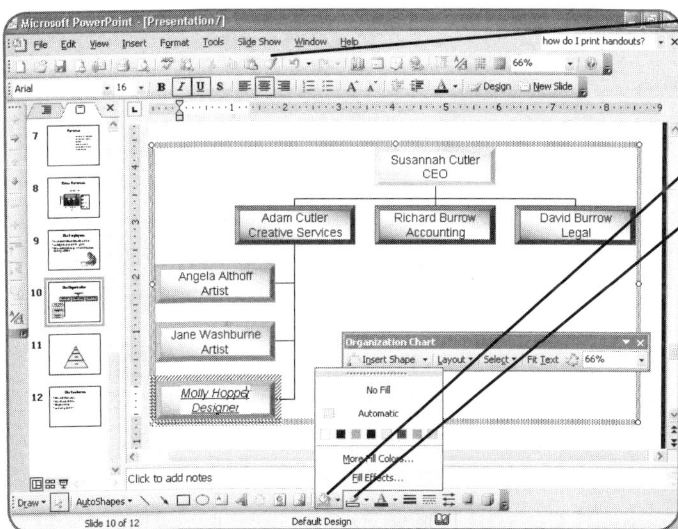

- Copy formatting from one box to another with Format Painter
- Choose a different fill color
- Choose a different border color

Part III Review Questions

1. What command can you select to align several graphics precisely in relation to one another? See "Aligning Graphics" in Chapter 8.
2. What command allows you to group several objects together and work with them as a whole? See "Grouping Graphics" in Chapter 8.
3. How can you edit the text you have entered for a piece of WordArt? See "Formatting WordArt" in Chapter 8.
4. What does the Washout image mode produce? See "Changing the Image Mode" in Chapter 9.
5. What key(s) can you press to move to the next cell in a table? See "Adding Text" in Chapter 10.
6. How can you add a background color to table cells? See "Adding Color to Cells" in Chapter 10.
7. Where do you type the data you need for a chart in PowerPoint? See "Entering Data for the Chart" in Chapter 11.
8. How can you switch between plotting the data by rows versus columns? See "Changing How the Data Is Plotted" in Chapter 11.
9. What command or button inserts a new diagram on a slide? See "Inserting a Diagram" in Chapter 12.
10. If you try to change the color of a box on a diagram, but the command is unavailable, what do you need to do? See "Manually Formatting the Diagram" in Chapter 12.

PART IV

Creating Special Effects

13

Animating the Slide Show

It's time to wake up your audience and roll a few objects across the screen during your slide show. How about a cool transition effect as each slide fades into the next slide? Or you could make bullet points fall from the sky as you introduce each point. The possibilities are endless. In this chapter, you'll learn how to:

- Use animation schemes to apply quick and easy slide transitions and animations
- Make slide elements march onto the slide in order
- Add cool effects so that one slide fades into the next slide

Using Slide Transitions

Moving from one slide to another is called a *slide transition*. It can be a simple replacement of one slide for the next, or you can set up fancier transitions that move between them.

1. **Select** the **slide(s)** to which you want to apply the transition effect. The slide(s) will be selected.

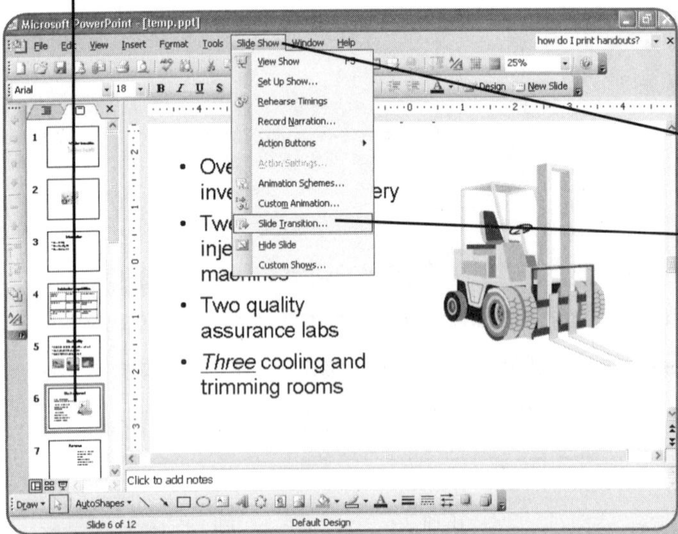

If you want to apply it to all slides, it does not matter which slide(s) you select.

2. **Click** on **Slide Show**. The Slide Show menu will appear.

3. **Click** on **Slide Transition**. The Slide Transition task pane will appear.

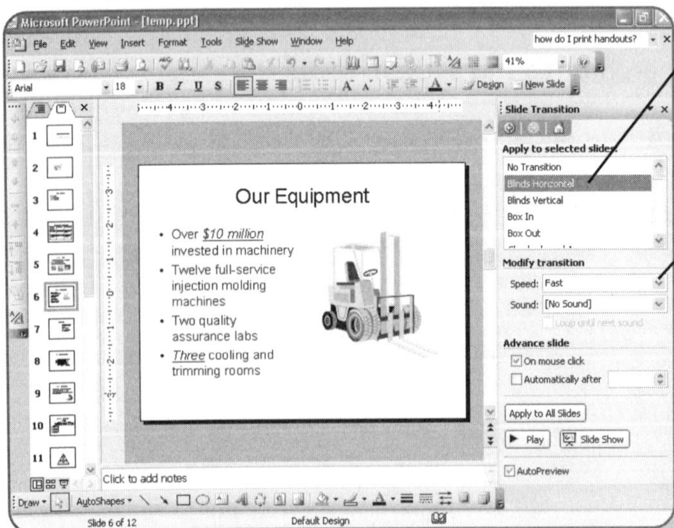

4. **Click** on a **slide transition**. The transition will be selected, and a preview of the transition will appear if the AutoPreview check box is selected.

5. **Click** the **Speed list box arrow** and select the speed at which you want the transition to play. The speed will appear in the list box.

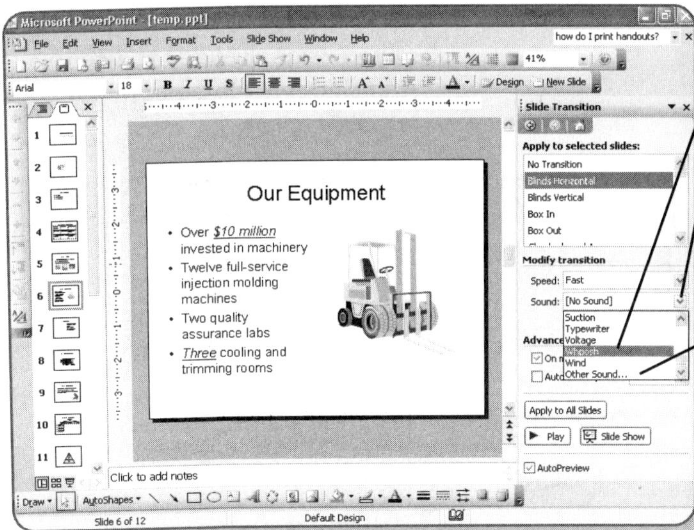

6. Click the **Sound list box arrow** and **select** a sound to play during a slide transition, if desired. The sound will appear in the list box.

> **TIP**
>
> If you want to play a sound that you have stored on your computer, select Other Sound from the bottom of the list.

> **NOTE**
>
> The first time you select a sound, a box may appear prompting you to install the Sound Effects feature. Click OK to do so.

7. Specify when the transition will occur:

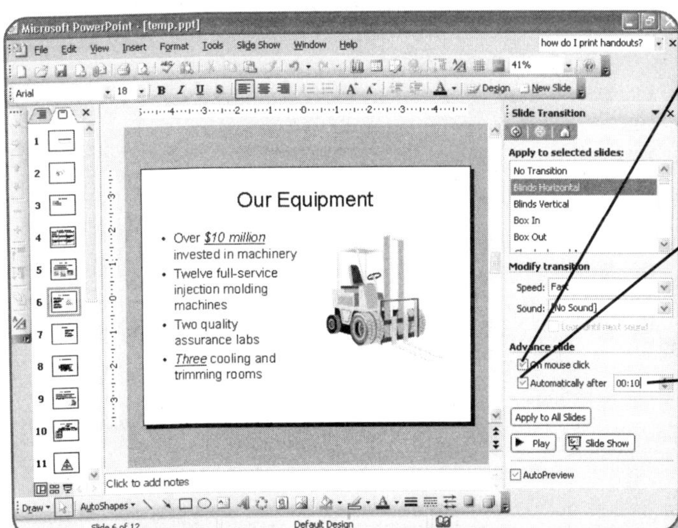

- **Mark** the **On mouse click check box** if you want the transition to occur when you click the left mouse button. It is marked by default.
- **Mark** the **Automatically after check box** if you want the transition to occur automatically after a specified time.
- **Enter** a **number of seconds** in the text box to specify the amount of time for the Automatically after setting.

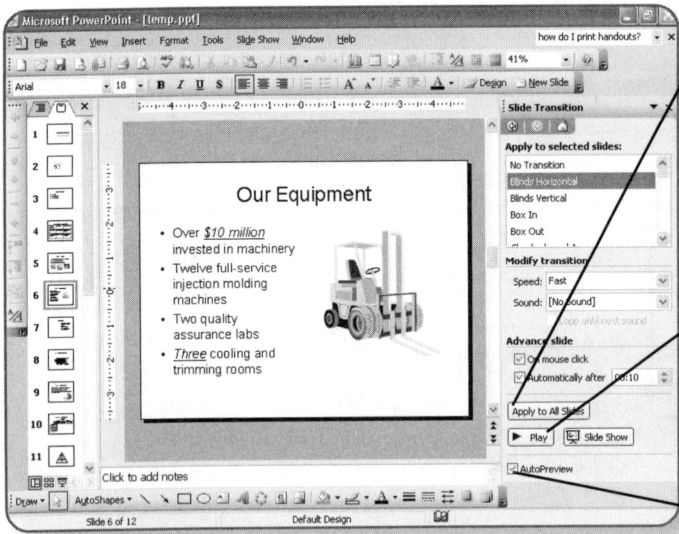

8. Click on **Apply to All Slides** if you want all slides to use this transition. It will be applied to all slides.

If you don't do this, it will apply only to the slides you selected in step 1.

9a. Click on **Play**. The transition effect will play in Normal view.

TIP

If you mark the AutoPreview check box, the transition will play without your having to click the Play button.

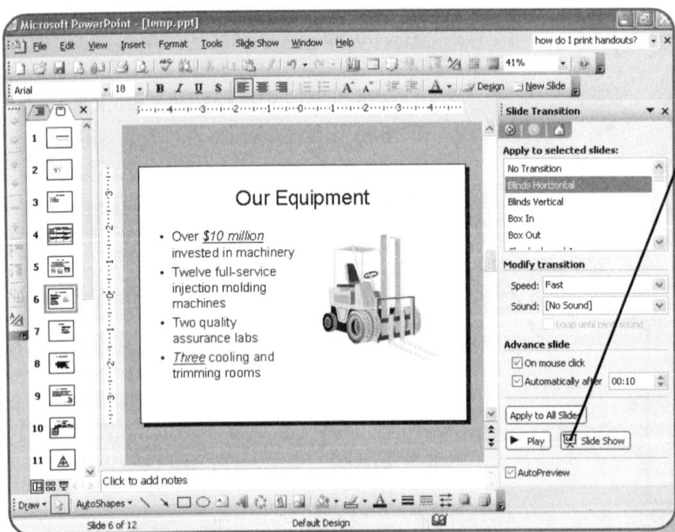

OR

9b. Click on **Slide Show**. The transition effect will play in Slide Show view.

Applying an Animation Scheme

Whereas a transition moves from one slide to another, an *animation* moves an individual object onto or off of the screen within a slide. PowerPoint comes with many preset animation schemes that are designed for ease of use. You can also create custom animations, as covered later in this chapter.

1. Display the **slide** to which you want to apply the animation. The slide will appear in Normal view. If you want to apply the animation to several slides, select the slides in Slide Sorter view.

2. Click on **Slide Show**. The Slide Show menu will appear.

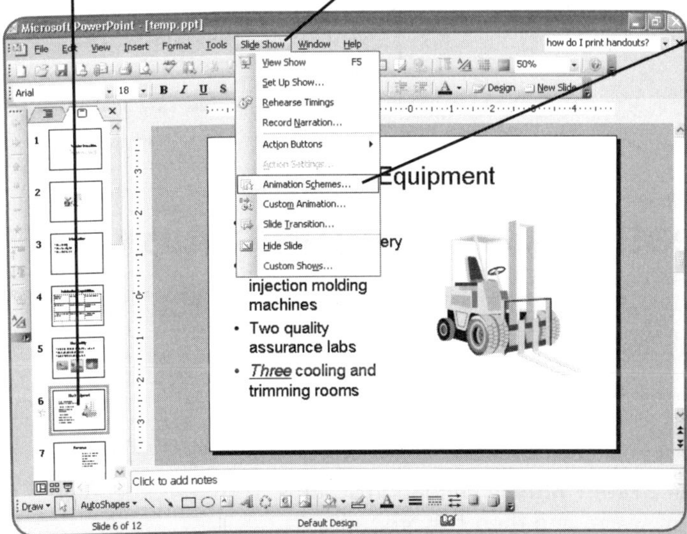

3. Click on **Animation Schemes**. The Slide Design task pane will appear, and the available slide animations will be listed.

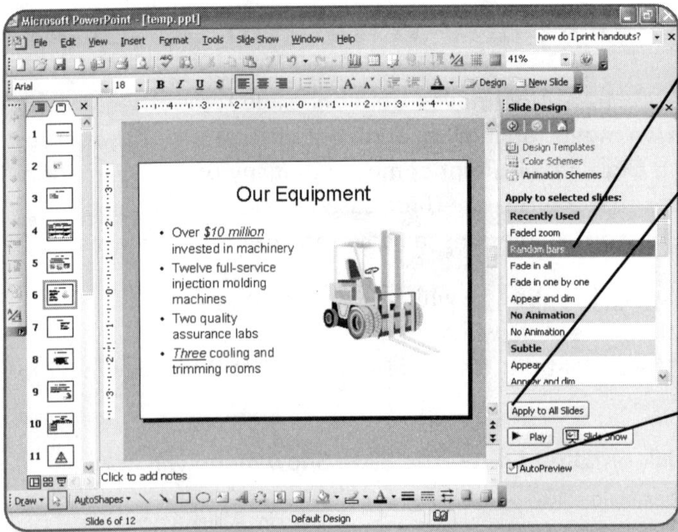

4. Click on an **animation scheme**. The animation will be applied to the selected slides.

5. Click on **Apply to All Slides** if you want every slide in the presentation to use the same animation scheme.

> **NOTE**
>
> Place a check mark in the AutoPreview check box if you want to watch the animation in action when you select the animation scheme.

Creating Custom Animation

Custom animation allows you to specify exactly what you want to animate and how it should be done.

> **TIP**
>
> You can start with an animation scheme from the preceding set of steps, and then customize it.

1. **Open** the **slide** that contains the element that you want to animate. The slide will appear in Normal view.

2. **Click** on **Slide Show**. The Slide Show menu will appear.

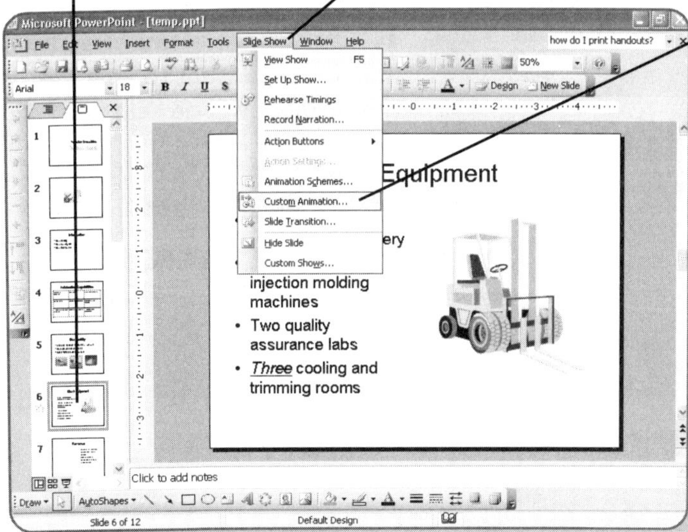

3. **Click** on **Custom Animation**. The Custom Animation task pane will appear.

If you applied an animation scheme previously, the animation for it will be shown.

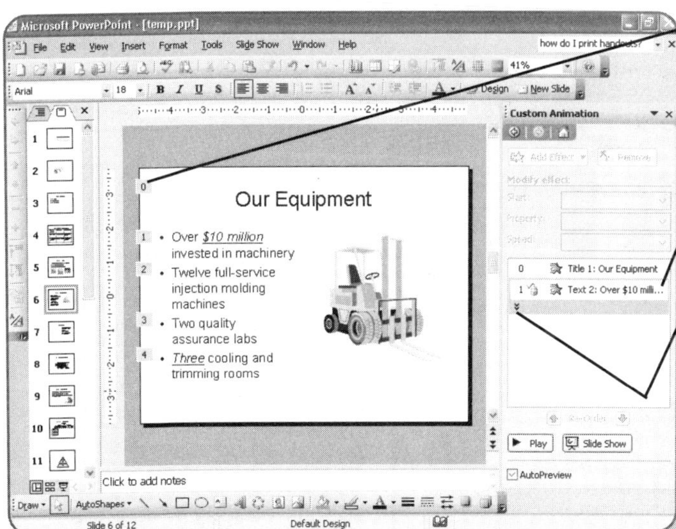

Each animated item has a number representing the order in which it will execute.

Each animated item appears in the Custom Animation list.

Groups of related items, such as individual bullet points in a list, are shown as a single item. Click the down arrow to display them.

Adding an Animation Effect

Start with a slide that does not already have any animation effects for this procedure.

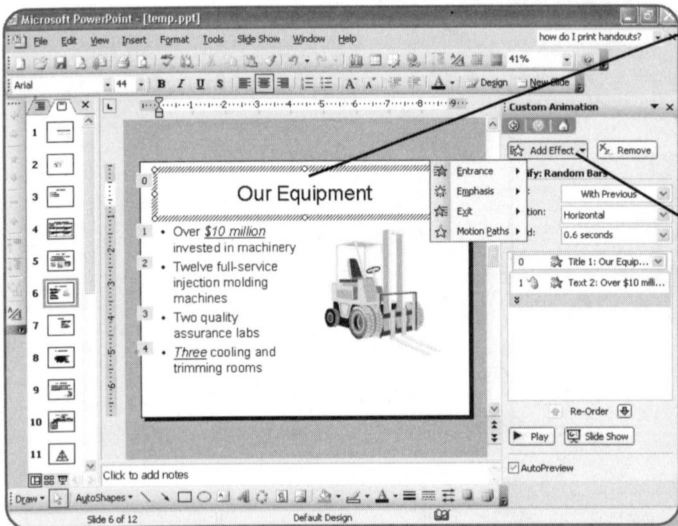

1. Click on the **element** on the slide that you want to animate. The element will be selected.

This could be a title, a bulleted list, or a graphic object.

2. Click on **Add Effect** on the task pane. A menu will appear.

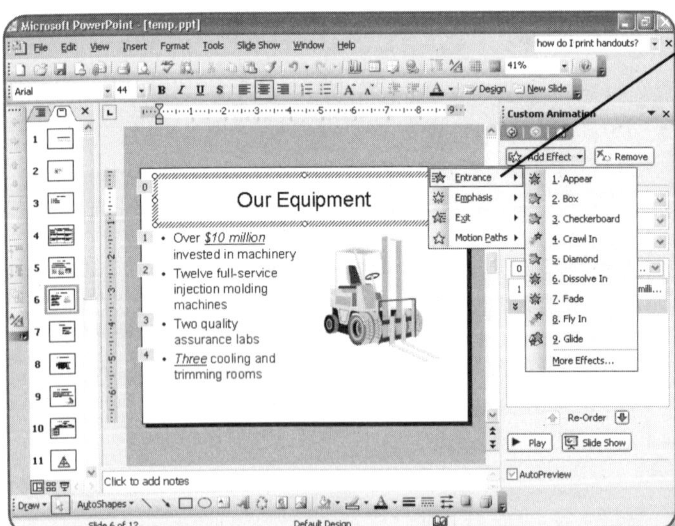

3. Point to a **category** of effects. A second menu will appear.

NOTE

Entrance effects control how the object enters the slide. *Emphasis effects* make it do something after its entrance. *Exit effects* control how it leaves the slide. A *motion path* is an advanced feature that enables you to specify exactly where the object travels.

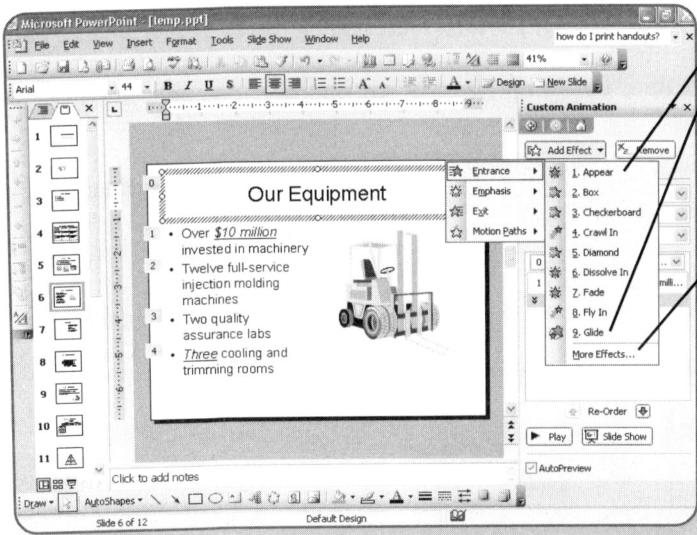

4a. Click on one of the **effects** shown on the menu. It will be applied to the object, and you are done.

OR

4b. Click on **More Effects**. A dialog box with a list of special effects will open.

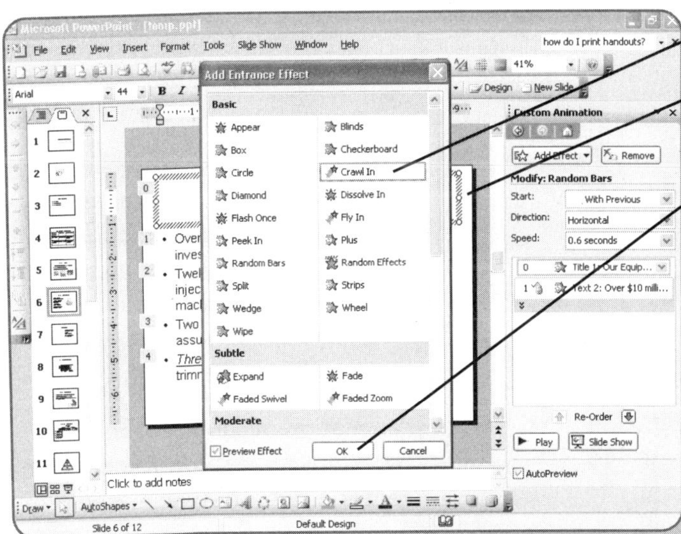

5. Click on an **effect**.

A preview of the effect will play in the Normal view.

6. Click on **OK** when you have selected an animation effect. The animation will be applied to the slide elements. You can now modify the animation.

Modifying an Animation

Do this on a slide that already has one or more animated objects.

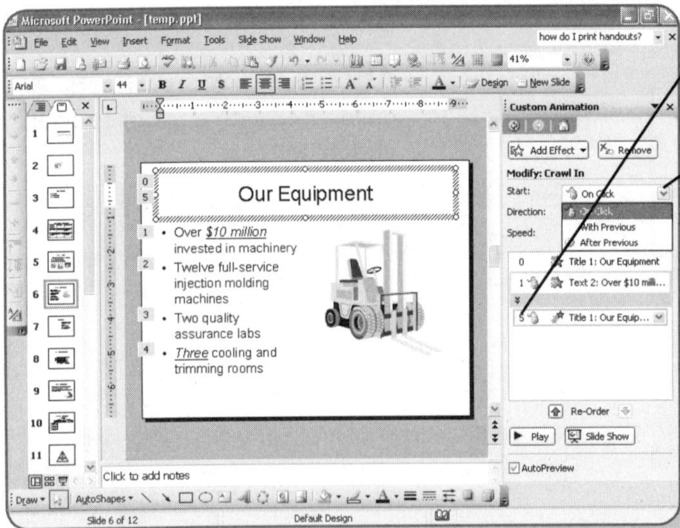

1. **Click** on the **animation effect** in the task pane. It will be selected.
2. **Select** an **event trigger** from the Start list. On Click is the most common.

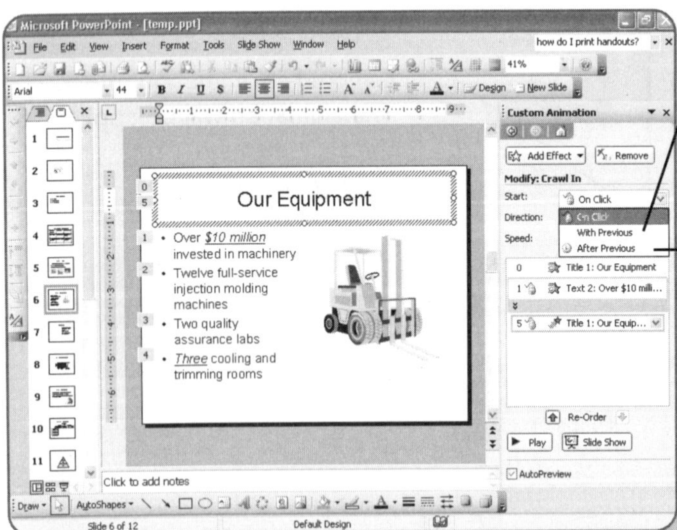

Use With Previous to make the animation occur simultaneously with the previous animation. If there is no previous animation on this slide, it will occur when the slide itself appears.

Use After Previous to make the animation occur after the previous animation. You can also enter a delay between them.

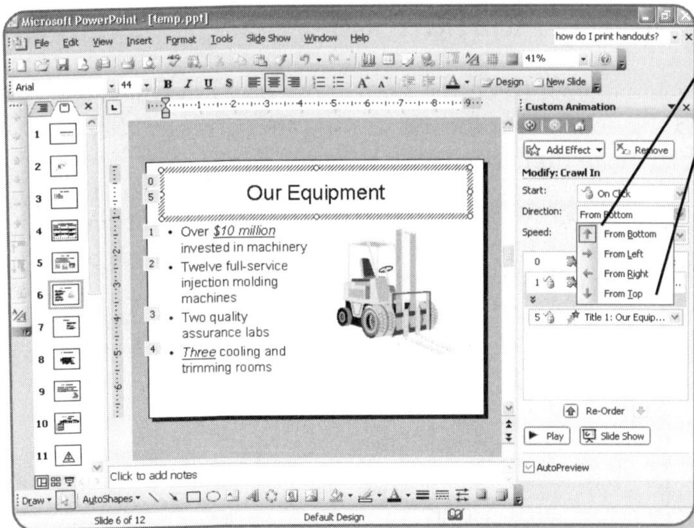

3. Select a **direction** from the Direction list.

The significance of Direction depends on the animation type. For example, if it is an entrance effect, the object will enter the slide from the chosen direction.

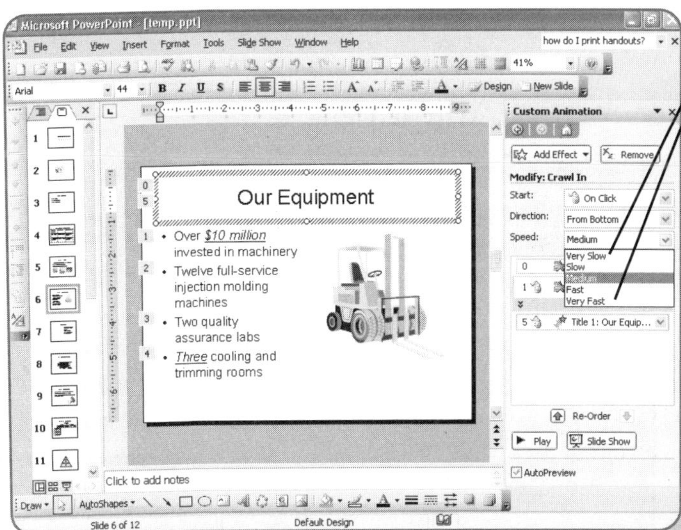

4. Select a **speed** from the Speed list.

TIP

You can also right-click the animation on the task pane and choose Effect Options to open a dialog box containing more choices. For example, you can enter a delay to be used with the After Previous event trigger, and you can specify a sound that should play with the animation.

Reordering Animations

Objects are animated on the slide in the order in which you created the animations for them. You can rearrange them on the list to make them occur in a different order.

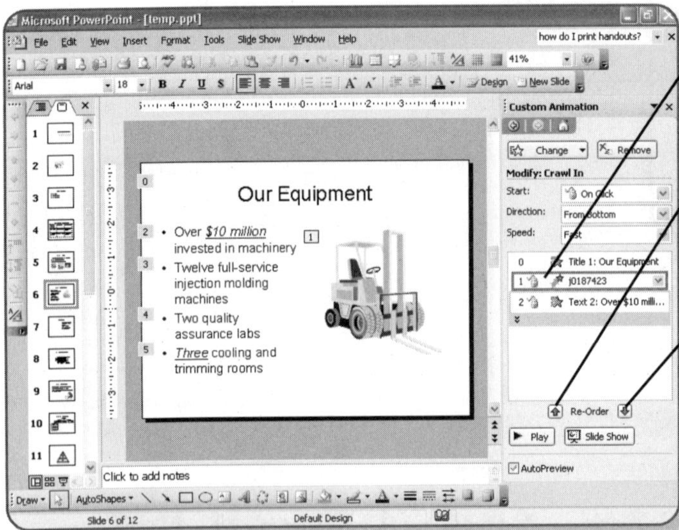

1. **Click** on the **animation** you want to move in the task pane. It will be selected.

2a. **Click** on the **Up button** to move it up on the list.

OR

2b. **Click** on the **Down button** to move it down on the list.

Removing an Animation

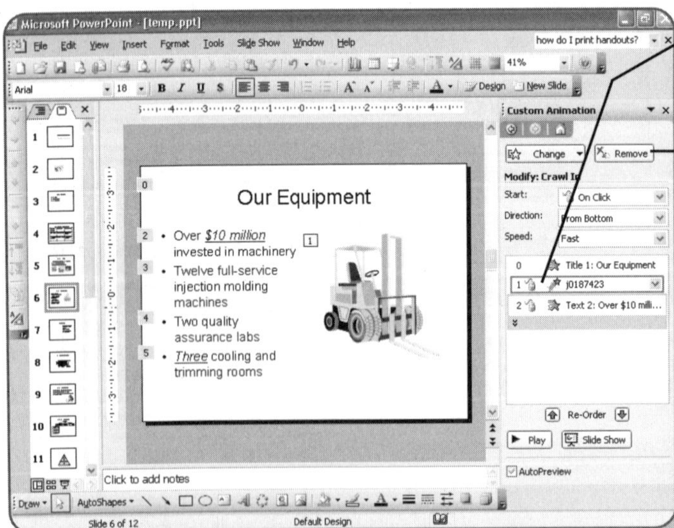

1. **Click** on the **animation** you want to remove. It will be selected.

2. **Click** on **Remove**. The animation will be removed.

14

Moving Along with Multimedia

Another way to make a slide show interesting and keep your audience's attention is to add music and video. You may have music that you've created using your computer's MIDI equipment and software, or you may have a music CD that you'd like to play. Also, if you have digital video files, it's easy to show videos during a slide show. In this chapter, you'll learn how to:

- Play a sound file as background music
- Listen to a CD while playing a slide show
- Watch movies during a slide show presentation

Adding Sound Clips to a Slide

PowerPoint lets you play a sound clip while a certain slide is displayed during a slide show. This could be a music clip, a sound effect, or any other sound recording in a common audio format such as WAV, WMA, or MP3.

These steps do *not* apply to using audio from a CD-ROM or using voiceover narration. See the specific sections on those topics later in this chapter.

1. **Display** the **slide** in Normal view that should receive the sound clip.

2. **Click** on **Insert**. The Insert menu will appear.

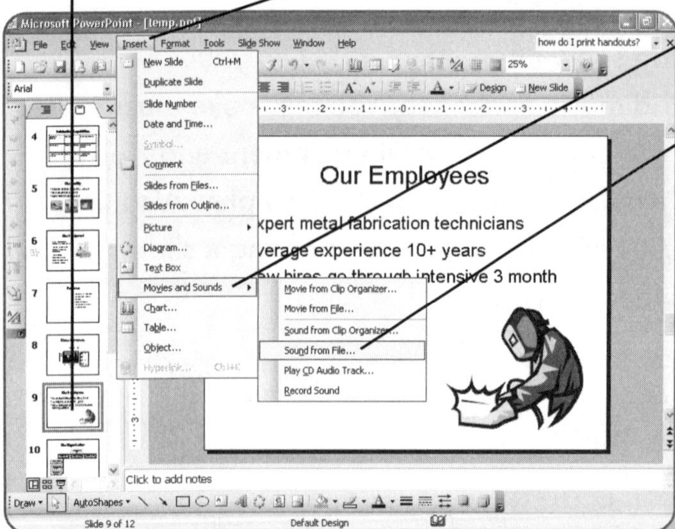

3. **Point to Movies and Sounds.** A second menu will appear.

4. **Click** on **Sound from File**. The Insert Sound dialog box will open.

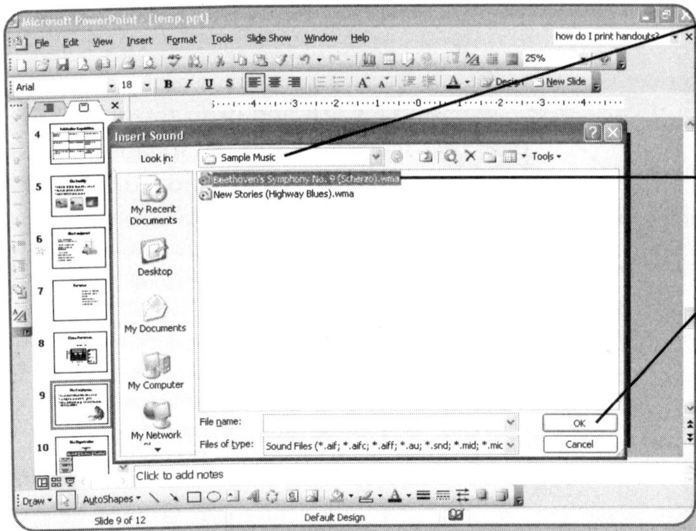

5. **Navigate** to the **folder** that contains the sound file. The folder's name will appear in the Look in list box.

6. **Click** on the **sound file**. The file will be selected.

7. **Click** on **OK**. A confirmation dialog box will open.

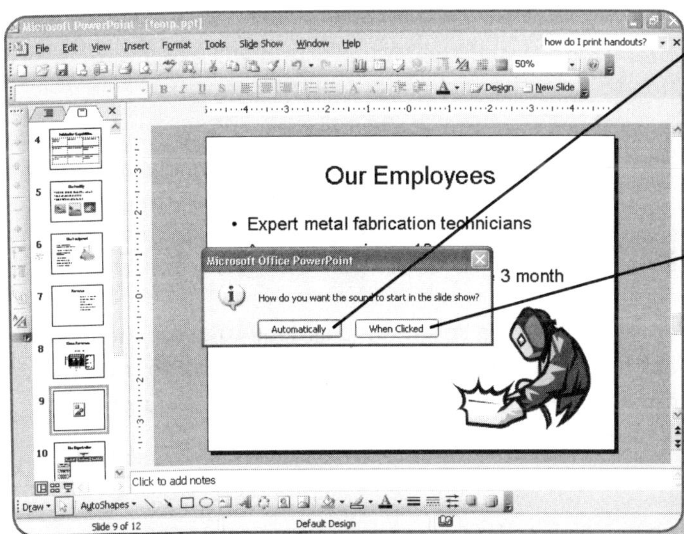

8a. **Click** on **Automatically** if you want the sound to play when the slide appears during the slide show.

OR

8b. **Click** on **When Clicked** if you want the sound to play only when its icon is clicked during the slide show.

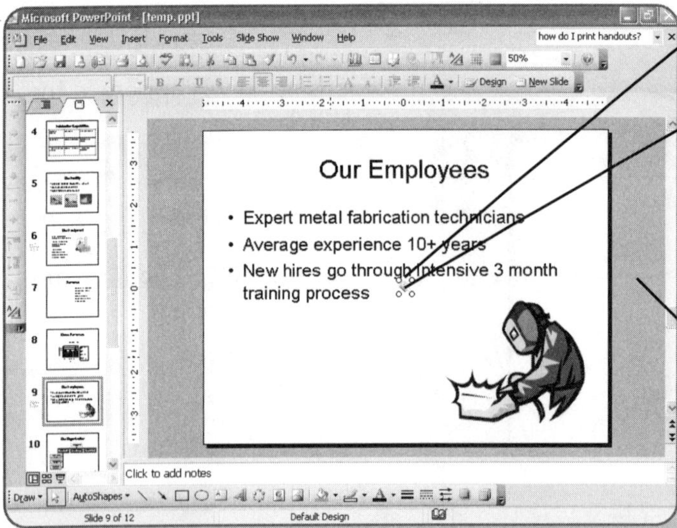

The sound icon appears in the center of the slide.

9. **Click** and **drag** the **sound icon** to a different location on the slide. The sound icon can be moved to any location on the slide.

TIP

If you don't want to see the sound icon on the slide, drag it off the slide.

TIP

You can use the Custom Animation task pane, as in Chapter 13, to specify when the sound will execute in relation to the other animations on the slide.

Attaching a Sound to an Object

Another way to place a sound on a slide is to associate it with an object on the slide. This could be a graphic, a text box, or anything else. Then, whenever that object is clicked or pointed to with the mouse, the sound will play.

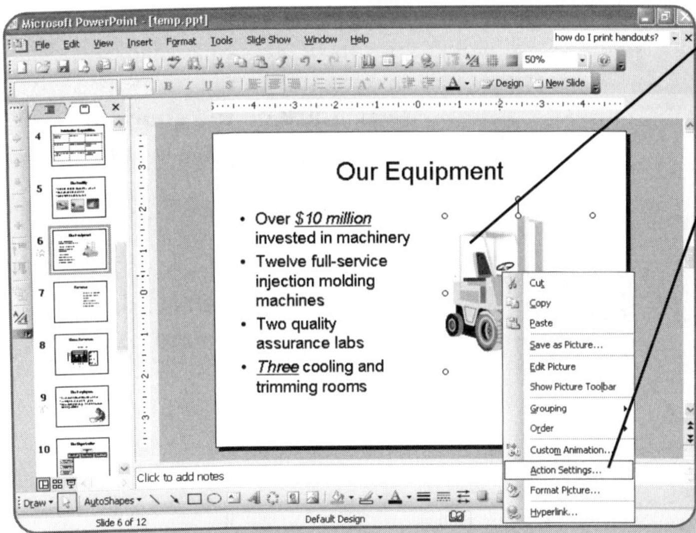

1. Right-click on the **object**. A menu will appear.

2. Click on **Action Settings**. The Action Settings dialog box will open.

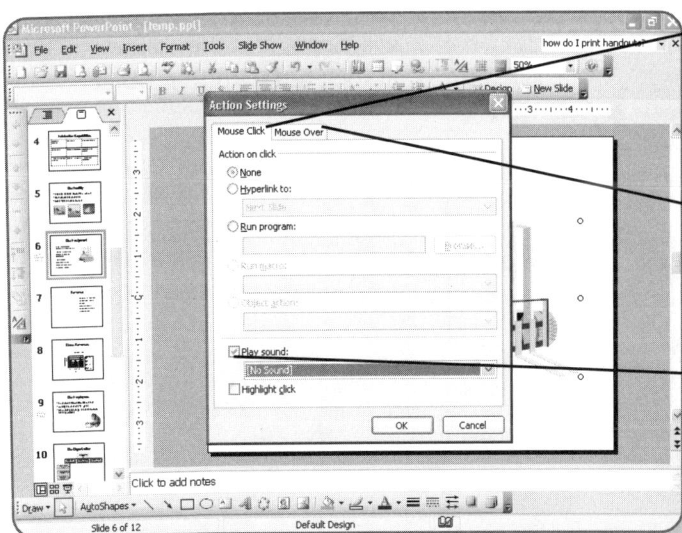

3a. Click on the **Mouse Click tab** if you want the sound to occur when the object is clicked.

OR

3b. Click on the **Mouse Over tab** if you want the sound to occur when the mouse touches the object.

4. Click on the **Play sound check box**. The drop-down list will become available.

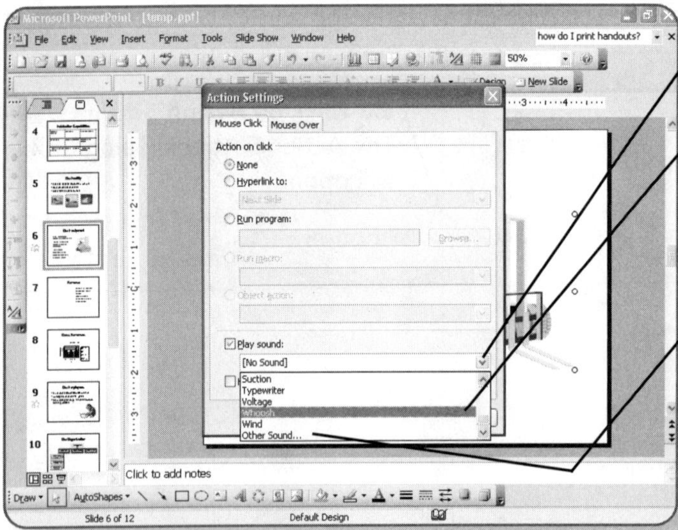

5. **Click** on the **down arrow**. The drop-down list will open.

6a. **Click** on the **sound** you want. It will appear in the Play sound box.

OR

6b. **Click** on **Other Sound** and browse for the sound you want.

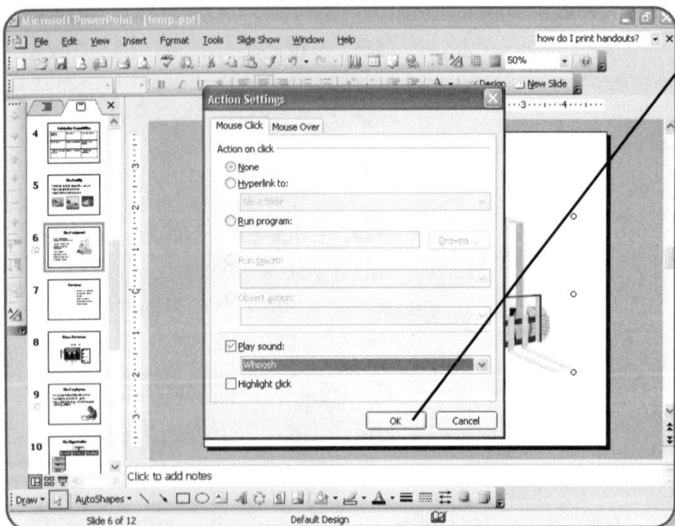

7. **Click** on **OK**. The dialog box will close, and the sound will be associated with that object.

Playing Audio CDs

Another way to play music while a slide is displayed during a slide show is to pop a music CD into the computer and let PowerPoint play the CD tracks that you specify.

> **NOTE**
>
> When you deliver the presentation, the same music CD will need to be in the computer's CD-ROM drive.

1. **Place** the **CD** that you want to play into the CD-ROM drive.
2. **Display** the **slide** for which you want to play the CD track. The slide will appear in Normal view.
3. **Click** on **Insert**. The Insert menu will appear.

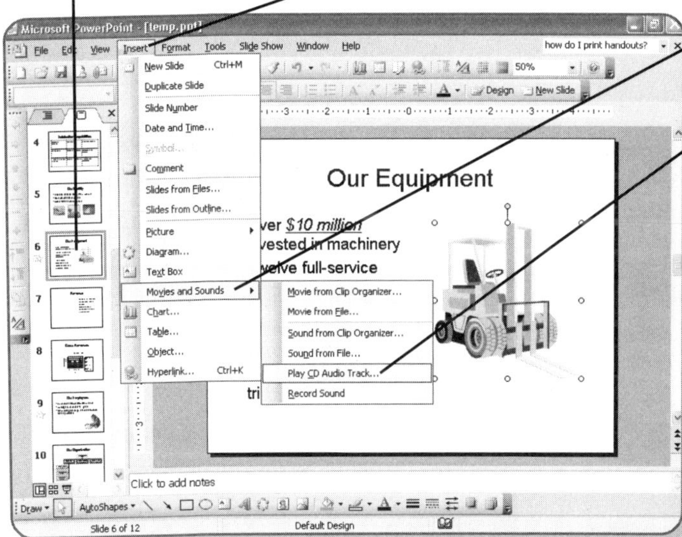

4. **Point to Movies and Sounds.** A second menu will appear.
5. **Click** on **Play CD Audio Track**. The Insert CD Audio dialog box will open.

6. **Click** in the **Start at track text box** and **type** the **track number** for the first track on the CD that you want to play.

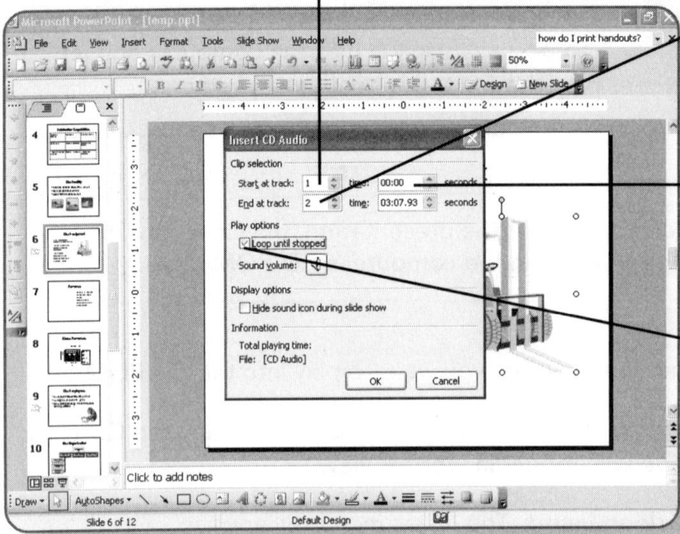

7. **Click** in the **End at track text box** and **type** the **track number** for the last track on the CD that you want to play.

You can select not only the starting and ending track, but also the number of seconds into them that you want to start.

8. **Click** on **Loop until stopped** if you want this same set of tracks to repeat until the presentation is over.

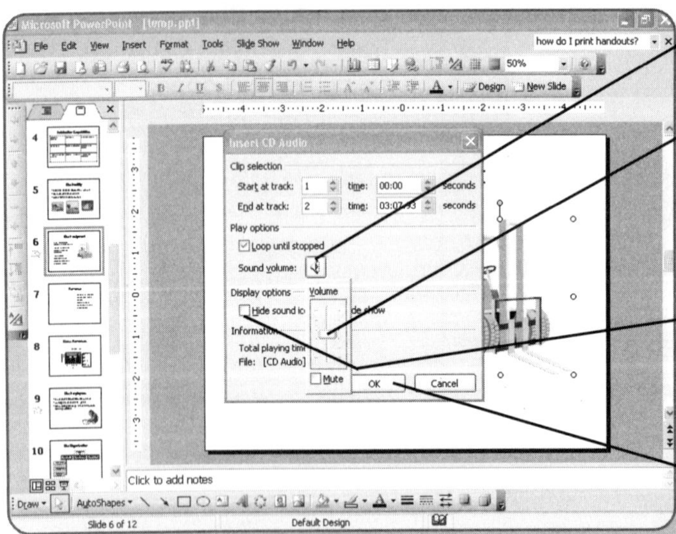

9. **Click** on the **Speaker icon**. A volume control will appear.

10. **Drag** the **volume slider bar** up or down. The volume of the clip will change (in relation to the system sound volume in general).

11. **Click** on **Hide sound icon during slideshow** if you do not want the CD icon to appear on the slide.

12. **Click** on **OK**. A confirmation dialog box will open.

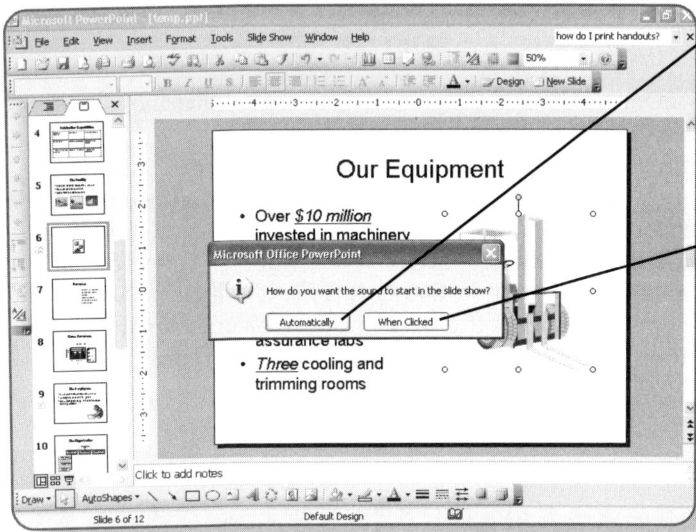

13a. **Click** on **Automatically**. The CD clip(s) will play automatically when the slide appears during the slide show.

OR

13b. **Click** on **When Clicked**. The CD clip(s) will play only when the CD icon is clicked during the slide show.

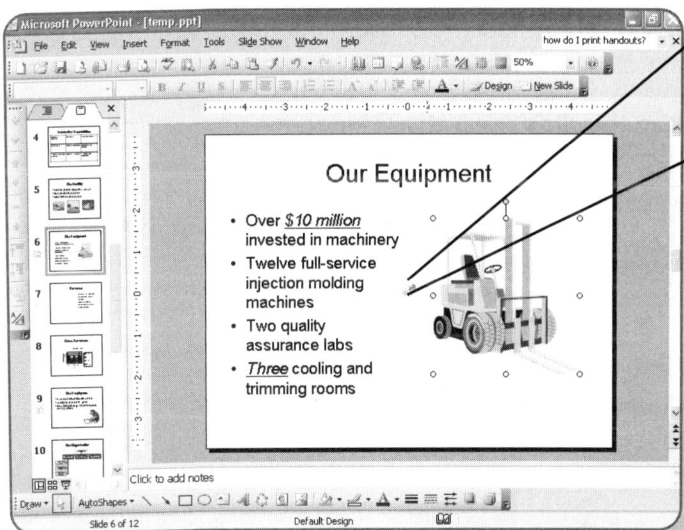

Unless you chose not to display the CD icon on the slide, it appears in the center of the slide.

14. **Click** and **drag** the **CD icon**. The CD icon will be moved to a different location on the slide.

NOTE

The CD clip will play only as long as that individual slide is onscreen. If you want the CD clip to play across multiple slides, you must do a bit of extra work. After adding the CD clip to the slide (as in the previous steps), go to Custom Animation and display the Effect Options for the CD clip, as described in Chapter 13. Then set Stop Playing After ____ Slides to 999. It will continue to play until the end of the presentation, or until it receives another instruction to play a CD clip on a later slide.

Adding Video Clips to a Slide

Digitized video files can also be used on PowerPoint slides to play a video during the slide show. For instance, you may have a product demonstration video that may be interesting to your slide show audience. Instead of playing the video on a separate display, just insert the video onto the slide.

1. **Open** the **slide** in which the video will appear. The slide will appear in Normal view.

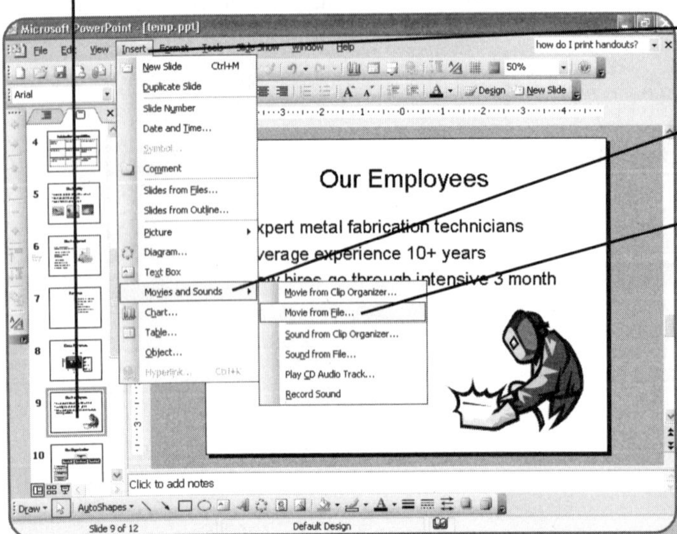

2. **Click** on **Insert**. The Insert menu will appear.
3. **Point to Movies and Sounds.** A second menu will appear.
4. **Click** on **Movie from File.** The Insert Movie dialog box will open.

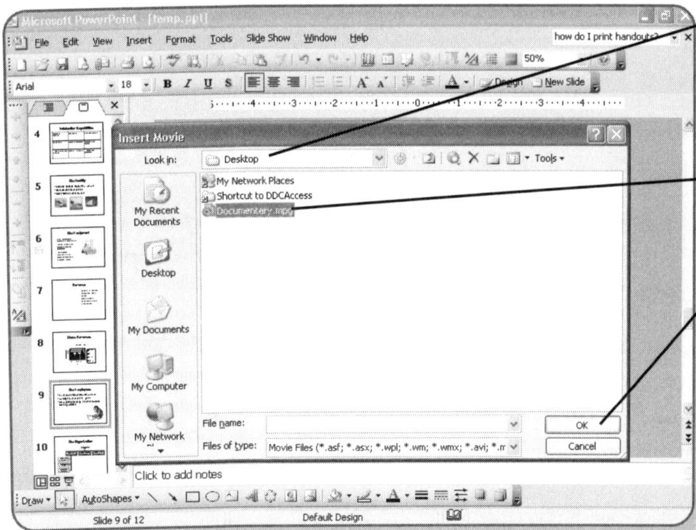

5. **Navigate** to the **folder** that contains the movie file. The folder's name will appear in the Look in list box.

6. **Click** on the **movie file**. The file will be selected.

7. **Click** on **OK**. A confirmation dialog box will open.

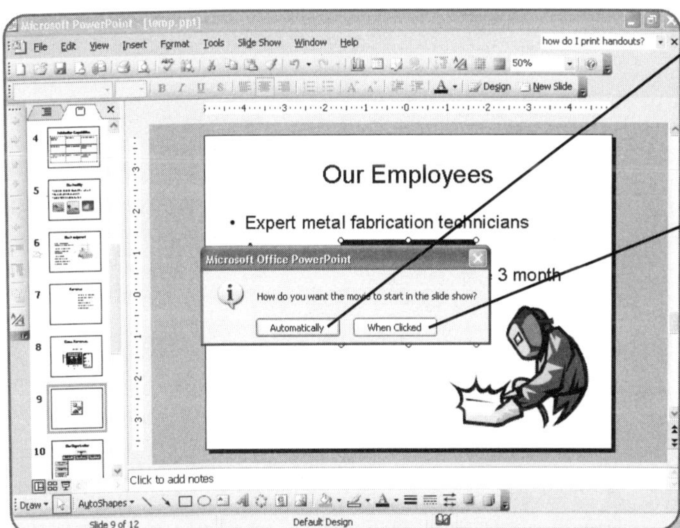

8a. **Click** on **Automatically** if you want the movie to play when the slide appears.

OR

8b. **Click** on **When Clicked** if you want the movie to start when you click on the movie icon.

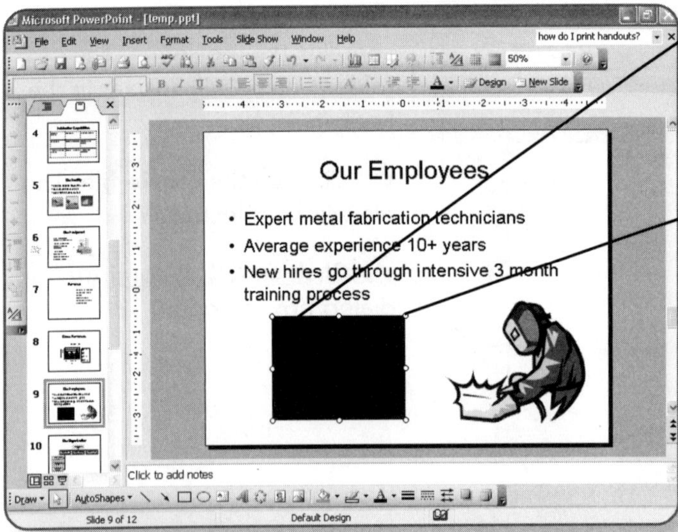

The first frame of the movie appears on the slide. In this case, the first frame is black because the movie starts by fading in.

9. **Click** and **drag** the **resize handles**. The movie clip window will be resized.

> ## NOTE
>
> You can fine-tune the way the movie plays by right-clicking it and choosing Edit Movie Object.

Part IV Review Questions

1. What command opens a task pane containing preset animation schemes? See "Applying an Animation Scheme" in Chapter 13.
2. How is a custom animation different from an animation scheme? See "Creating Custom Animation" in Chapter 13.
3. How do you change the speed at which text moves across a slide during a slide show? See "Modifying an Animation" in Chapter 13.
4. How do you apply a transition between one slide and another during a slide show? See "Using Slide Transitions" in Chapter 13.
5. Is it possible to play a sound file when you move from one slide to another during a slide show? See "Using Slide Transitions" in Chapter 13.
6. How can you hide the icon for a sound clip on a slide? See "Adding Sound Clips to a Slide" in Chapter 14.
7. When you attach a sound to an object, it can be set to execute when either of two things happens. What are they? See "Attaching a Sound to an Object" in Chapter 14.
8. How must you set the custom animation in order for an audio CD to play across multiple slides? See "Playing Audio CDs" in Chapter 14.
9. How do you resize the video clip window on a slide? See "Adding Video Clips to a Slide" in Chapter 14.
10. What does it mean if the video clip box is black when placed on the slide? See "Adding Video Clips to a Slide" in Chapter 14.

PART V

Getting Ready for the Show

15

Working with Other Office Applications

One of the nice parts about Microsoft Office is how seamless it is to transfer content between its various applications. For example, it's easy to use an Excel chart in PowerPoint, a PowerPoint outline in Word, or any other combination. There are several ways of getting content from place to place, depending on how you want it to behave. It can stand alone in its destination location, or it can retain a link either to its original data file (linking) or to the application that created it (embedding). In this chapter, you'll learn how to:

- Copy items using the Office Clipboard
- Use Smart Tags to specify how items are copied
- Drag and drop items between Office applications
- Link and embed items

Using the Office Clipboard

The Office Clipboard is an enhanced version of the Windows Clipboard. Instead of being able to store only one item at a time, the Office Clipboard can store up to 24 items that you can copy between all Office programs (not just within PowerPoint).

Displaying the Clipboard

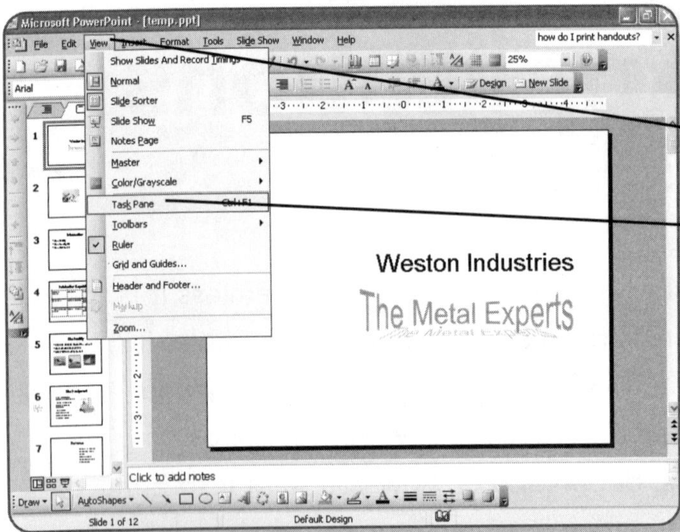

1. **Click** on **View**. The View menu will appear.

2. **Click** on **Task Pane** if there is not already a checkmark beside it. The Task Pane will appear.

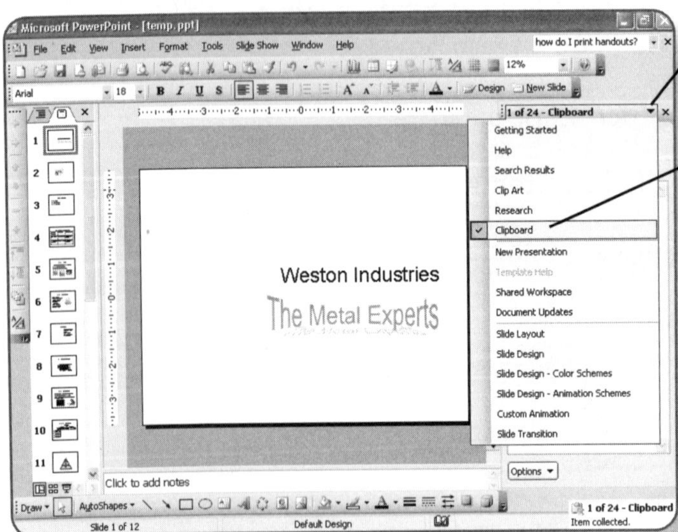

3. **Click** on the **Task Pane down arrow**. A list of available task panes will appear.

4. **Click** on **Clipboard**. The Clipboard task pane will appear.

Copying and Pasting with the Clipboard

You can copy and paste between applications or within the same one. The application you copy from is the *source application*; the one you copy to is the *destination application.*

1. **Select** the **data** that you want to add to the Clipboard. It may be in PowerPoint or some other application.

> **NOTE**
>
> You can select any amount of text, an object, or more than one object. To select multiple objects, hold down Ctrl as you click on each one.

2. **Click** on the **Copy button** or press Ctrl+C. The item will be copied to the Office Clipboard.

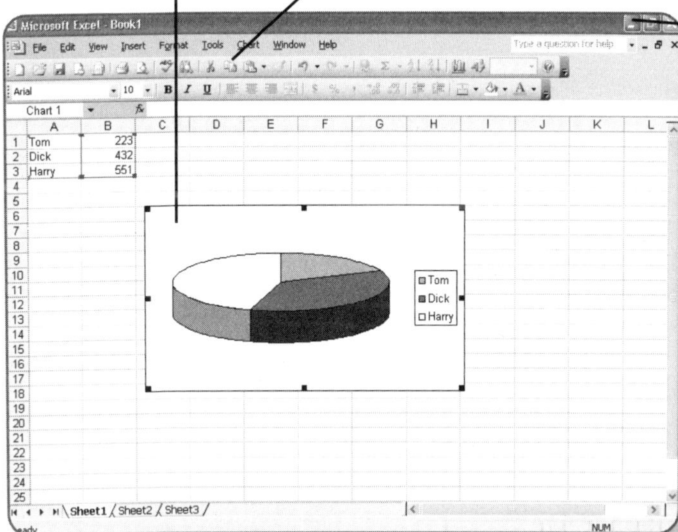

3. **Minimize** the **source application window** if you are copying between applications.

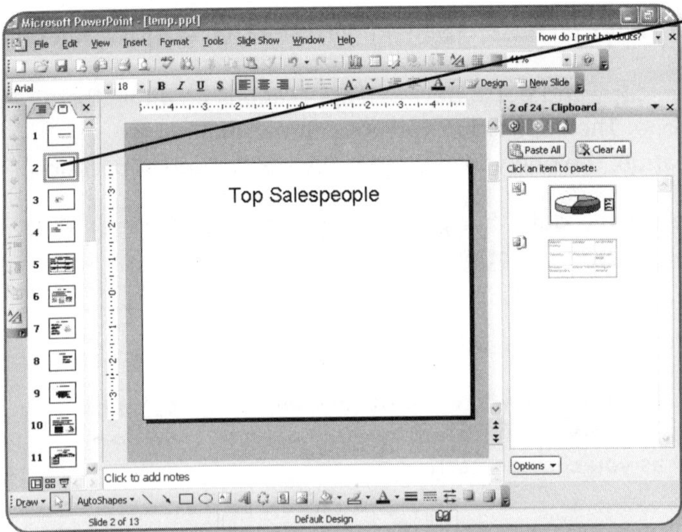

4. Display the **slide** (in PowerPoint) on which you want to paste. The slide will appear in Normal view.

5. If you're pasting text, **click** in the **text box** where you want to paste. The insertion point will appear there.

> ### NOTE
>
> Step 5 is necessary only when you're pasting text. If you're pasting a graphical object, it will appear on the center of the slide, and you can then drag it where you want it.

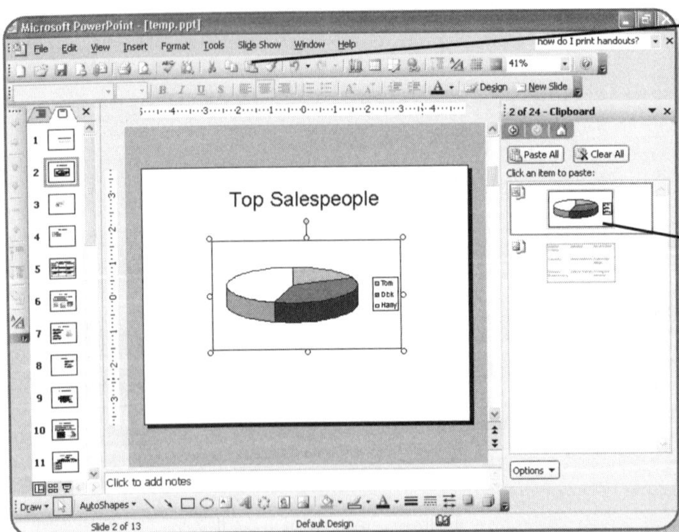

6a. Click on the **Paste button**. The most recently copied item will be pasted from the Clipboard.

OR

6b. Click on the **item** in the Clipboard task pane that you want to insert. A copy of the item will appear on the slide. Use this method if you want to paste an item other than the one you most recently copied.

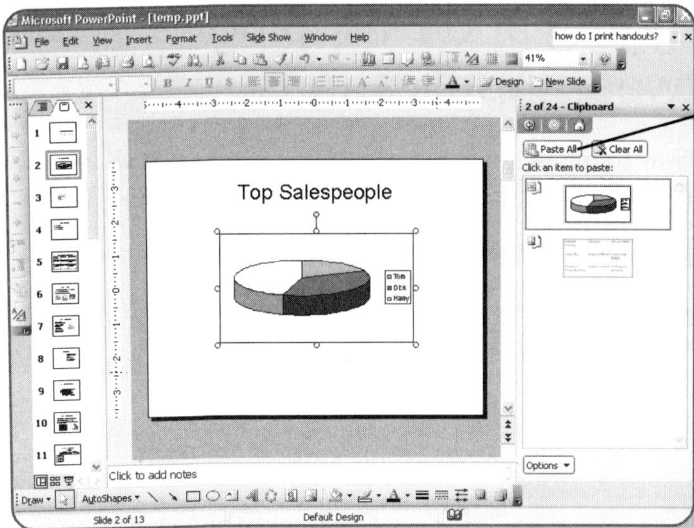

TIP

If you want to paste everything in the Clipboard to the slide, click on Paste All.

Keeping the Source Formatting When Pasting

If you are pasting text, it takes on the formatting of the destination by default. A Smart Tag icon appears next to the pasted text. You can use that icon to return the pasted text to its original formatting, if needed.

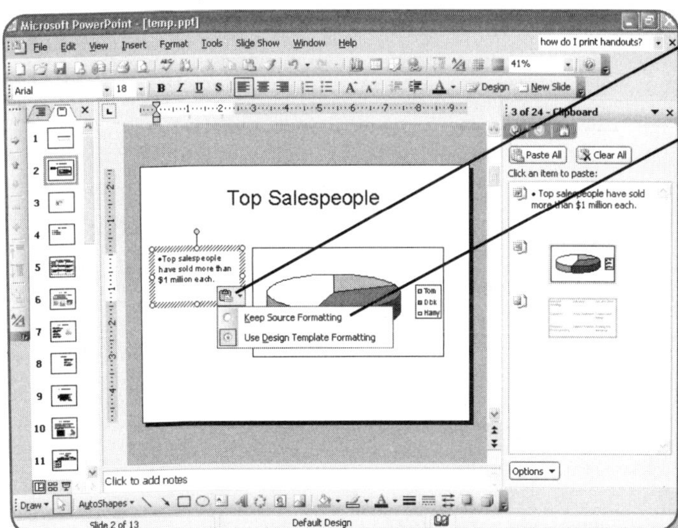

1. **Click** on the **Smart Tag icon.** A menu will appear.

2. **Click** on **Keep Source Formatting** if you want to retain the original formatting of the text. The text format will change back to the way it appeared in the Office application from which it was copied.

Dragging and Dropping Between Applications

A fast way to move items between two programs is to use the drag-and-drop method.

1. **Open both applications.**

2. **Resize** and **arrange** the **application windows** so that both are visible at once.

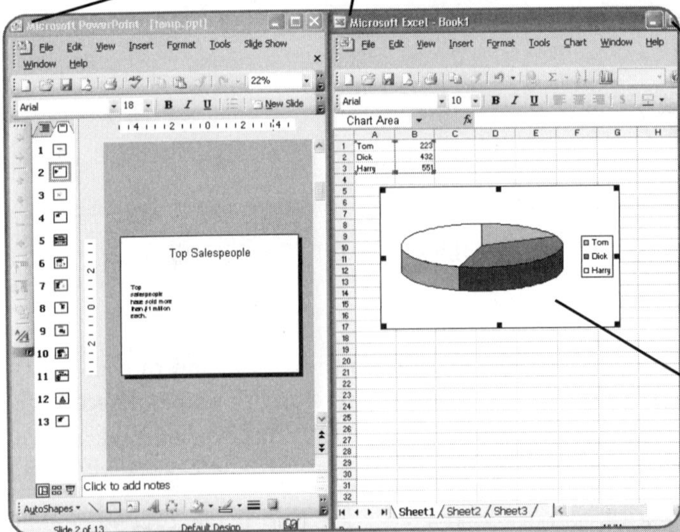

NOTE

To accomplish step 2, click the Restore button in a window so that it is no longer maximized, and then drag its border to resize it or drag its title bar to move it.

3. **Select** the **item(s)** that you want to copy. The items will be selected.

4. **Press** and **hold** the **Ctrl key**. This will cause whatever is dragged to be copied, rather than moved.

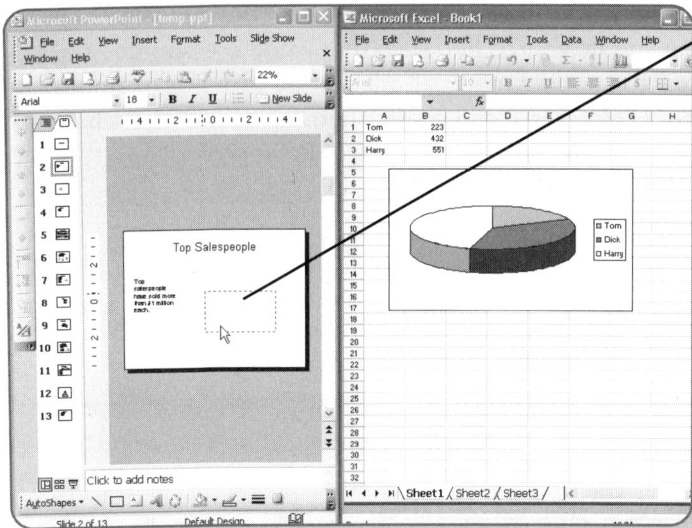

5. **Drag** the **object** from the source application to the destination application. The mouse pointer will show a box on it as you drag.

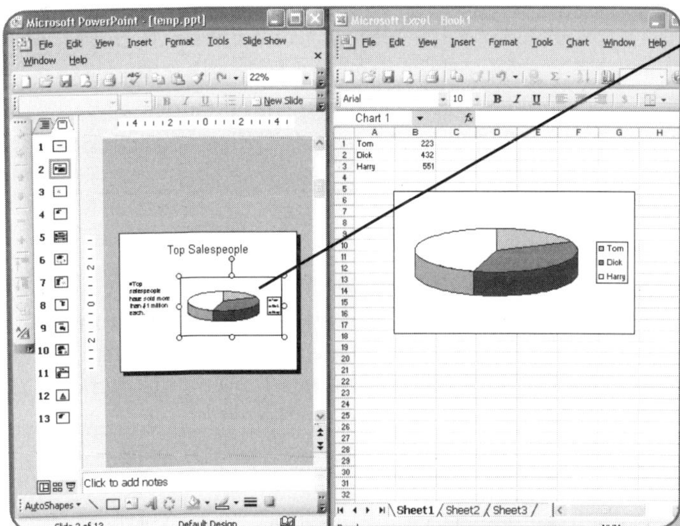

6. **Release** the **mouse button** at the desired location in PowerPoint. The object will be copied.

Linking Content

Linking is a way of retaining a connection between the copied material and its source file, such that when the source changes, the copied material will change too. For example, you could link to an Excel chart. Then, whenever that chart changed in Excel, it would change in PowerPoint too.

> **NOTE**
>
> The link will be updated when the PowerPoint file is opened *only* if the file to which it is linked is available. Otherwise, the last update will appear.

Linking Part of a File

You can link just a part of another file, such as the chart from an Excel workbook, or you can link an entire file.

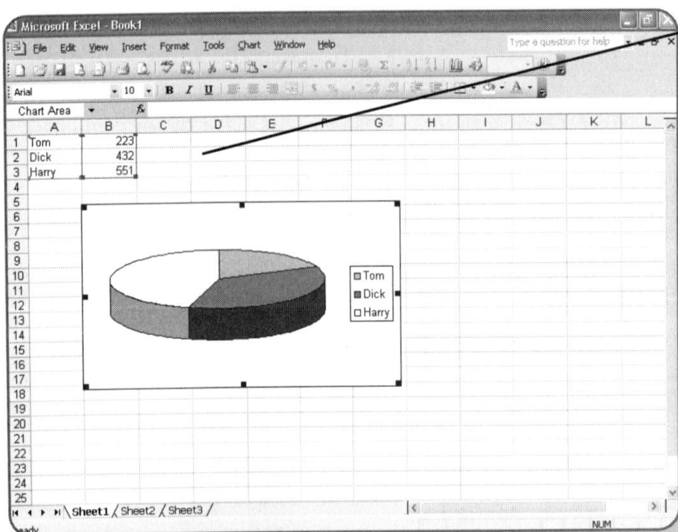

1. Open the **file** containing the object to be linked. It can be in any application that supports linking. (That includes all Microsoft Office applications.)

> **NOTE**
>
> The file in step 1 must have been saved. That is, it must have a name. Otherwise, there will be no file name to link to.

2. Select the **portion of the file to be copied**. This could be a single object, a range of text or cells, or any other amount of data.

3. Click on the **Copy button**, or press **Ctrl+C**. The data will be copied to the Clipboard.

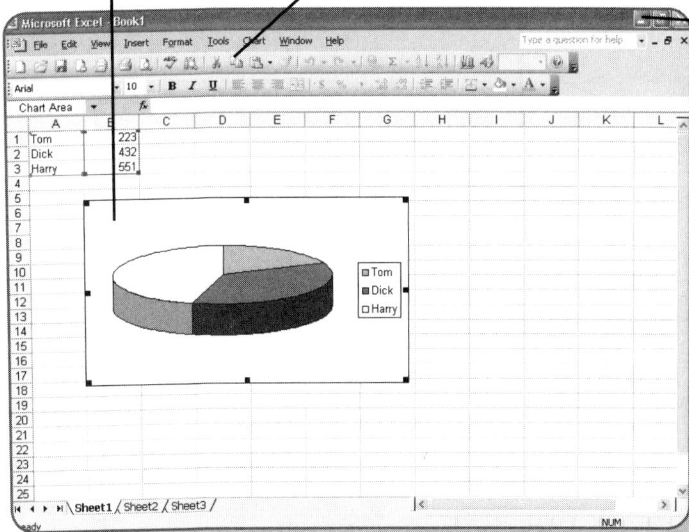

4. Minimize the **source application**.

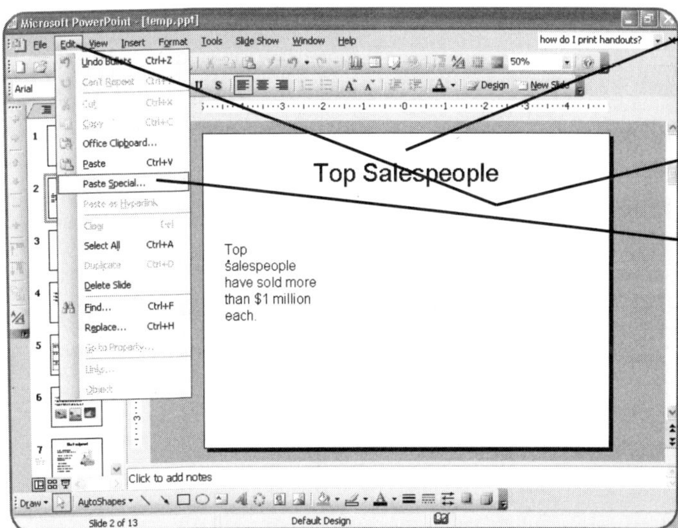

5. Display, in PowerPoint, the **slide** on which the linked object should appear.

6. Click on **Edit**. The Edit menu will appear.

7. Click on **Paste Special.** The Paste Special dialog box will open.

8. **Click** on **Paste Link**. The As list will change to show only linkable object types.

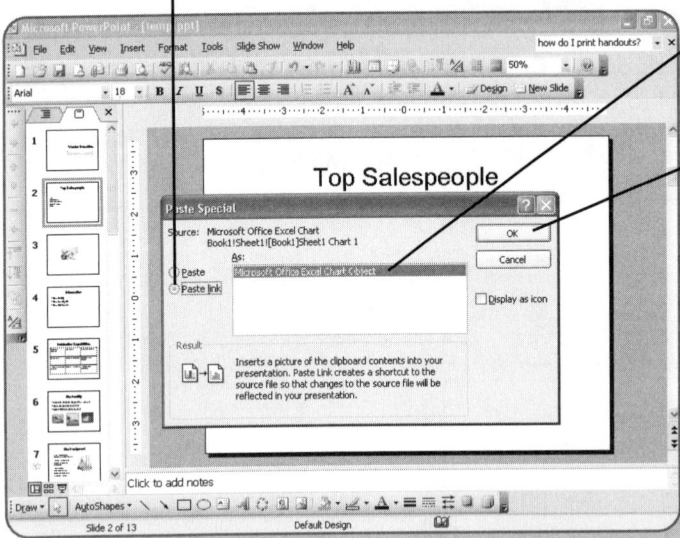

9. **Click** on the **desired object type**. In most cases, there will be only one choice.

10. **Click** on **OK**. The link will be pasted, and the object will appear on the slide.

> **NOTE**
>
> If you want to test the link, restore the source application's window and make a change to the data. Then restore PowerPoint and observe that the change has been made in PowerPoint too.

Linking an Entire File

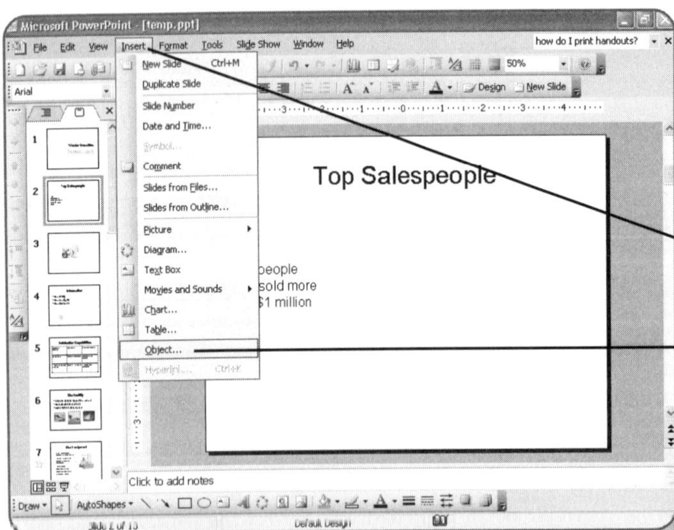

This method is useful if the content you want to link to is an entire file by itself, such as a graphic file.

1. **Click** on **Insert**. The Insert menu will appear.

2. **Click** on **Object**. The Insert Object dialog box will open.

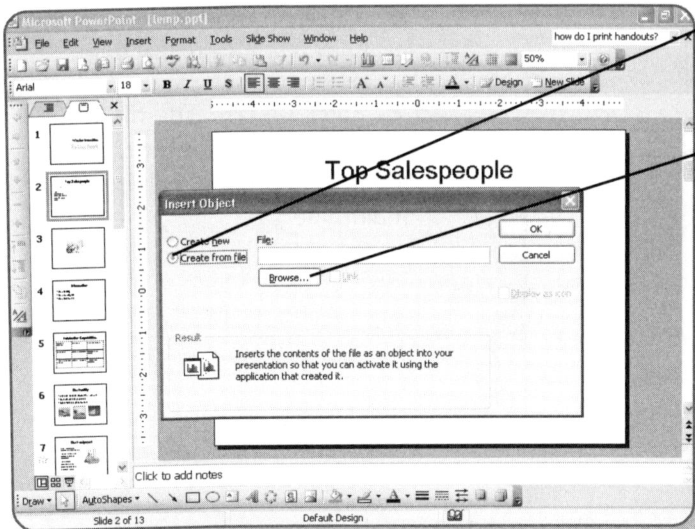

3. Click on **Create from file**. The File text box and Browse button will appear.

4. Click on **Browse**. The Browse dialog box will open.

5. Choose the **folder** in the Look in box. The folder's contents will appear.

6. Click on the **file** you want. A preview of it will appear.

7. Click on **OK.** The file's name and path will appear in the Insert Object dialog box.

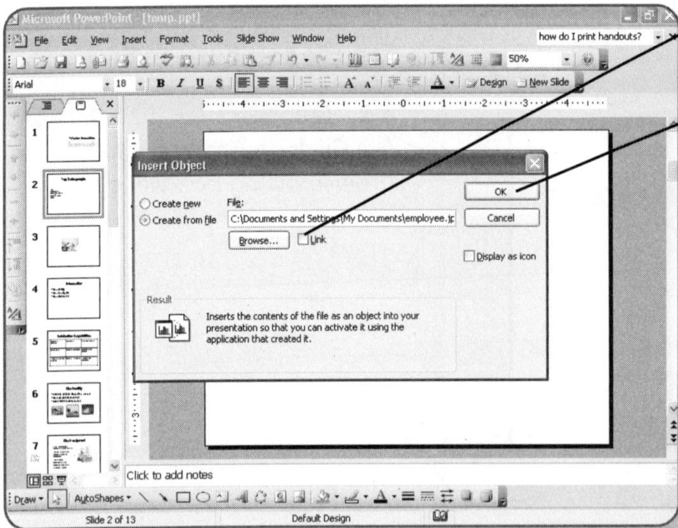

8. Click on the **Link check box**. A check will be placed in it.

9. Click on **OK**. The file will appear as slide content, and a link to the original will be maintained.

Changing the Link Update Method

You can change a link's properties so it can be updated either manually or automatically. Updating manually is a good choice when the source file is not always available.

1. Click on **Edit**. The Edit menu will appear.

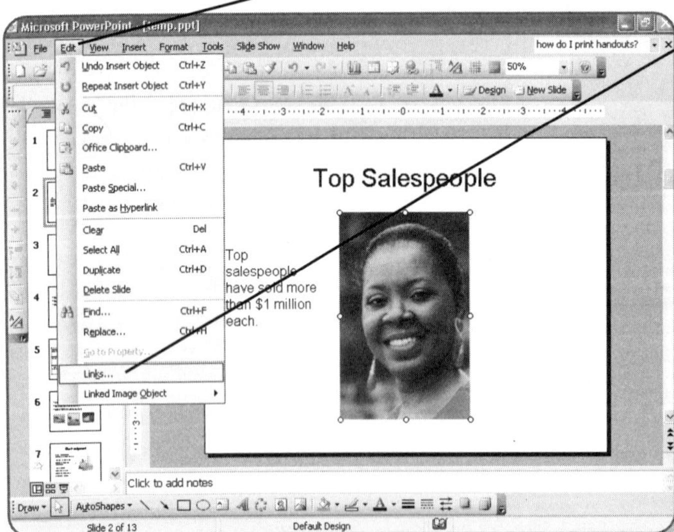

2. Click on **Links**. The Links dialog box will open.

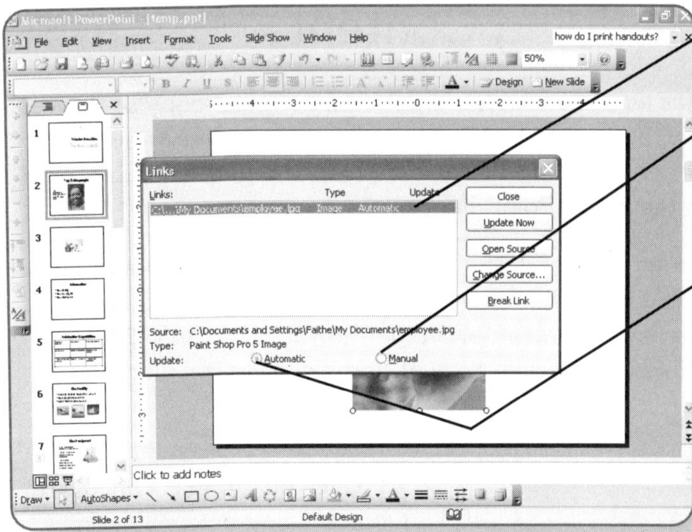

3. Click on the **link** you want to change. It will be highlighted.

4a. Click on **Manual** to set it to manual updating.

OR

4b. Click on **Automatic** to set it to automatic updating.

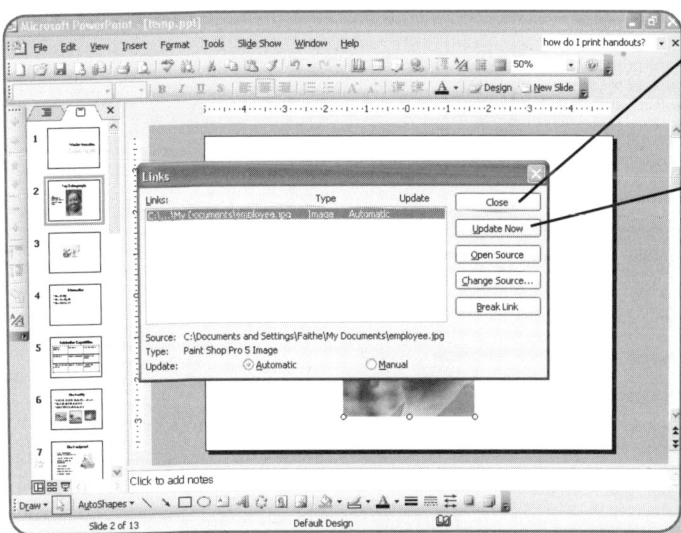

5. Click on **Close**.

> **NOTE**
>
> With manual updating, you must initiate the update. To do so, return to the Links dialog box, select the link, and click Update Now.

Embedding Content

Whereas linking maintains a link to an original copy of the data file, embedding maintains a link only to the original application (not a particular data file). The data itself is stored only in the PowerPoint file.

Embedding is useful when you have no need for an externally updatable data file, but you want to place some type of content in your presentation that PowerPoint can't create. This could be a certain type of graphic, chart, or diagram.

1. **Click** on **Insert**. The Insert menu will appear.

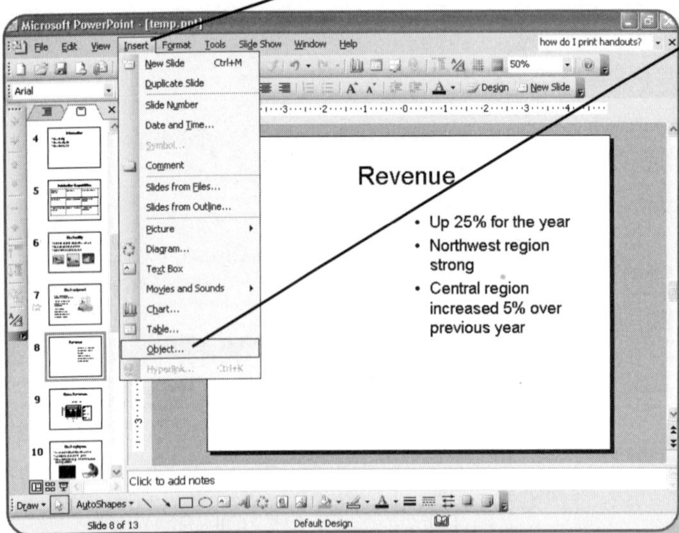

2. **Click** on **Object**. The Insert Object dialog box will open.

3. Click on the **object type** you want to create. It will be selected.

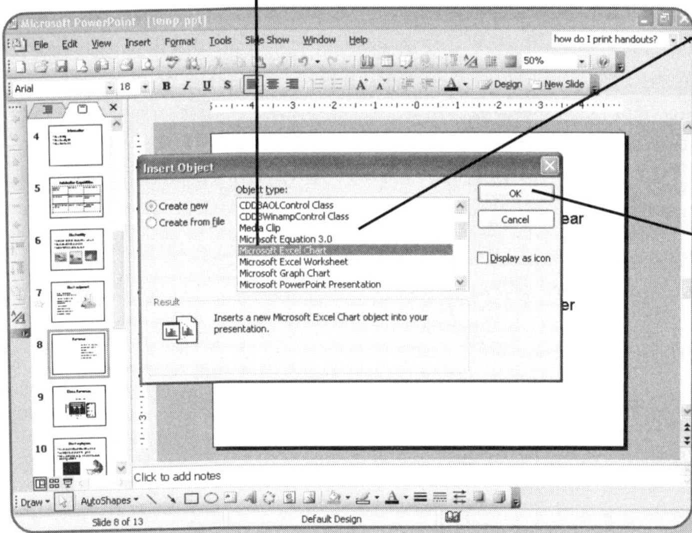

The object types listed here represent the OLE-compliant applications installed on your computer. Your list may be different than the one shown here.

4. Click on **OK**. The controls for creating that object will appear.

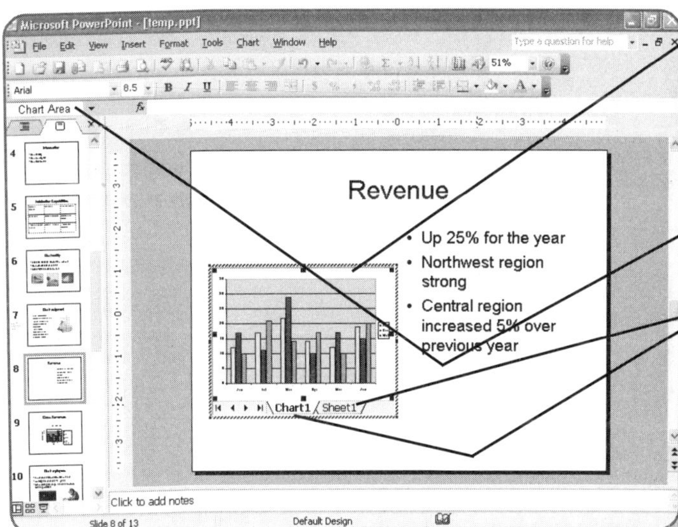

Depending on the object type chosen, a separate window may appear, or the controls may appear within the PowerPoint window.

5. Use the **controls that appear** to create the content.

For example, here an Excel chart and worksheet appears. Click the Sheet1 tab to edit the data, and use the Chart menu to change the chart's features.

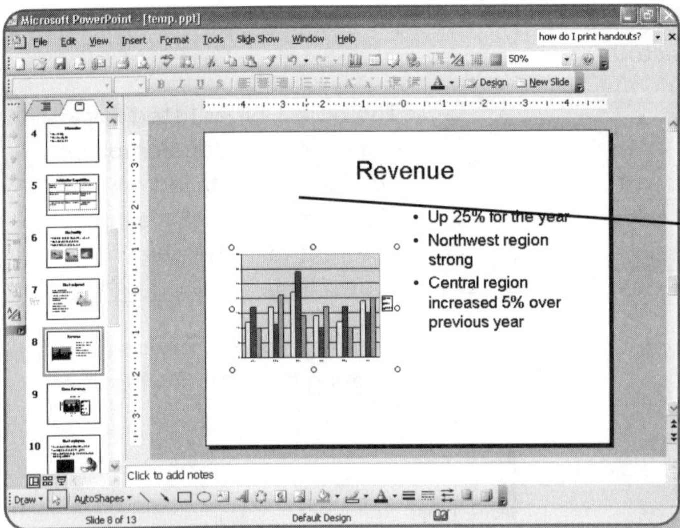

Returning to PowerPoint

If you're using an application from within the PowerPoint window:

Click on the **slide's background**. PowerPoint will return to normal operation.

OR

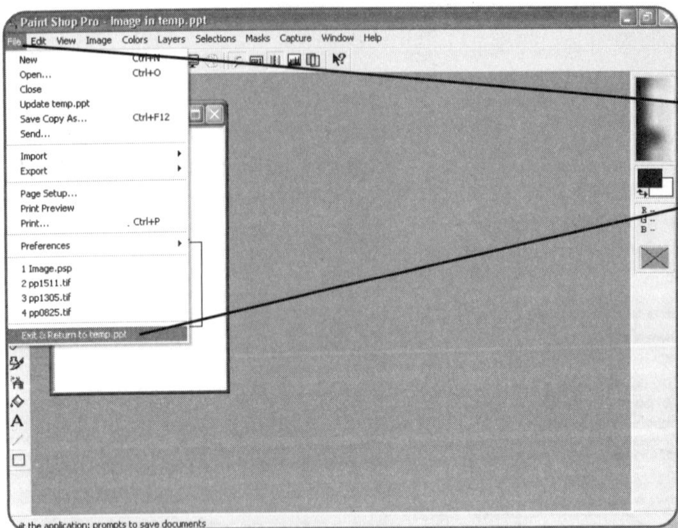

If you're using an application that appears as a separate window:

1. **Click** on **File.** The File menu will appear.
2. **Click** on **Exit & Return to [*presentation*].** The application will close, and PowerPoint will display the object.

Editing an Embedded Object

1. **Double-click** on the **object** on the PowerPoint slide. Its application's controls will appear so you can edit it.

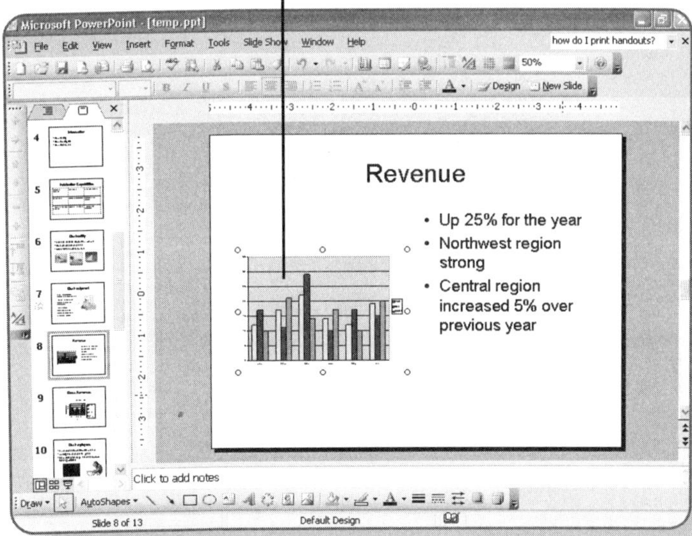

2. **Make changes** to the object.

3. **Return** to **PowerPoint**, as in the preceding steps.

16

Adding the Final Touches to Your Presentation

You've finished creating your presentation. Now it's time to add a few items that will help you when you deliver it. If you'll be delivering it in front of an audience, you'll want to use notes. You'll also need to practice. To prepare for potential questions from the audience, you may want to hide a few slides up your sleeve. Self-running presentations (such as kiosks) that use voice-over narration are more effective than those without accompanying sounds. In this chapter, you'll learn how to:

- Create speaker notes
- Customize the Notes Master
- Use hidden slides
- Rehearse and set timings

Using Notes

When you're giving a presentation, cue cards are a handy item. Not only do they help relieve anxiety caused by stage fright, but they also enhance a presentation. You can develop notes and print them with a copy of the slide to help keep your presentation on course. To provide your audience with more information, print a notes page that they can take home.

Adding Notes to a Slide

1. Click on the **Normal View button**. Your slide will appear in Normal view.

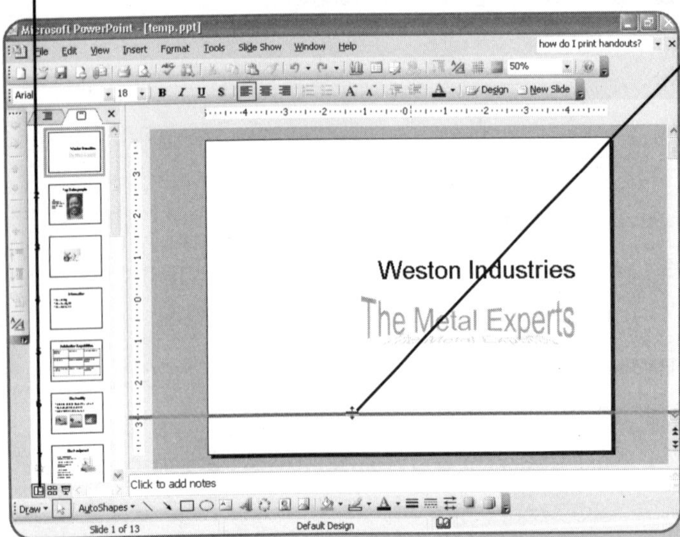

2. Click and **drag** the **bar** up to the middle between the Slide pane and the Notes pane. The mouse pointer will turn into a double arrow, and an outline of the bar will show how the pane size will be changed.

3. Release the **mouse button**. The two panes will be resized, and you'll have more room to work in the Notes pane.

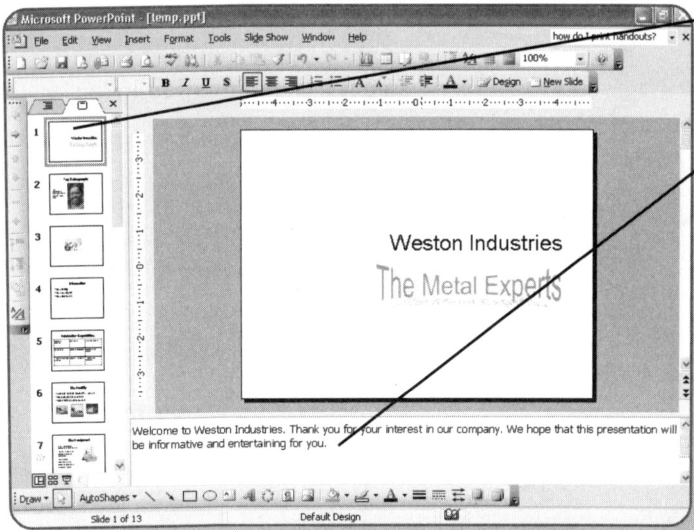

4. **Display** the **slide** to which you want to add the notes. The slide will appear in the Slide pane.

5. **Click** inside the **Notes pane** and **type notes** as desired. These notes can be anything that will help you remember what you need to say, or that will provide additional background as needed during the presentation.

> **TIP**
>
> When a presentation is displayed as Web pages, notes can be shown on a page along with the corresponding slide.

Working in Notes Page View

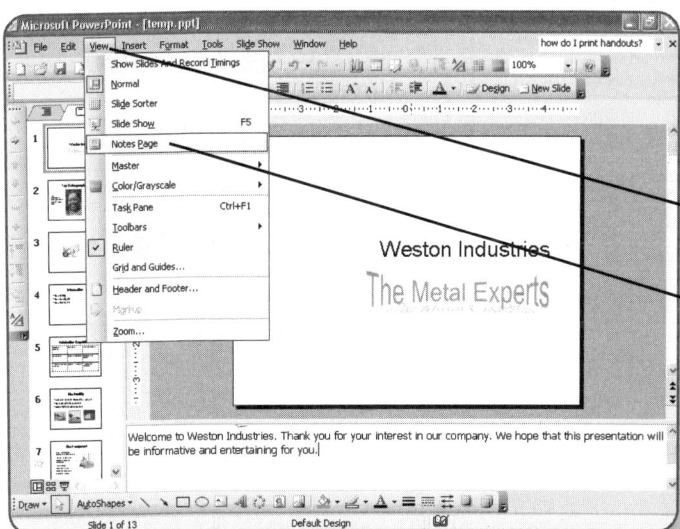

Notes Page view is a special view designed specifically for typing and editing notes. It displays each slide as it will appear when you print Speaker Notes.

1. **Click** on **View**. The View menu will appear.

2. **Click** on **Notes Page**. The Notes page for the slide will appear. This is actually a preview of what the Notes page will look like when printed.

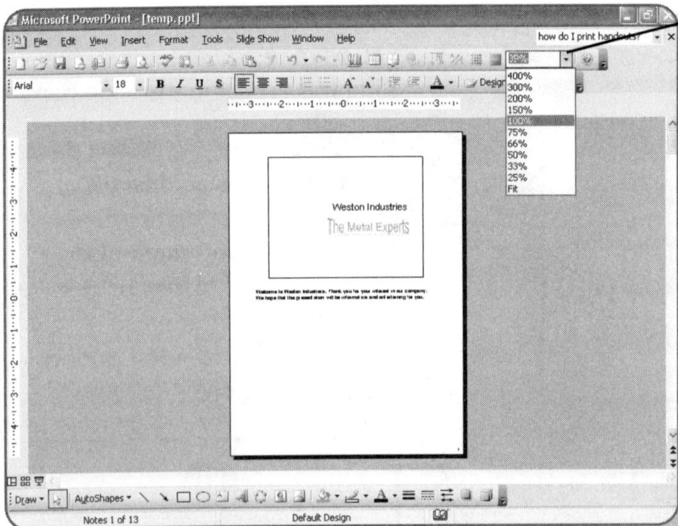

3. Click on the **down arrow** next to the Zoom button and select a magnification level.

4. Edit the **notes**. The notes will appear below a sample of the slide.

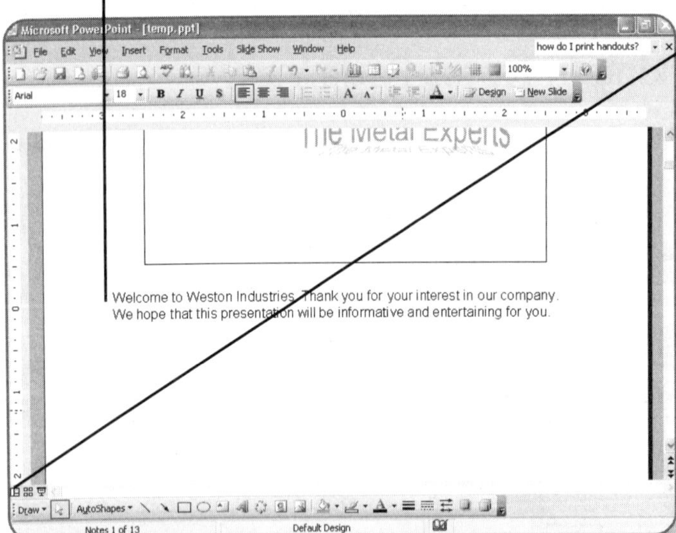

5. Click on the **Normal View button**. The selected slide will appear in Normal view. You won't see the images that you added to the Notes page in the Notes pane.

Working with the Notes Master

You worked with the Slide Master in Chapter 6, "Changing the Presentation's Look." Like the Slide Master, the Notes Master is where you can set the basic format and look for all the Notes pages in your presentation.

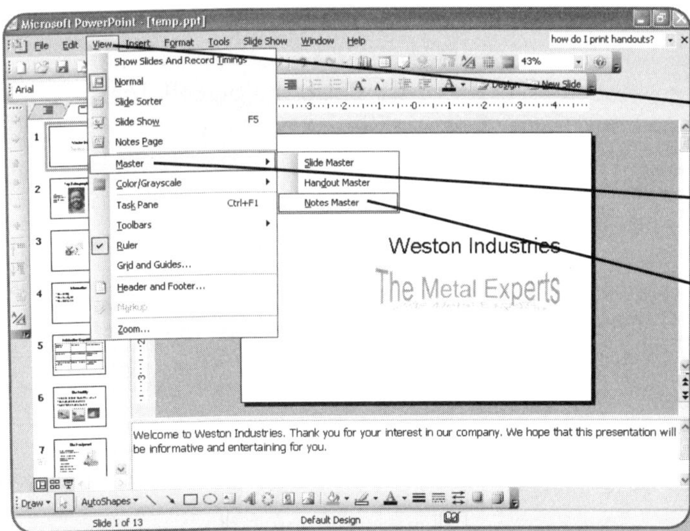

1. **Click** on **View**. The View menu will appear.

2. **Point to Master**. A submenu will appear.

3. **Click** on **Notes Master**. The Notes Master page will appear.

Removing a Placeholder

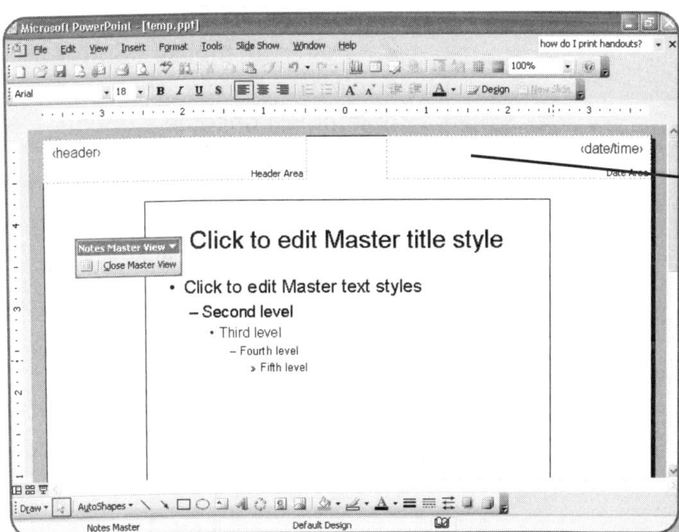

The Notes Master has several placeholder boxes. You can delete any placeholders that you do not want.

1. **Click** on the **placeholder to remove**. The placeholder will be selected.

2. **Press** the **Delete** key. The placeholder will disappear.

Moving a Placeholder

1. **Click** on a **placeholder's border**. It will be selected.

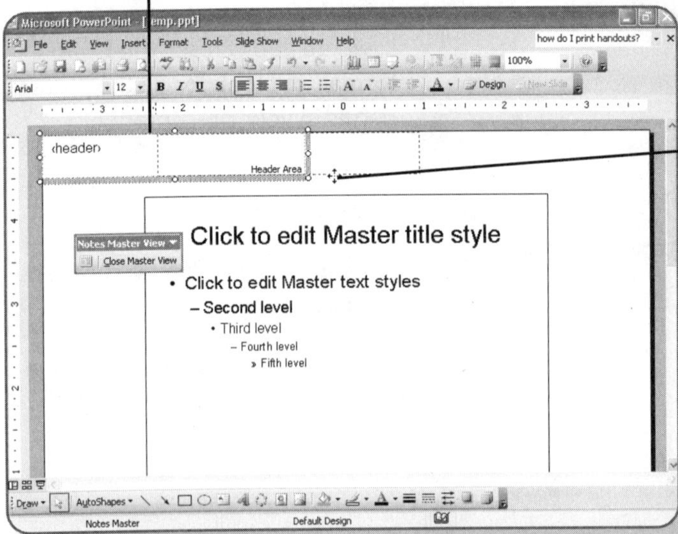

2. **Point** the **mouse pointer** at the border, but not on a selection handle.
3. **Drag** the **placeholder** to a different location.

Resizing a Placeholder

1. **Click** on the **placeholder's border**. It will be selected.

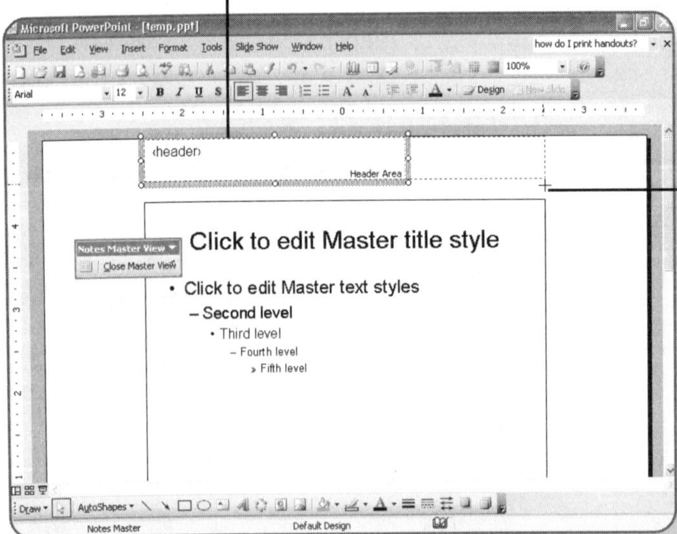

2. **Point** the **mouse pointer** at a selection handle. The mouse pointer will become a double-headed arrow.
3. **Drag** the **selection handle** to change the size of the placeholder box.

Restoring Deleted Placeholders

1. Click on the **Notes Master Layout button**. The Notes Master Layout dialog box will open. Any placeholders that have been deleted will appear as empty check boxes.

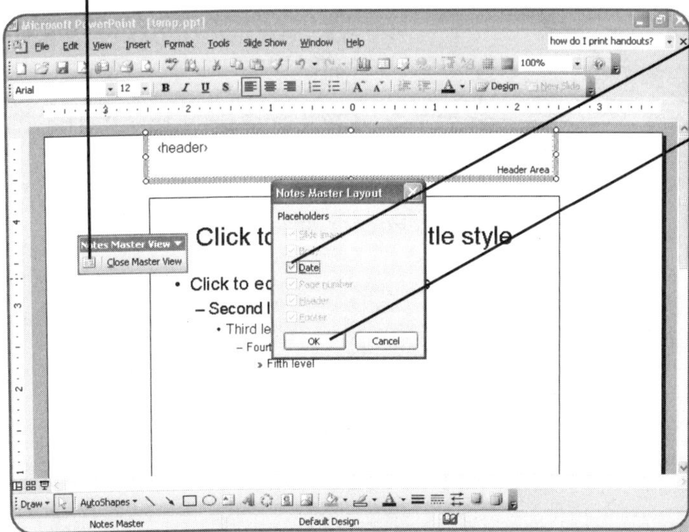

2. Click in a **check box** for a placeholder you want to restore.

3. Click on **OK**. The placeholder will be restored on the Notes Master.

Editing Headers and Footers

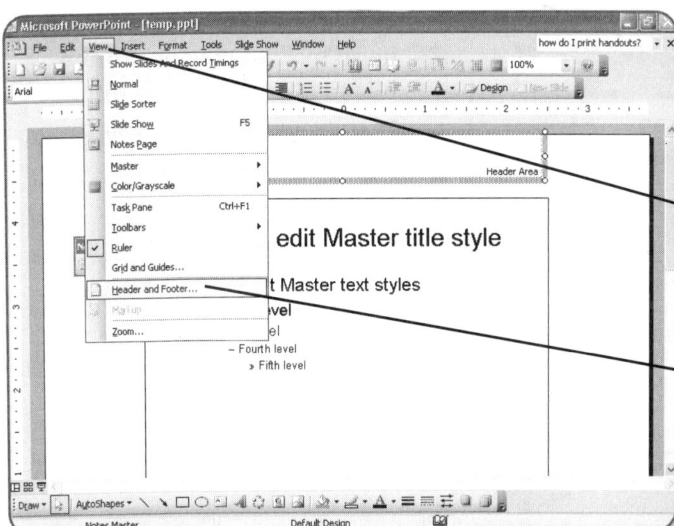

The preceding procedures worked with the placeholders for the header and footer elements. Now you will specify what text should appear in them.

1. Click on **View** to add information to the Header and Footer areas. The View menu will appear.

2. Click on **Header and Footer**. The Header and Footer dialog box will open, and the Notes and Handouts tab will be on top.

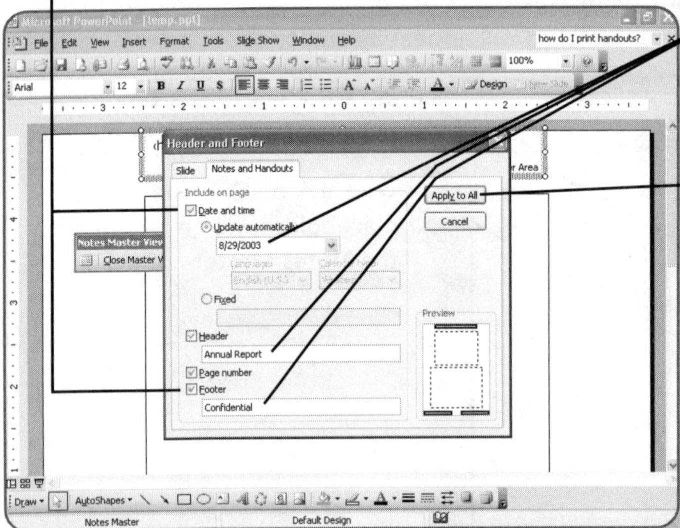

3. **Mark** the **check boxes** for the placeholder items you want to appear, and **clear** the **check boxes** for the placeholders you don't want to appear.

4. **Type** any **text** that you want to appear in those areas, or specify automatic entry (as with Date and time).

5. **Click** on **Apply to All**. The information you've typed will appear in the Header and Footer areas.

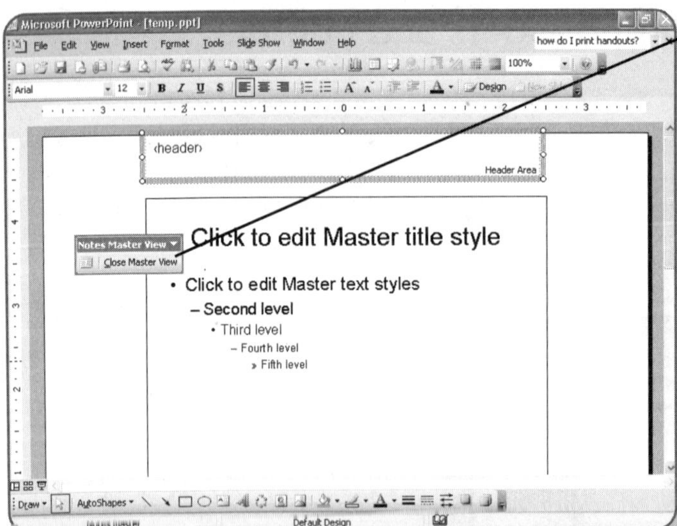

6. **Click** on the **Close Master View button** on the Notes Master View toolbar when you finish making changes to the Notes Master. You will return to the view you were using previously.

Printing Your Notes

1. **Click** on **File**. The File menu will appear.

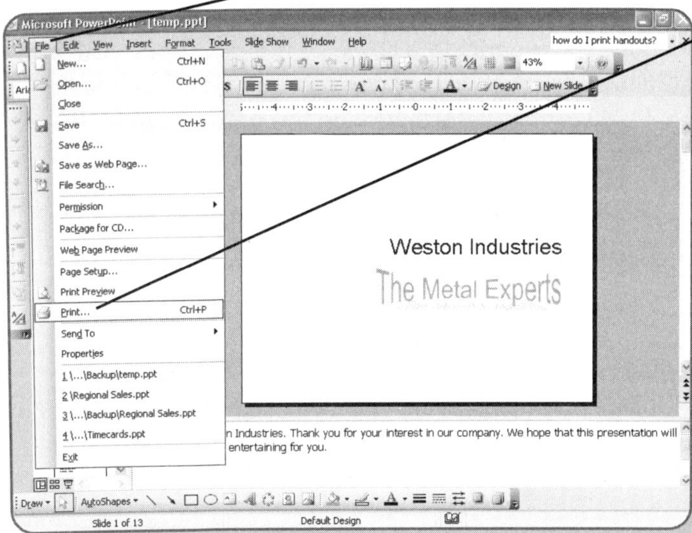

2. **Click** on **Print**. The Print dialog box will open.

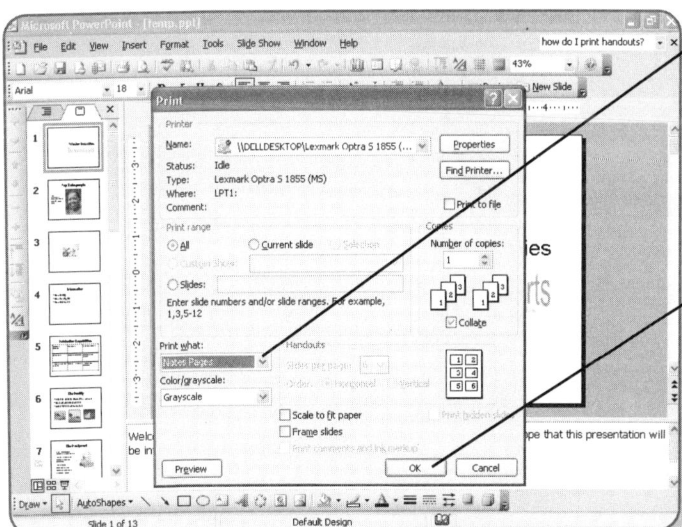

3. **Click** on the **down arrow** next to the Print what list box, and **click** on **Notes Pages**. The option will appear in the list box.

4. **Change** any other **options** as needed.

5. **Click** on **OK**. The Notes pages will be printed.

Using Hidden Slides

At some point during a presentation, you'll probably receive questions from your audience. Before you deliver your presentation, try to anticipate some of the questions you'll be asked. Make slides that will answer the questions, or provide additional background information in the notes. Your audience will think that you're brilliant!

Hiding a Slide

This same procedure both hides and unhides slides.

1. **Display** the **slide** that you want hidden. The slide will appear in Normal view.

2. **Click** on **Slide Show**. The Slide Show menu will appear.

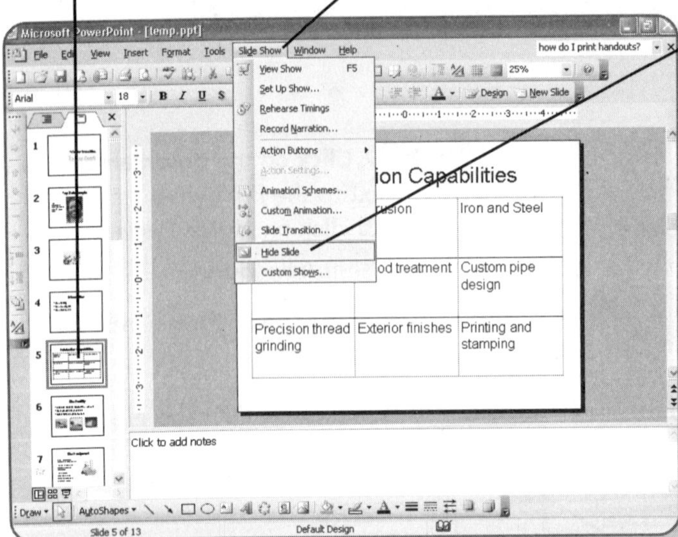

3. **Click** on **Hide Slide**. The slide will be hidden until you ask for it during your slide show.

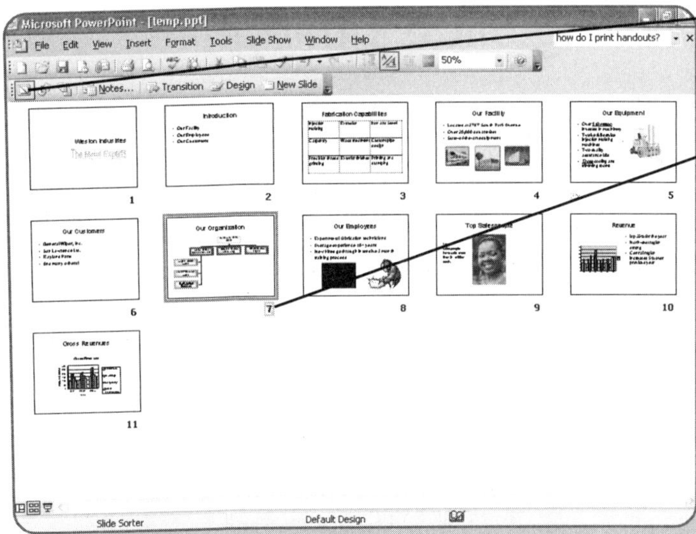

There is a Hide Slide button on the toolbar in Slide Sorter view that hides and unhides slides.

A hidden slide has a Hidden indicator around its slide number.

Using Hidden Slides During a Slide Show

Start in the slide show (in Slide Show view). See Chapter 17, "Creating Audience Handouts," for help.

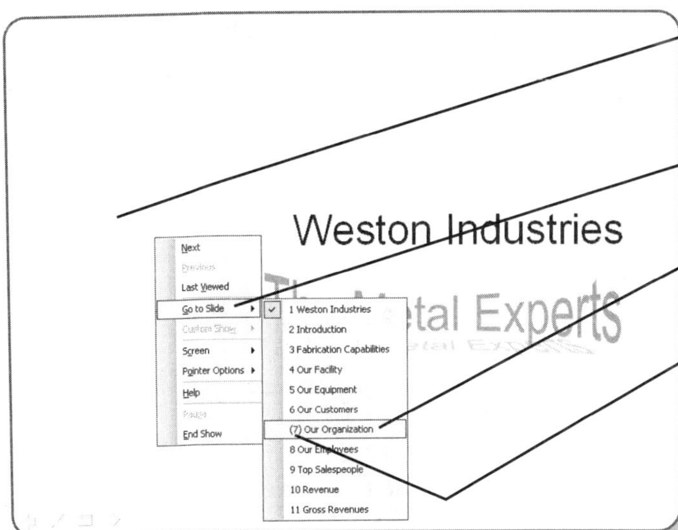

1. **Right-click** on the **slide** that is showing in Slide Show view. A shortcut menu will appear.
2. **Point to Go to Slide.** A submenu will appear.
3. **Click** on the **slide to display**. The slide will appear.

A hidden slide has parentheses around its slide number.

Recording Slide Timings

You can set up your presentation so that the slides advance manually (on a mouse click), and/or so that they advance automatically after a certain amount of time.

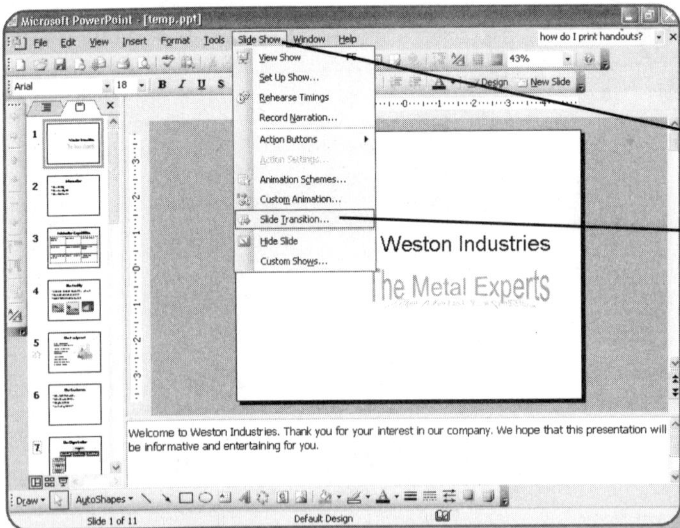

Most of the timing settings are assigned from the Slide Transition task pane.

1. **Click** on **Slide Show**. The Slide Show menu will open.
2. **Click** on **Slide Transition**. The Slide Transition task pane will appear.

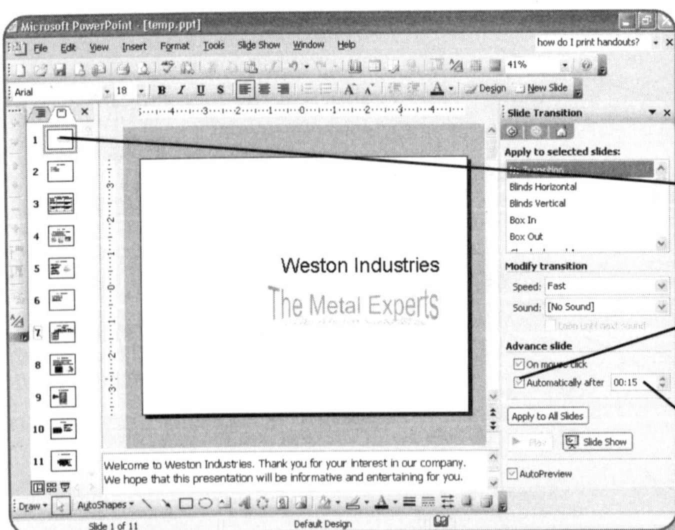

Setting the Timing for an Individual Slide

1. **Display** the **slide** for which you want to set the transition timing.
2. **Click** on the **Automatically after check box**. A check will be placed in the check box.
3. **Enter** a **number of seconds** in the Automatically after text box. The number will appear in the box.

Setting the Same Timing for All Slides

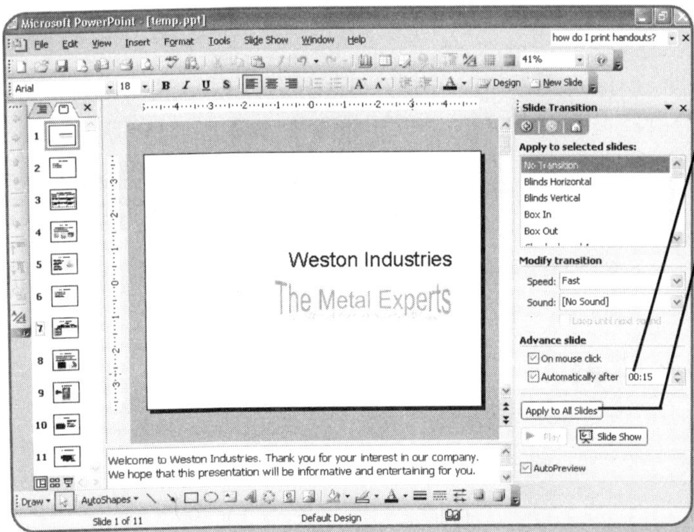

1. **Set** the **timing** for one slide, as in the preceding steps.

2. **Click** on **Apply to All Slides.** The same timing will be assigned to every slide in the presentation.

Recording Custom Timings for Each Slide

If you are not sure how much time to allocate for each slide, you can play the slide show and rehearse your speech as it runs. PowerPoint will record the amount of time you spend on each slide.

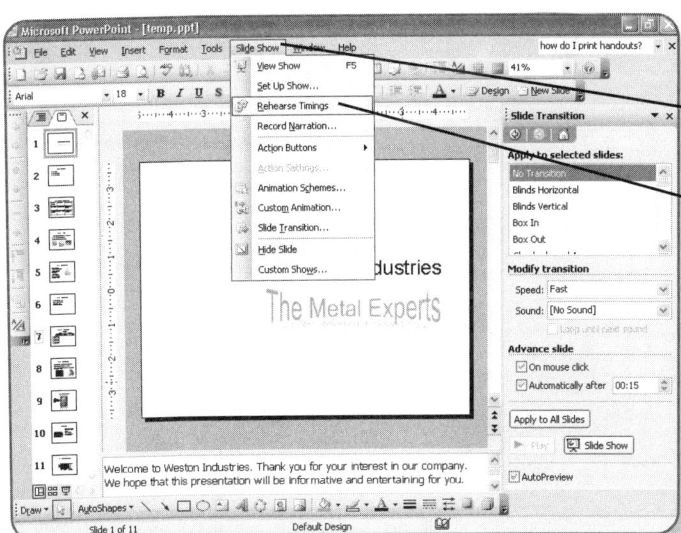

1. **Click** on **Slide Show.** The Slide Show menu will open.

2. **Click** on **Rehearse Timings.** The presentation will open in Slide Show view with a Rehearsal toolbar.

3. Speak, or do whatever it is you are going to do during the actual show, to help gauge when to move to the next slide.

4. Click on the **Next button**, or **click the mouse**. The next slide will appear. The Rehearsal toolbar will keep a count of the seconds spent on each slide.

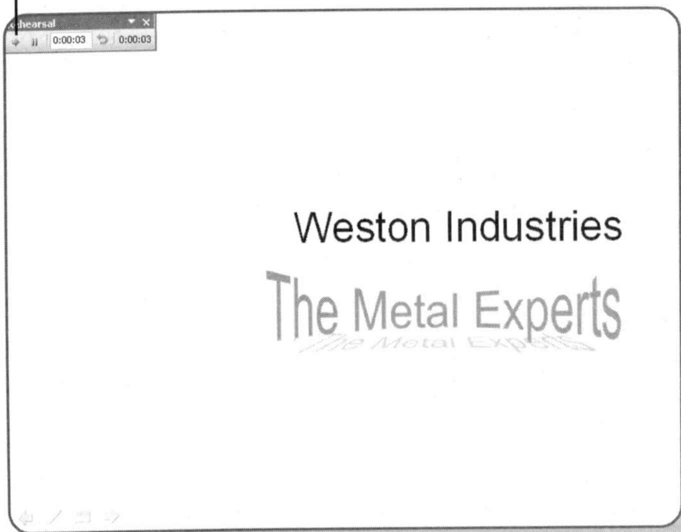

5. Repeat steps 3 and 4 until you reach the end of the slide show.

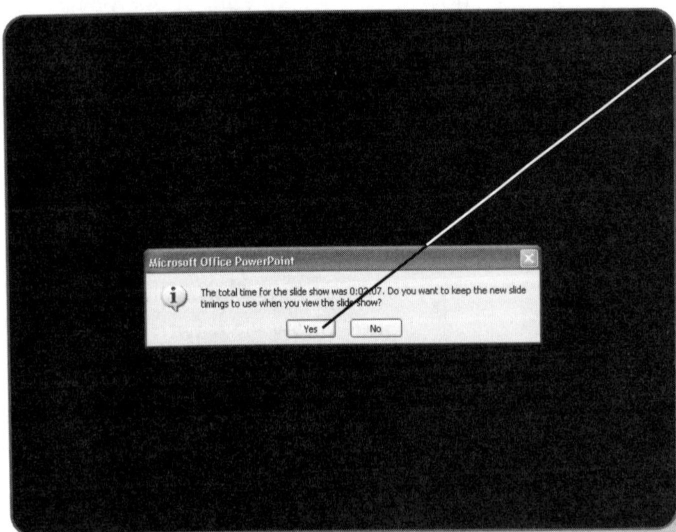

6. Click on **Yes** to keep the slide timings. Slide Show view will exit.

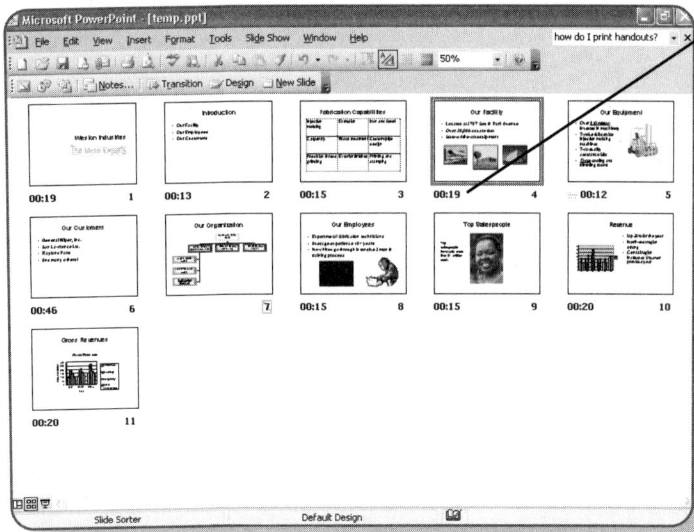

PowerPoint will reappear in Slide Sorter view, and the transition time for each slide will appear beneath it.

17

Creating Audience Handouts

Most presentations are designed primarily for display on some type of screen, whether it's a computer screen, a slide projector screen, or some other large format. However, you may also want to print a hard copy of the presentation slides for your audience to refer to. In this chapter, you will learn how to:

- Print audience handouts
- Format handouts with the Handout Master
- Export audience handouts to Word

Printing Handouts

PowerPoint can print handouts in a variety of styles, from one to nine slides per page. These layouts are ready to go from the Print dialog box.

1. **Click** on **File**. The File menu will appear.

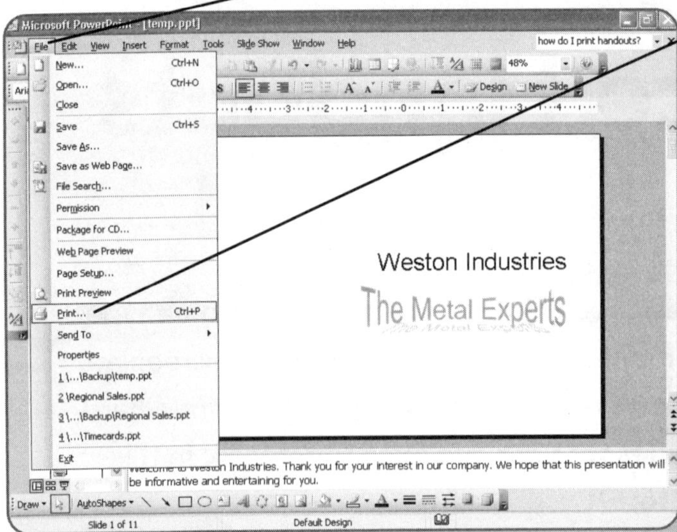

2. **Click** on **Print**. The Print dialog box will open.

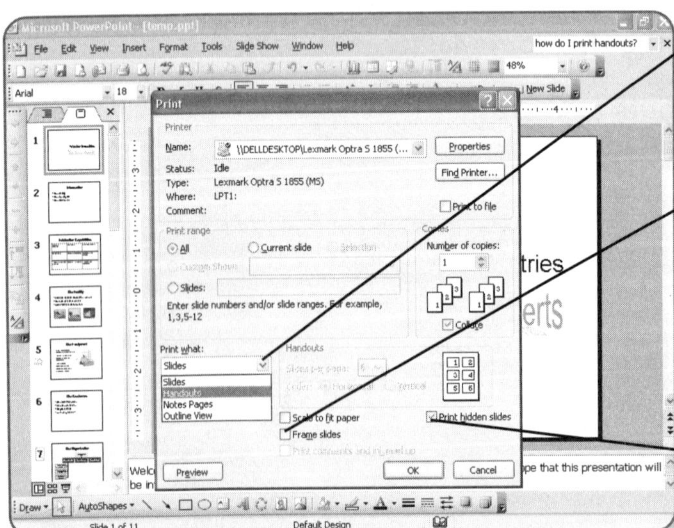

3. **Click** the **down arrow** next to the Print what list box and **click** on **Handouts**. The option will appear in the list box.

4. **Click** on the **Frame slides check box** to check or clear it as desired. If checked, it will place a black border around each slide image on the printout. This can be useful for slides with a white background.

5. **Click** on the **Print hidden slides check box** to check or clear it as desired.

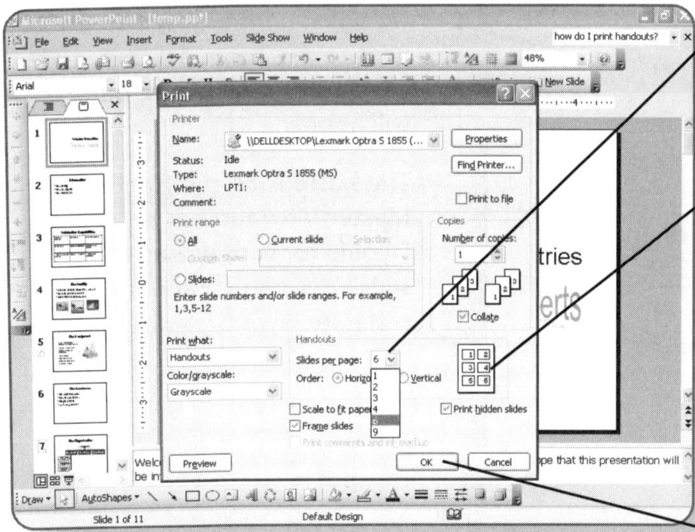

6. **Click** the **down arrow** next to Slides per page, and **click** the **number of slides** you want on each handout page.

The sample next to the box will change to show the chosen layout.

7. **Select** any **other options** as needed. For example, choose a page range or a number of copies, as you learned in Chapter 3, "Learning About Presentations."

8. **Click** on **OK**. The handouts will be printed.

Formatting Handouts with the Handout Master

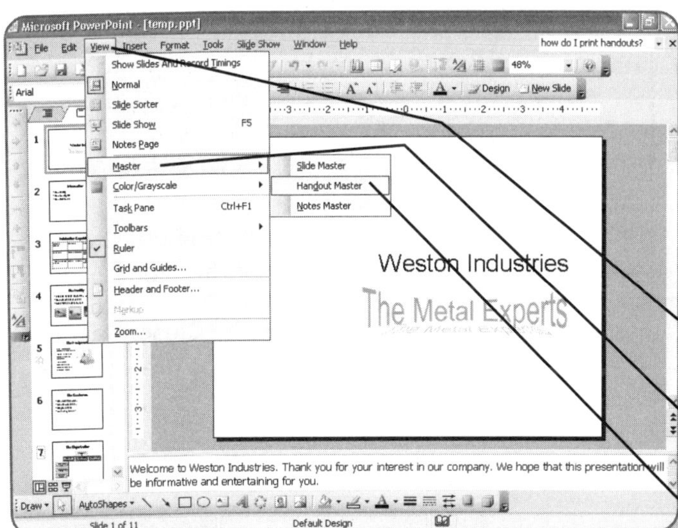

The handouts that are printed with certain numbers of slides per page are controlled by the Handout Master. It works much like the Slide Master (Chapter 6, "Changing the Presentation's Look") and the Notes Master (Chapter 16, "Adding the Final Touches to Your Presentation").

1. **Click** on **View**. The View menu will appear.

2. **Click** on **Master**. A submenu will appear.

3. **Click** on **Handout Master**. The Handout Master will appear.

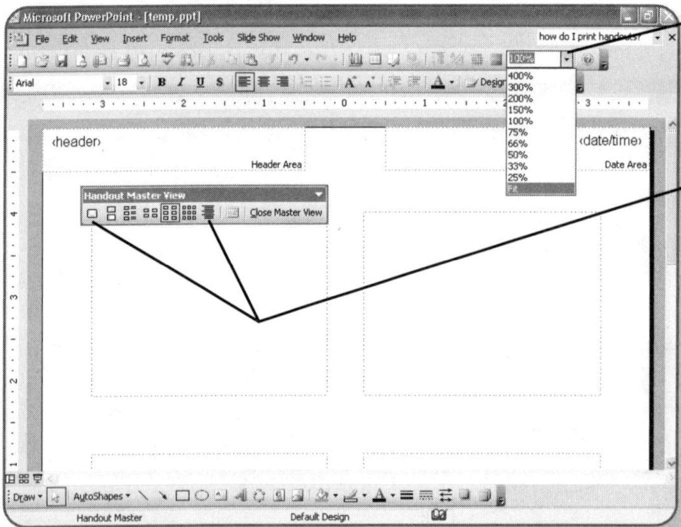

4. **Click** on the **down arrow** next to the Zoom list box, and **click** on **Fit**. The entire page will appear.

The buttons on the Handout Master View toolbar represent layouts for various numbers of slides per page. Each is a separate layout.

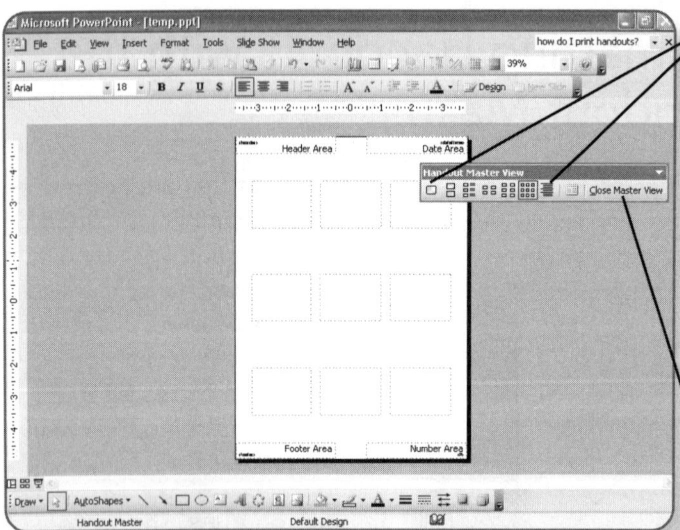

5. **Click** on a **button** on the Handout Master View toolbar. The display will change to show the layout for the chosen number of slides per page.

6. **Make** any **changes** to the layout. For example, you can change the font used in placeholder boxes, delete the placeholders, or move them. You cannot change the size or positioning of the slide boxes.

7. **Click** on the **Close Master View button**. The presentation will appear in the previous view in which you were working.

Exporting Handouts to Microsoft Word

As you saw in the preceding section, PowerPoint doesn't have many options for customizing the handout layout. You can get more freedom to change the layout by exporting the handouts for a particular presentation to Word and working with them there.

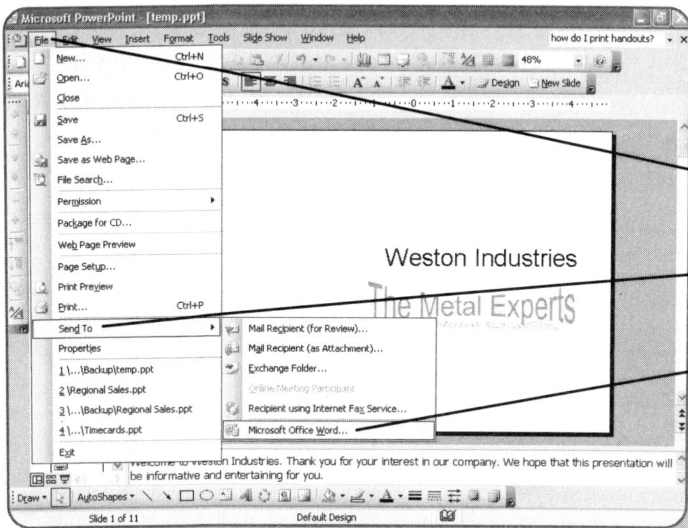

1. **Click** on **File**. The File menu will appear.
2. **Point** to **Send to**. A submenu will appear.
3. **Click** on **Microsoft Office Word**. The Send To Microsoft Office Word dialog box will open.

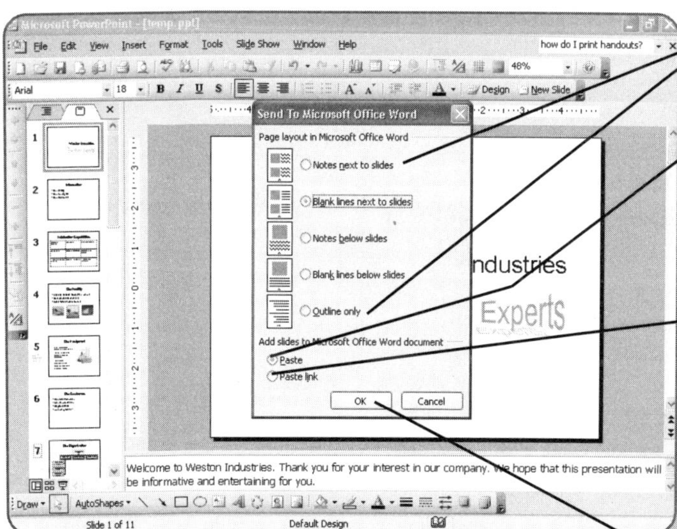

4. **Click** on one of the **layouts**. It will be selected.

5a. **Click** on **Paste**. Copies of the slides will be exported to Word.

OR

5b. **Click** on **Paste link**. The material exported into Word will retain a link with the PowerPoint presentation. This is useful if you want to reprint the handouts from Word after making more changes in PowerPoint.

6. **Click** on **OK**. The handouts will be displayed in Word.

7. **Make any changes** in Word as needed. You can edit text, change the fonts, resize the slide images, and so on.

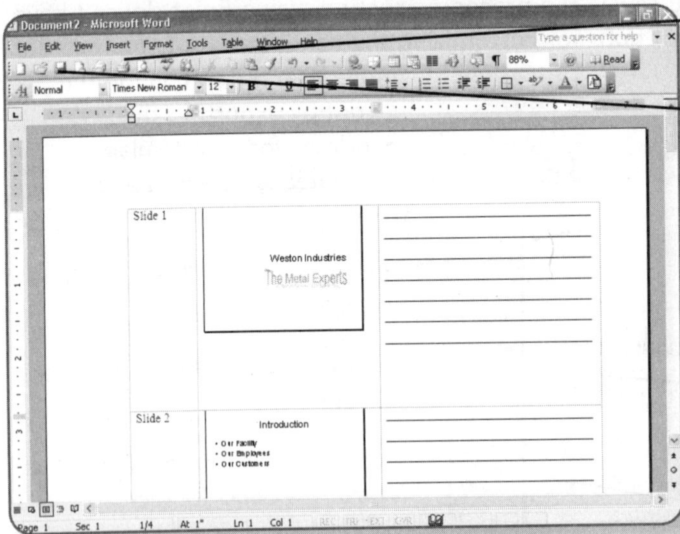

8. **Click** on the **Print button** to print the handouts from Word.

9. **Save** your **work** in Word if you want to save the file for later reprinting. The procedure is the same as saving in PowerPoint. See Chapter 3.

18

Delivering the Presentation

You're ready to give your presentation in front of a live audience. Each slide contains just the right content and is formatted so that your audience can see it clearly. You've rehearsed and rehearsed until your voice is hoarse. Your handouts are printed and stashed away in your briefcase. Now it's time to give the presentation in front of a live audience! In this chapter, you will learn how to:

- Present the show with Slide Show view
- Navigate between slides
- Use the pen in Slide Show view

Presenting a Live Slide Show

To start your live show, simply enter Slide Show view.

1. **Click** on **View**. The View menu will appear.

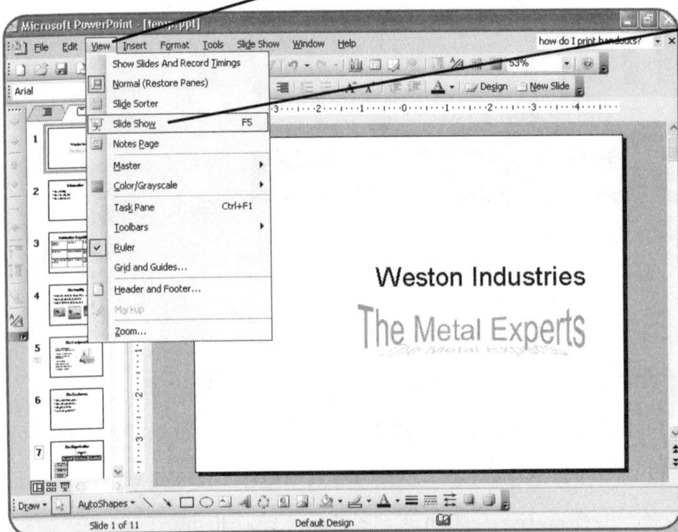

2. **Click** on **Slide Show**. The slide show will begin.

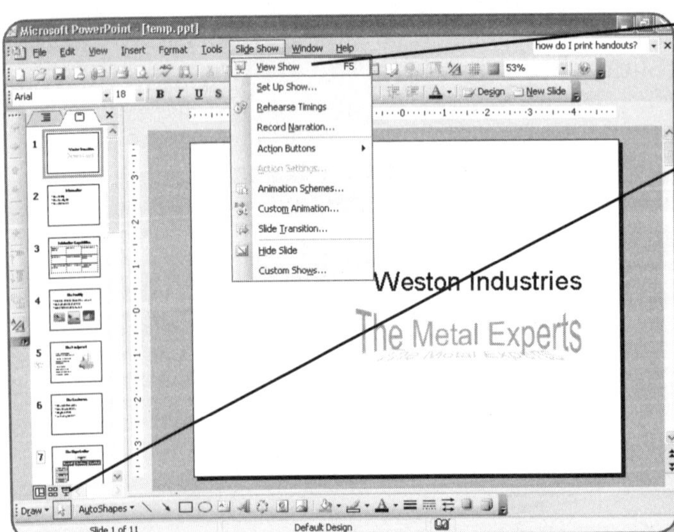

You can also open the **Slide Show** menu and choose **View Show**, or **press F5**.

You can also click the **Slide Show View button**. This starts the show at the selected slide, not necessarily at the beginning.

Moving Between Slides

To move between slides with the keyboard or mouse:

- Click the **left mouse button**, or press **Enter** or the **right arrow**, to move forward.
- Press the **Backspace key** or the **left arrow** to move backward.

You can also use an on-screen menu system.

1. **Right-click** anywhere in Slide Show view. A menu will appear.

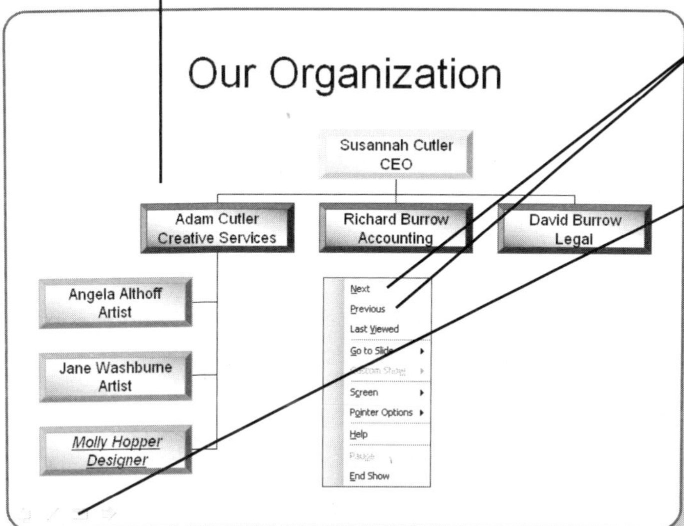

2a. **Click** on **Next** or **Previous**.

> **NOTE**
>
> When you move the mouse, the icons in the bottom-left corner appear. Clicking this one opens the same menu as right-clicking.

OR

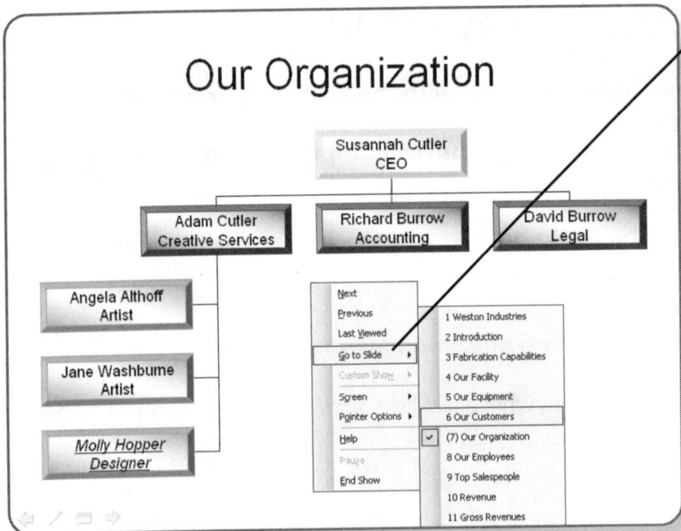

2b. Point to **Go to Slide** and then **click the slide** to display.

> **NOTE**
>
> When you reach the last slide, a black screen will appear with a message prompting you to press any key to return to PowerPoint. You can also end a show early by pressing the Esc key.

Pausing the Presentation

Pausing is useful if you have automatic advance timings set up and you need to stop for a discussion.

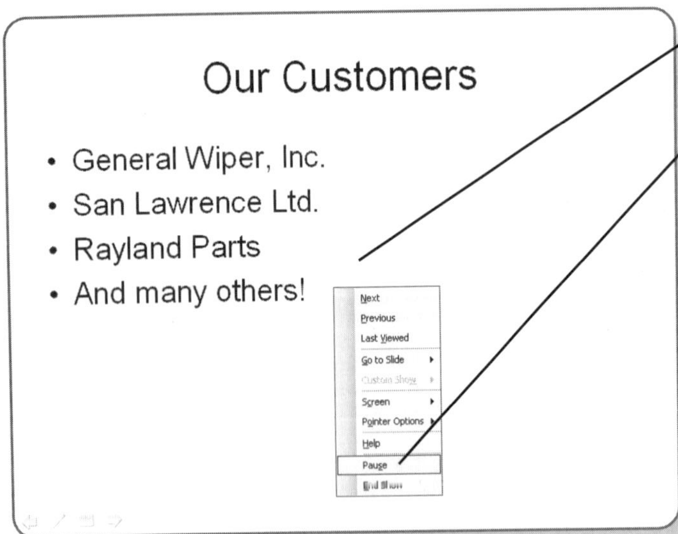

1. **Right-click** on the **slide**. A menu will appear.
2. **Click** on **Pause**. Automatic advance will be stopped.

> **NOTE**
>
> There is no shortcut key for the Pause command. The natural choice would be P, but P is used for "Previous" and takes you to the previous slide.

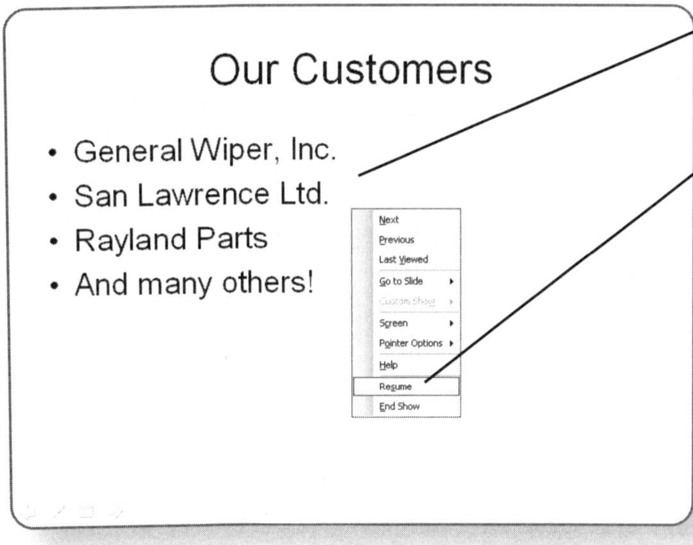

3. **Right-click** on the **slide** again when you are ready to resume. A menu will appear.

4. **Click** on **Resume**. Automatic slide advance will resume.

Blanking the Screen

You can blank out the screen temporarily during the presentation. This might be useful if you want to pause for an extended discussion but don't want to turn off the projector.

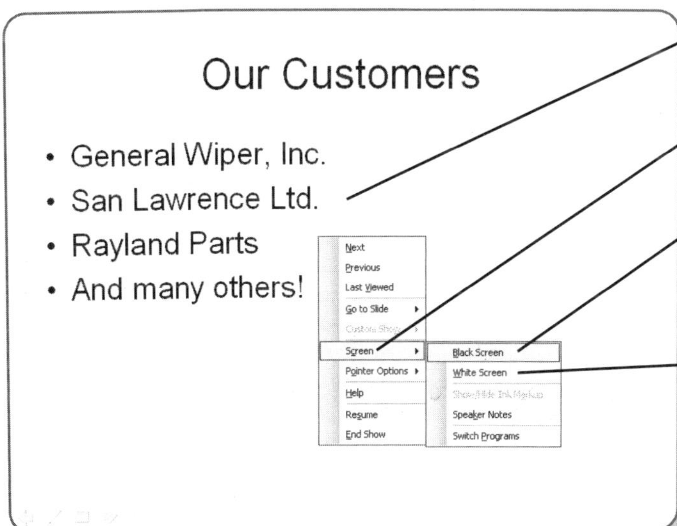

1. **Right-click** on the **slide**. A menu will appear.

2. **Point** to **Screen**. A submenu will appear.

3a. **Click** on **Black Screen.** The screen will become solid black.

OR

3b. **Click** on **White Screen**. The screen will become solid white.

4. **Click** the **mouse** or **press** a **key**. The presentation will resume.

Using the Pen in Slide Show View

The pen feature enables you to annotate the slides—that is, to write on them. If you have a tablet and stylus for computer use, you can use it for the annotation. Otherwise, you can click and drag to create lines and writing (although many people find it awkward to write with the mouse).

Writing with the Pen Tool

1. Move the **mouse**. The menu buttons in the bottom-left corner will appear.

2. Click on the **Pen** button. A menu will appear.

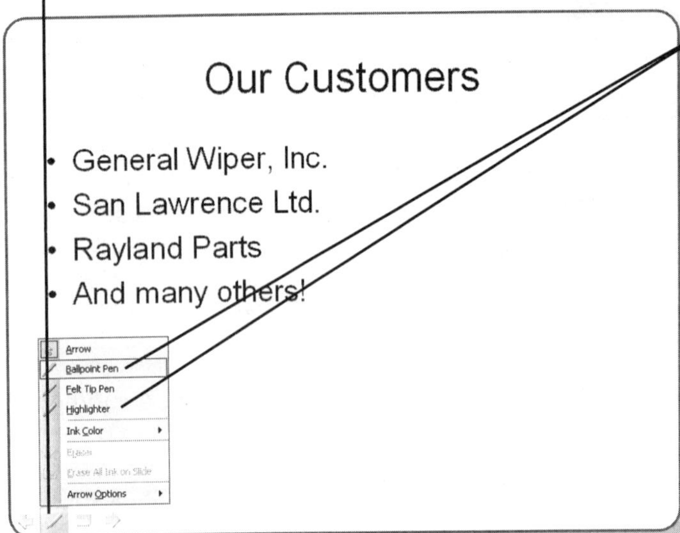

3. Click on the **type of pen** you want. The menu will close and the pointer will change to a colored dot.

Ballpoint and Felt Tip are two thicknesses of solid ink. Highlighter is semitransparent ink.

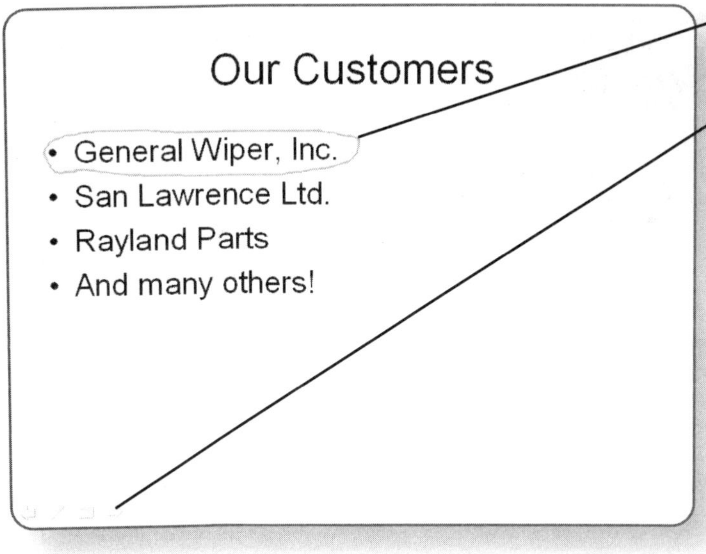

4. **Drag** on the **slide** to draw or write your annotations.

5. **Click** on the **Next button**, or press **Enter** or the **right arrow key**, to advance to the next slide.

The pen will stay active when you're moving between slides.

6. **Click** on the **Pen button**. The menu will appear.

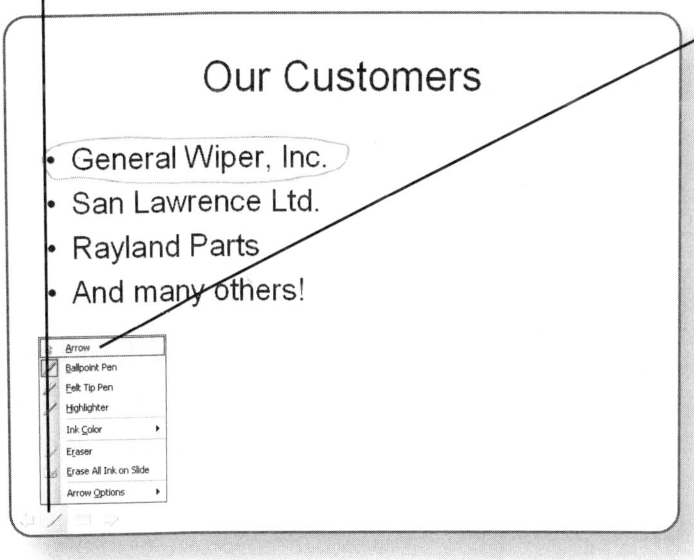

7. **Click** on **Arrow**. The mouse pointer will be restored to a normal arrow.

8. **Continue advancing** through the presentation to the end, or press **Esc** to end early. A message will appear, asking whether you want to save your annotations.

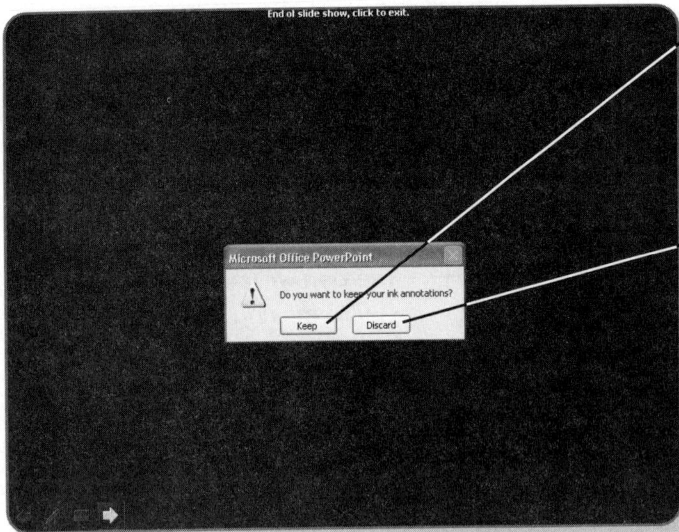

9a. Click on **Keep**. The drawings will be converted to AutoShapes and transferred to the slides. See the next section.

OR

9b. Click on **Discard**. The annotations will not be kept.

Working with Saved Annotations

Saved annotations appear as free-form AutoShape drawings on the slides. You can delete them, move them, and so on, just like ordinary AutoShape objects.

1. Display a **slide** containing annotations.

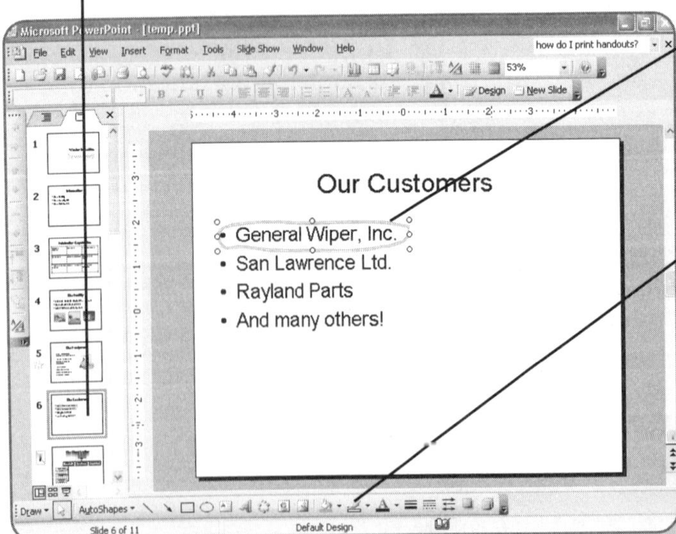

2. Click on the **annotation line**. It will be selected.

3. Modify it as desired. You can:

- Press Delete to delete it.
- Change its color with the Line Color button.
- Drag it to a different spot on the slide.

Changing the Pen Color

You can select any color for the pen during the presentation, and you can change it to a different one at any time.

1. **Move** the **mouse**. The buttons in the bottom-left corner of the screen will appear.

2. **Click** on the **Pen button**. A menu will appear.

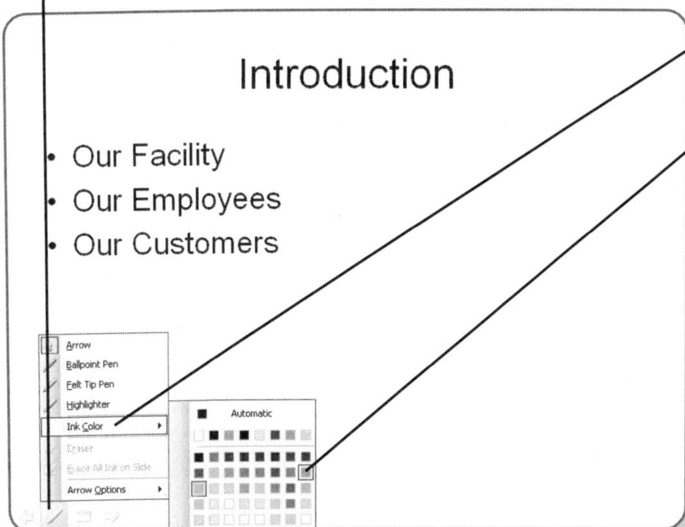

3. **Point** to **Ink Color**. A submenu will appear.

4. **Click** on a **color**. Future pen usage will be in that color.

19

Creating a Self-Running Presentation

Some presentations must be delivered remotely, either because the people you want to reach aren't available to sit through a live lecture, or because you want to use the presentation on the Web or some other widely distributed medium. There are some special considerations when you're preparing such a show, and this chapter will deal with them. In this chapter, you will learn how to:

- Create hyperlinks
- Create action buttons for navigation
- Add voice-over narration recordings

Creating Hyperlinks

> **TIP**
>
> Perhaps the easiest way to create a hyperlink to a Web site or e-mail address is simply to type its address in any text box. Then press Enter or the spacebar, and PowerPoint converts it into a working hyperlink automatically.

A *hyperlink* is a link from one location or document to another. When the user clicks a hyperlink, the destination document appears. You are probably familiar with hyperlinks on Web pages from using the Internet. You can also create hyperlinks on PowerPoint slides. These hyperlinks can point to other slides in the presentation, to e-mail addresses, or to other files stored anywhere on a network or on the Internet.

A hyperlink can be attached to any object, including any amount of text or a graphic object. For example, the user could click on underlined text as a hyperlink, or click on a graphic that is a hyperlink.

Hyperlinking to Another Slide in the Presentation

You would not normally hyperlink from one slide to the next one, because simply clicking the mouse will move to the next slide. However, you might hyperlink in order to jump around in the order (for example, to skip a certain set of slides), or to jump to a hidden slide.

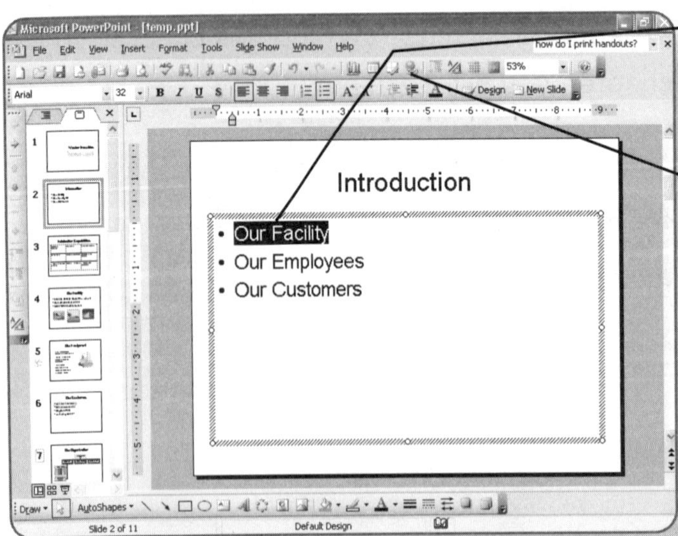

1. **Select** the **text** or **graphic** that you want to use as the hyperlink. The text or graphic will be selected.
2. **Click** on the **Insert Hyperlink button**. The Insert Hyperlink dialog box will open.

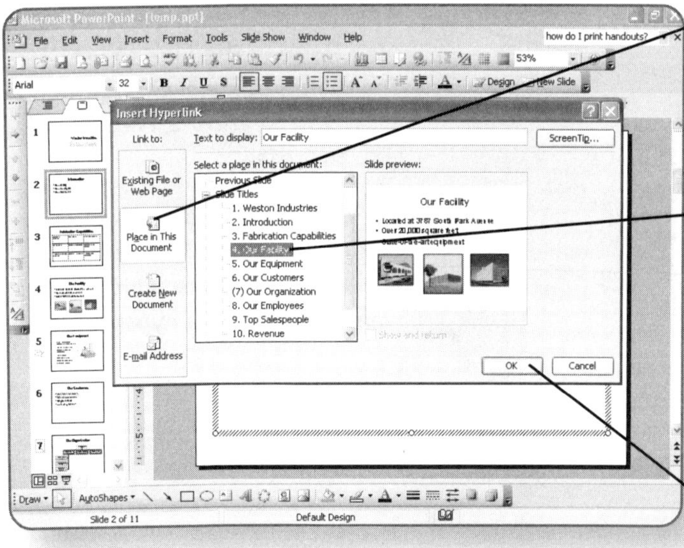

3. Click on **Place in This Document** in the Link to list. A list of slides found in the presentation will appear in the center of the dialog box.

4. Click on the **slide** in the Select a place in this document list box that you want to appear when a visitor clicks on the hyperlink. The slide will be selected, and a preview of the slide will appear in the Slide preview box.

5. Click on **OK**. The hyperlink will be created.

Creating Hyperlinks to Web Sites

A hyperlink to a Web site will open a Web browser when the user clicks on it, taking the user away from your PowerPoint presentation.

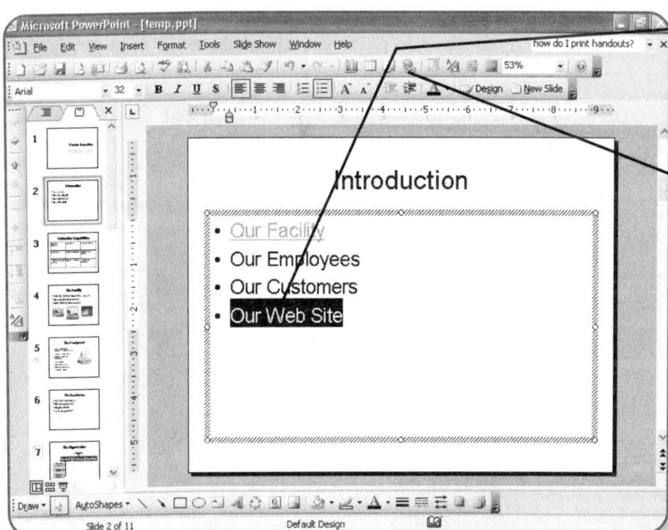

1. Select the **text** or **image** that will be used as the hyperlink. The text will be selected.

2. Click on the **Insert Hyperlink button**. The Insert Hyperlink dialog box will open.

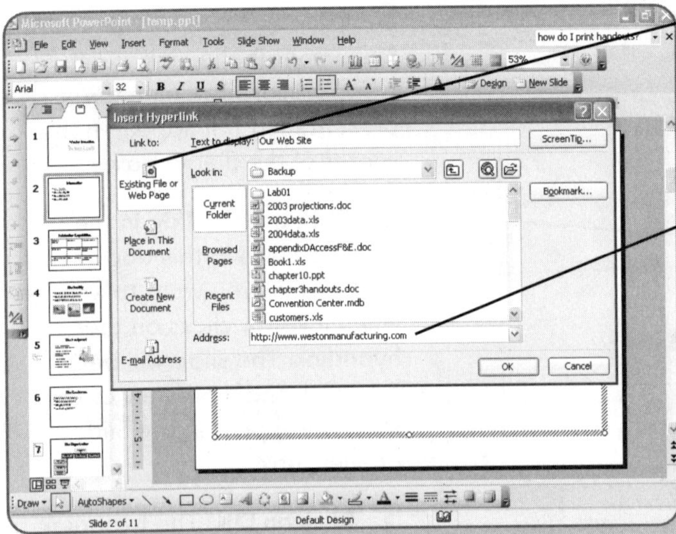

3. Click on **Existing File or Web Page** in the Link to list. The dialog box will change to allow you to enter a Web page's URL address.

4. Click in the **Address text box** and **type** the **URL address** of the Web page to which you want to create the hyperlink.

If you don't know the URL address, and if it's a page you've visited recently using your Web browser, click on Browsed Pages and select from the list.

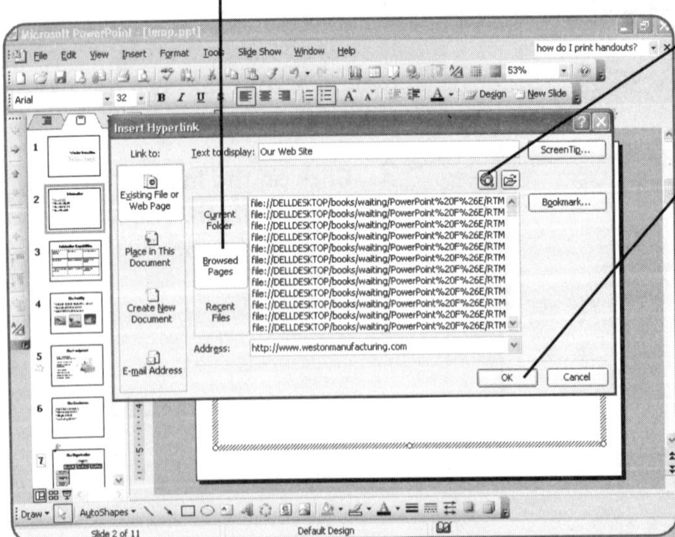

You can also click on the Browse the Web button to browse for the page in Internet Explorer.

5. Click on **OK**. The hyperlink will be created.

Creating an E-Mail Hyperlink

To give your audience an easy way to contact you, place an e-mail hyperlink on one of the slides. When people click on the e-mail hyperlink, a new message window will open from their default e-mail program. Your e-mail address (or any other address you specify) will appear in the To field. They just need to type a message and send it to you.

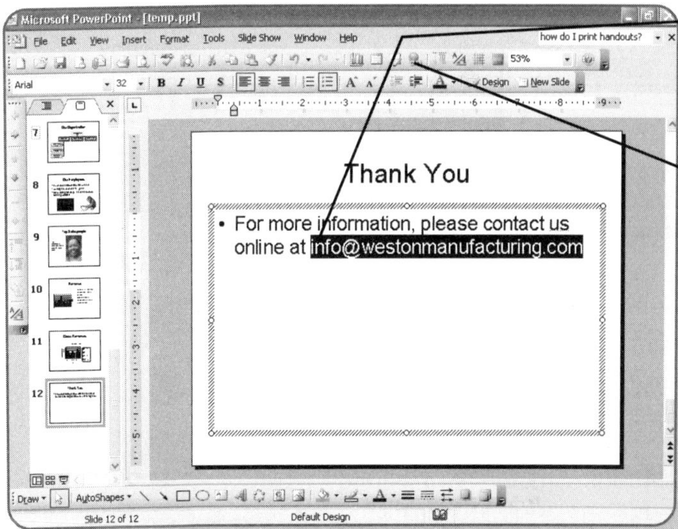

1. Select the **text** or **image** that you want to use as the e-mail hyperlink. The item will be selected.

2. Click on the **Insert Hyperlink button**. The Insert Hyperlink dialog box will open.

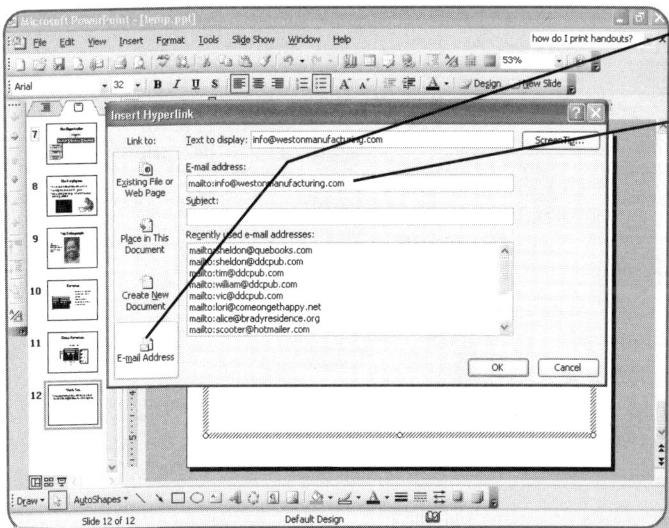

3. Click on **E-mail Address** in the Link to list.

4. Click in the **E-mail address text box** and **type** the **e-mail address** to which you want to create the link.

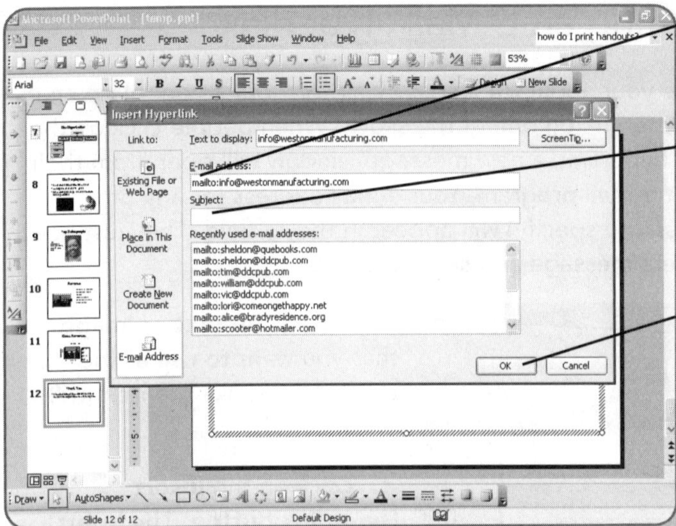

You do not have to type mailto: at the beginning; PowerPoint adds this automatically.

If you want e-mail sent from this link to contain a specific message header, type it in the Subject text box.

5. **Click** on **OK**. The e-mail hyperlink will be created.

Editing Hyperlinks

After creating a hyperlink, you may want to edit its display text or edit the address to which it links.

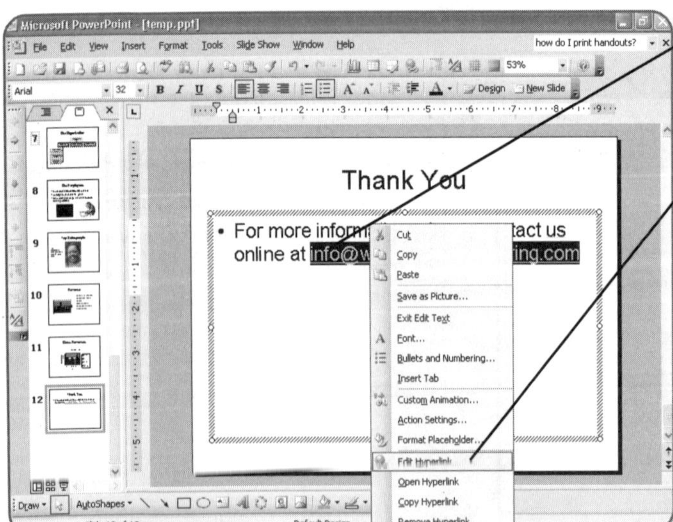

1. **Right-click** on the **hyperlinked text** or **object**. A menu will appear.

2. **Click** on **Edit Hyperlink**. The Edit Hyperlink dialog box will open.

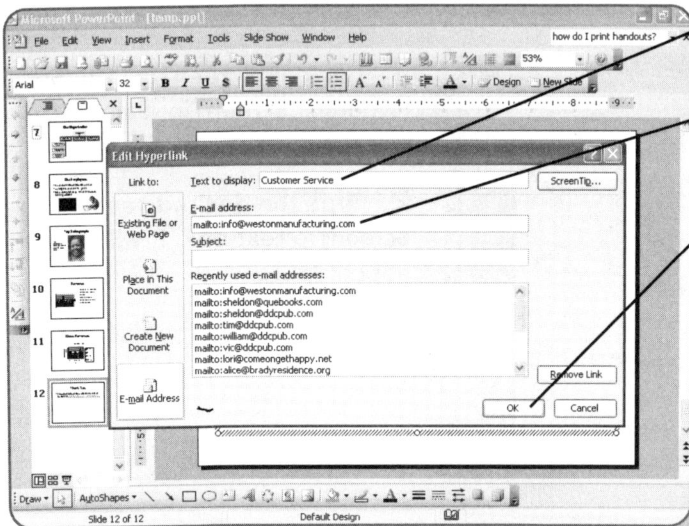

3. Edit the **text to display** in PowerPoint, if desired.

4. Edit the **address of the hyperlink,** if desired.

5. Click on **OK**. The dialog box will close and your changes will be made.

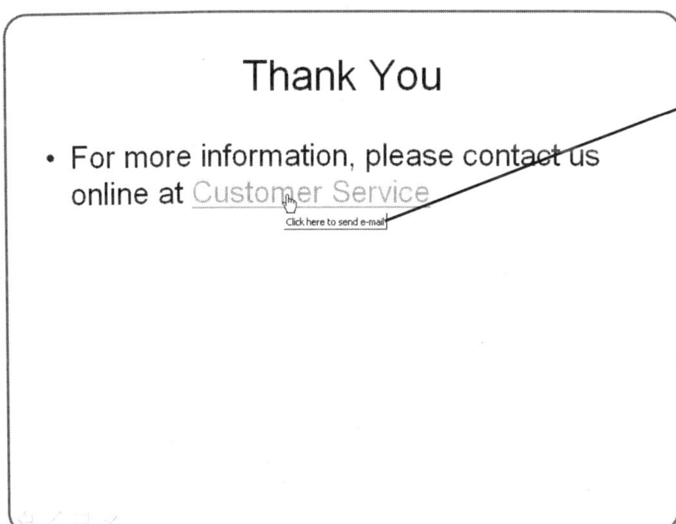

Using a ScreenTip

A *ScreenTip* is a box that pops up when the user points at the hyperlink. It can contain any text you like. Some people use it to show the URL if the display text shows something different.

From the Insert Hyperlink or Edit Hyperlink dialog box:

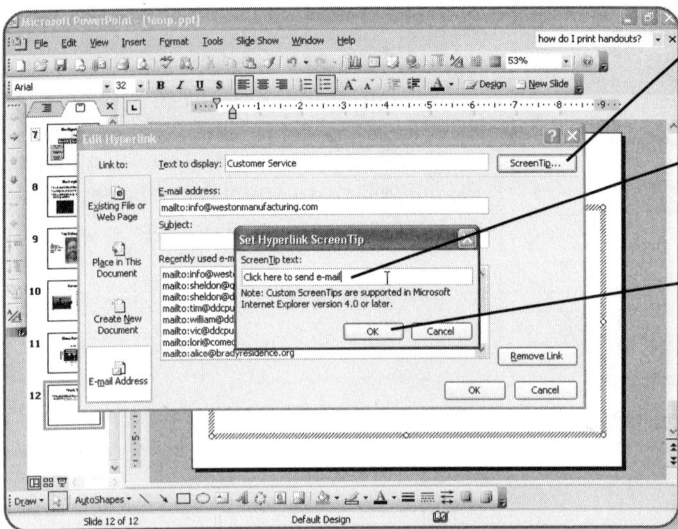

1. **Click** on **ScreenTip**. The Set Hyperlink ScreenTip dialog box will open.
2. **Type** the **desired text** in the ScreenTip text box. It will appear there.
3. **Click** on **OK**. The dialog box will close.

Creating Action Buttons

An *action button* is a graphic that is specifically designed for use as a hyperlink. Action buttons enable the person watching the presentation to move between slides by clicking on graphical buttons onscreen.

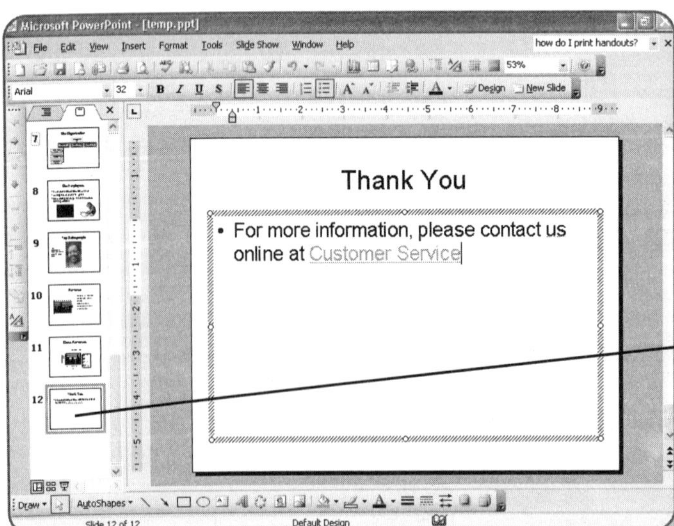

You can place an action button on an individual slide (for example, as a jump point to a hidden slide), or you can place it on the Slide Master so that the same button appears on all slides.

1. **Open** the **slide** on which you want to place the action buttons. The slide will appear in Normal view.

> **NOTE**
>
> If you want to place the button on all slides, display the Slide Master in step 1.

2. **Click** on **Slide Show**. The Slide Show menu will appear.

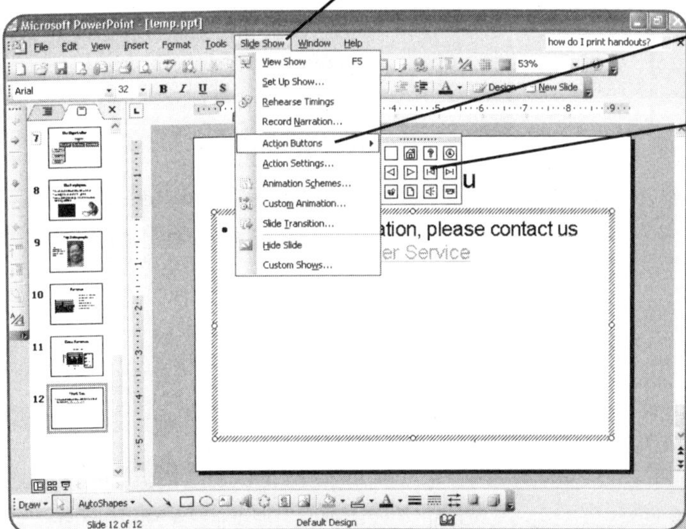

3. **Point to Action Buttons.** A submenu will appear.

4. **Click** on the **button** that you want to insert into the slide. The mouse pointer will turn into crosshairs.

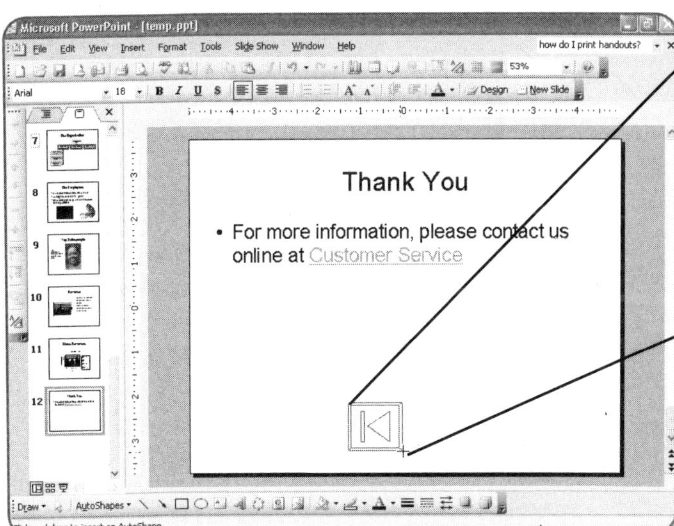

5a. **Click** on the **mouse pointer** where you want to place the navigation button. The button will appear in a predefined size, and the Action Settings dialog box will open.

OR

5b. **Click and drag** the **mouse pointer** to the exact size and shape you want for the button. When you release the mouse, the button will appear, and the Action Settings dialog box will open.

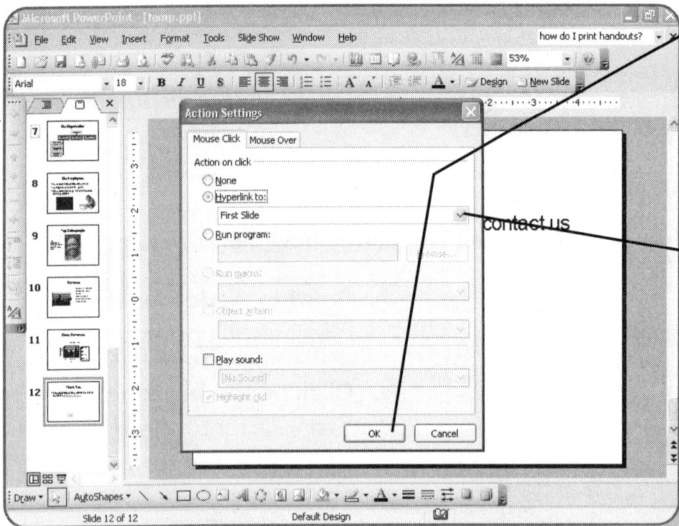

6. Click on **OK** to accept the default hyperlink. The button will be used as a hyperlink to the specified page.

> **TIP**
>
> If you want to change the slide that the button links to, click the down arrow next to the Hyperlink to list box and select a different slide.

Action buttons are treated just like AutoShapes for the purposes of formatting.

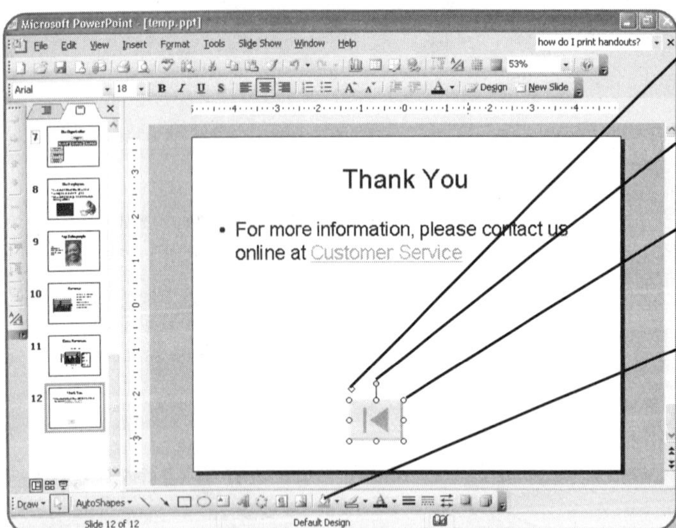

- Change its bevel width by dragging the yellow diamond.
- Rotate the button by dragging the green circle.
- Change the button's size and shape by dragging a selection handle.
- Change the fill color with the Fill Color button.

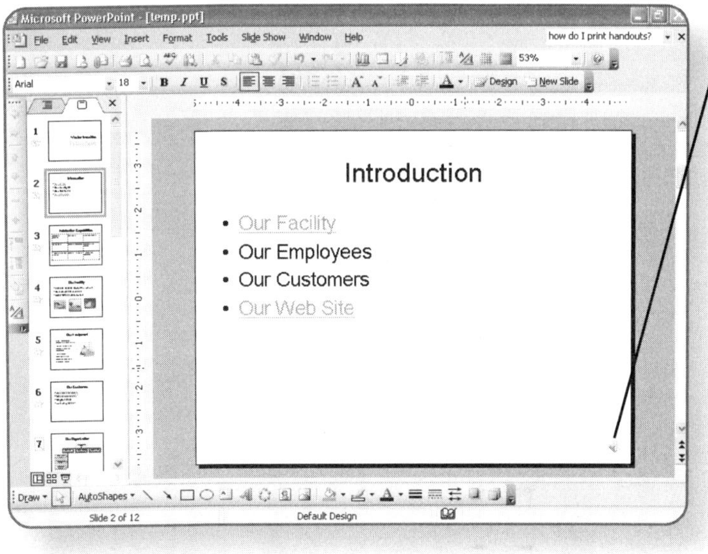

In Normal view, you will see a sound icon in the corner of each slide. You can double-click that sound icon to hear the recorded narration.

20

Publishing to the Web or CD

PowerPoint includes some features that make it easy for you to share a self-running or user-interactive presentation with others. You can save a presentation in Web format and make it available on any Web site, or you can copy it to a writeable CD and then duplicate and distribute the CD. In this chapter, you will learn how to:

- Save a presentation in Web format
- Create a self-running presentation on a CD

Publishing the Presentation in Web Format

Publishing in Web format is useful when you are trying to reach an audience over a network. This can include the Internet or an internal corporate intranet. The main advantage of this distribution method is that the people viewing it do not need PowerPoint installed on their PCs—or even a Windows-based operating system.

1. **Click** on **File**. The File menu will appear.

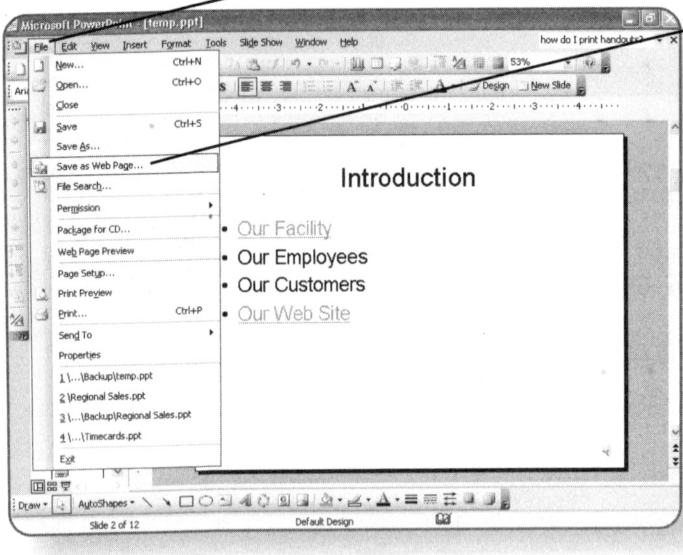

2. **Click** on **Save as Web Page**. A special version of the Save As dialog box will open.

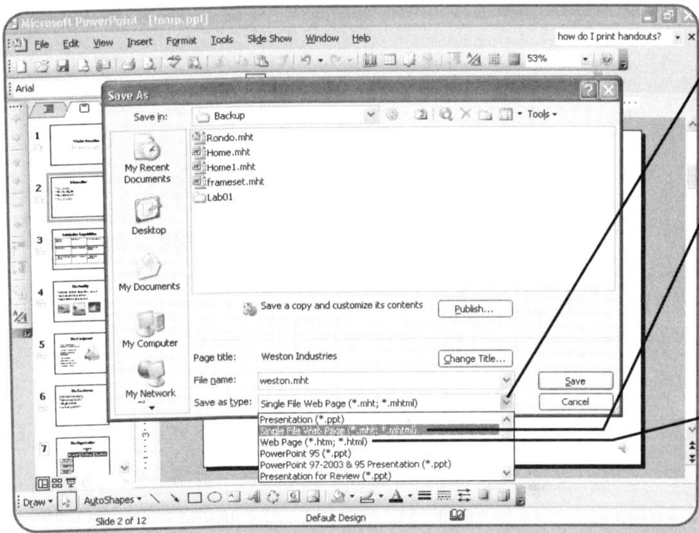

3. Click on the **down arrow** next to Save as type and **select** the **type of file** you want.

The default file format, Single File Web Page, puts the entire presentation into a single file. This is convenient, especially for attaching to e-mails. However, some older Web browsers may not be able to display such a file.

Web Page creates a single Web page as a starting point and a folder of support files containing the graphics. This is the "traditional" way of storing Web pages and is universally accepted.

4. Click on **Change Title**. The Set Page Title dialog box will open.

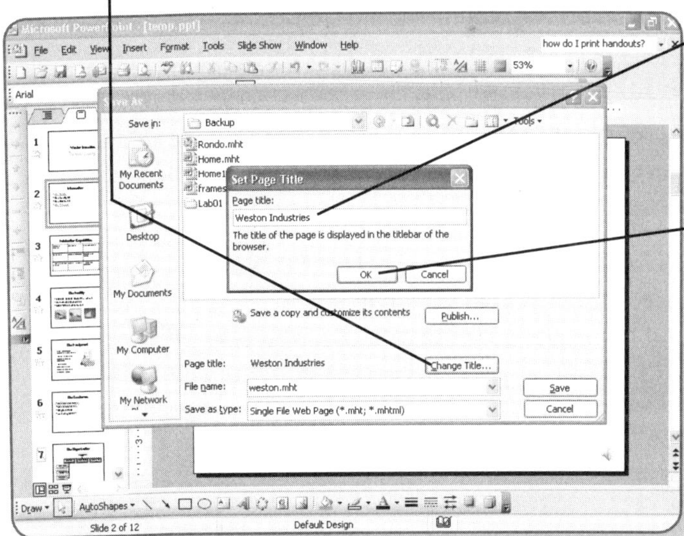

5. Enter the **title** you want in the Page title box. This title will appear in the user's Web browser when he or she displays the presentation later.

6. Click on **OK**. The title will appear next to Page title in the Save As dialog box.

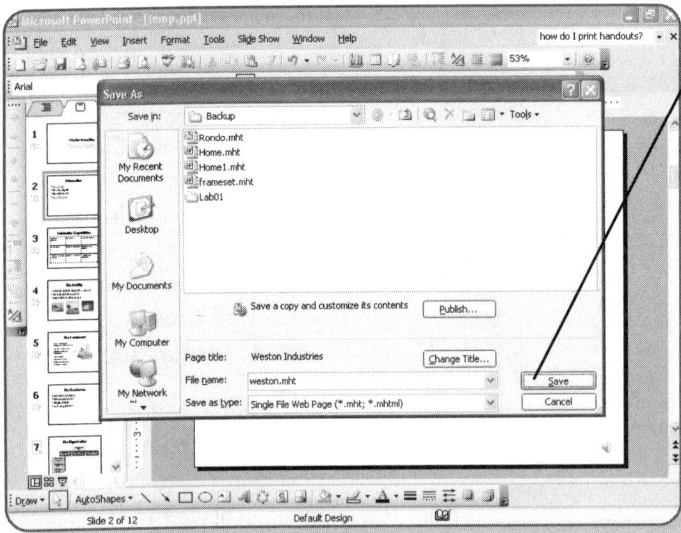

7. Click on **Save**. The presentation will be saved in Web format.

> **NOTE**
>
> You can save the file in any location (as you learned in Chapter 3, "Learning About Presentations"). You can also save it directly to a Web server by entering the URL for the Web address in the File name box, or by going through My Network Places. That is beyond the scope of this book, however.

Publishing a Presentation to CD

A new feature in PowerPoint 2003 is the ability to create a self-contained CD that contains the presentation and a copy of a utility called PowerPoint Viewer. This utility enables any computer to display a PowerPoint presentation even if PowerPoint isn't installed.

For this feature to write directly to a CD, you must have a writeable or rewriteable CD drive and an operating system that supports writing to CD (such as Windows XP). If you don't have them, you can still package the presentation for CD and save the package to your hard disk. You can then copy the files to another disk later.

1. Click on **File**. The File menu will appear.

2. Click on **Package for CD**. The Package for CD dialog box will open.

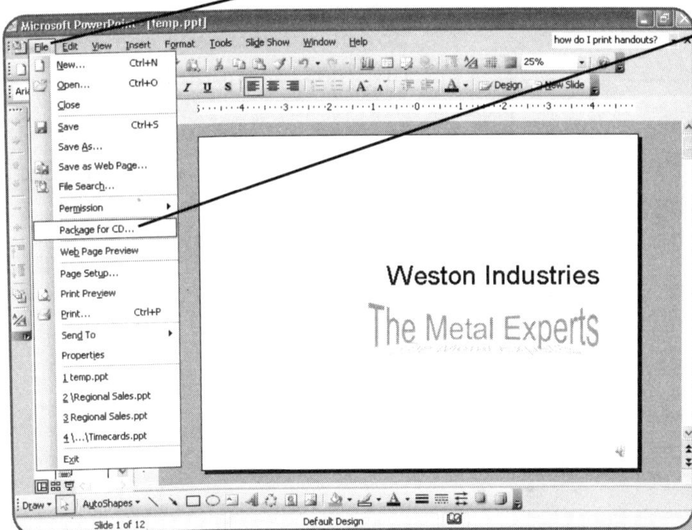

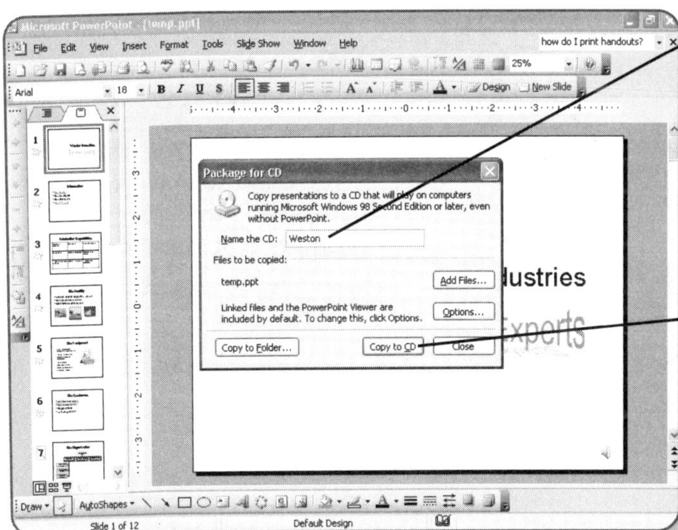

3. Type a **name** for the CD in the Name the CD box. This name will appear beneath the CD icon in My Computer when the disc is inserted into a computer.

4. Insert a **blank writeable CD** into your CD-R or CD-RW drive.

5. Click on **Copy to CD**.

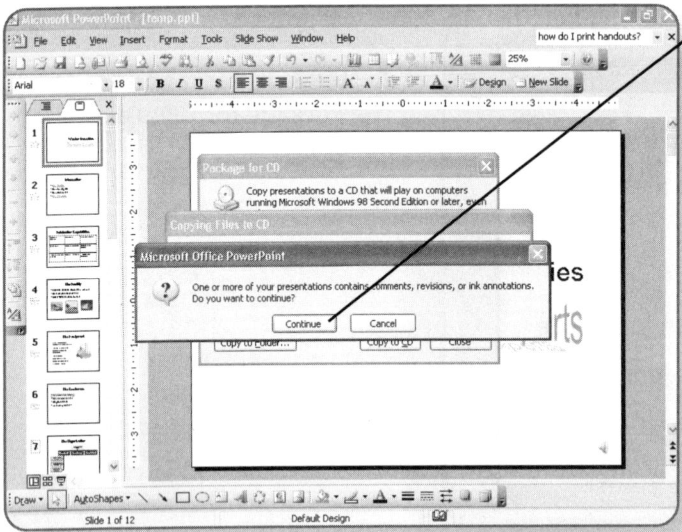

6. **Click** on **Continue,** if needed. You will see this dialog box only if you have comments, revisions, or annotations.

The needed files will be transferred to the CD. When the process is finished, the CD will be ejected from the drive (on most systems).

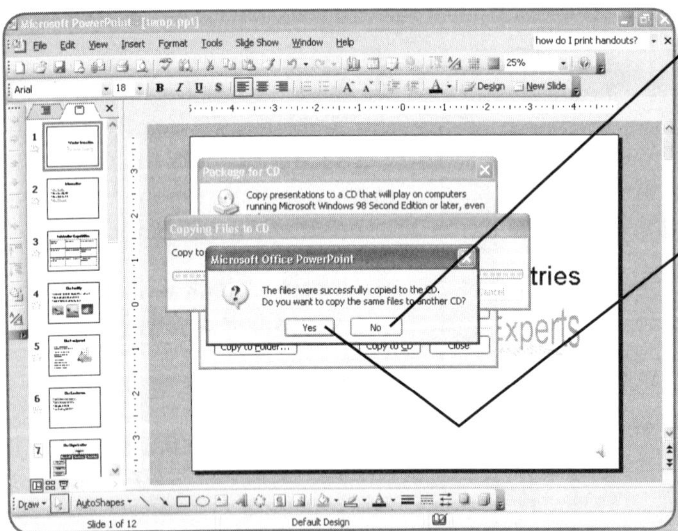

7. **Click** on **No**. The Package for CD dialog box will reappear.

> **NOTE**
>
> You can click on Yes in step 7 if you need to make extra copies, and then follow the prompts that appear.

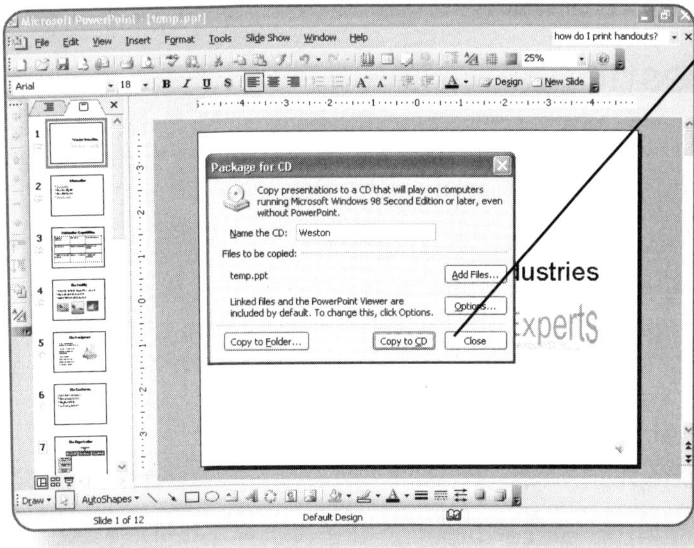

8. Click on **Close**. The Package for CD dialog box will close.

Part V Review Questions

1. What is the purpose of the icon that appears in the bottom-right corner of a pasted selection? See "Keeping the Source Formatting When Pasting" in Chapter 15.
2. When you're linking an entire existing file in PowerPoint, what menu command do you use? See "Linking an Entire File" in Chapter 15.
3. In what two views can you type speaker notes for a slide? See "Using Notes" in Chapter 16.
4. How do you restore a deleted placeholder in the Notes Master? See "Restoring Deleted Placeholders" in Chapter 16.
5. How can you change the automatic-advance timing for an individual slide? See "Setting the Timing for an Individual Slide" in Chapter 16.
6. What is something you can do with handouts exported to Word that you cannot do with handouts within PowerPoint? See "Exporting Handouts to Microsoft Word" in Chapter 17.
7. What key can you press on the keyboard to move to the previous slide during a slide show? See "Moving Between Slides" in Chapter 18.
8. How would you make the screen solid black temporarily during a presentation? See "Blanking the Screen" in Chapter 18.
9. When does a hyperlink's ScreenTip appear? See "Using a ScreenTip" in Chapter 19.
10. What program is included on presentation CDs that makes it possible for people who don't have PowerPoint to view a presentation? See "Publishing a Presentation to CD" in Chapter 20.

A

Using Shortcut Keys

Shortcut keys are a quick and efficient way to execute commands. They increase productivity and decrease the strain caused by excessive mouse usage. Shortcut keys are common to all Microsoft Windows and Office applications, and many of them are common between applications.

This appendix introduces many commonly used shortcut keys. Keep this guide close at hand and practice using the shortcut keys. You'll find that with a little time and patience, you'll be using the keyboard as naturally as you once used the mouse. In this appendix, you'll learn how to:

- Display shortcut keys in the ScreenTips
- Work with presentations
- Navigate the Help system
- Edit text
- Organize an outline
- Move around in a table or presentation

Showing Shortcut Keys in ScreenTips

The menu system lists the shortcut key for a command on the right side of the menu. Shortcut keys can also be displayed in the ScreenTips. When you enable this option, you'll see the shortcut key for a command when you hold the mouse pointer over a toolbar button.

1. **Click** on **Tools**. The Tools menu will appear.

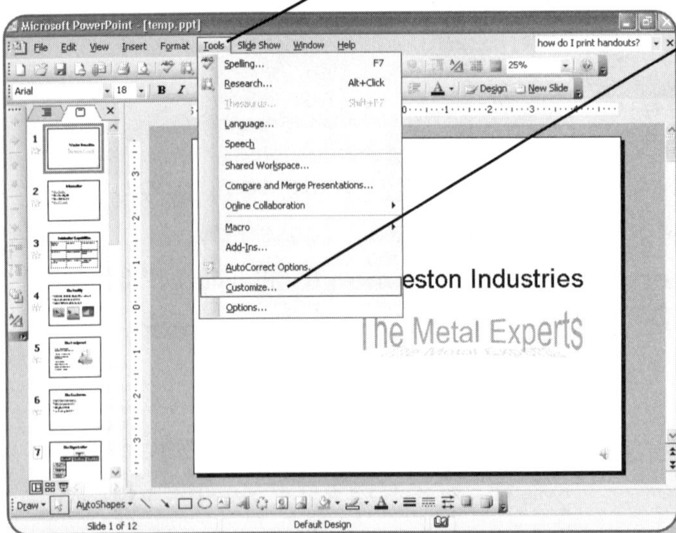

2. **Click** on **Customize**. The Customize dialog box will open.

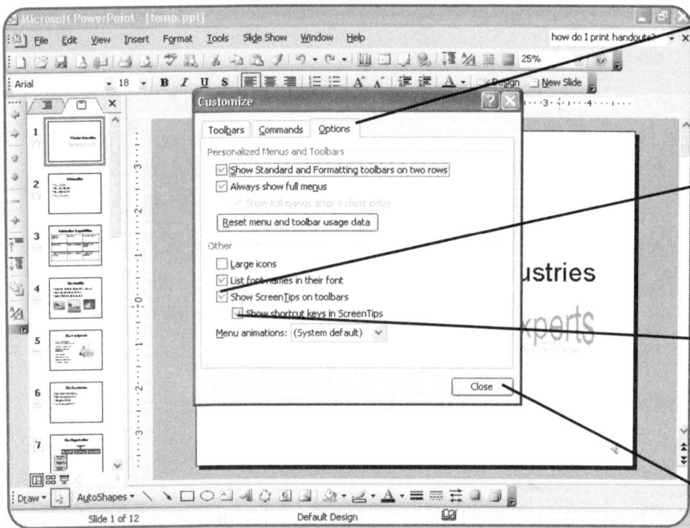

3. **Click** on the **Options tab** if it is not selected when the dialog box opens. The Options tab will come to the front.

4. **Click** in the **Show ScreenTips on toolbars check box**, if it is not selected. A check will be placed in the check box.

5. **Click** in the **Show shortcut keys in ScreenTips check box**. A check will be placed in the check box.

6. **Click** on **Close**. The dialog box will close.

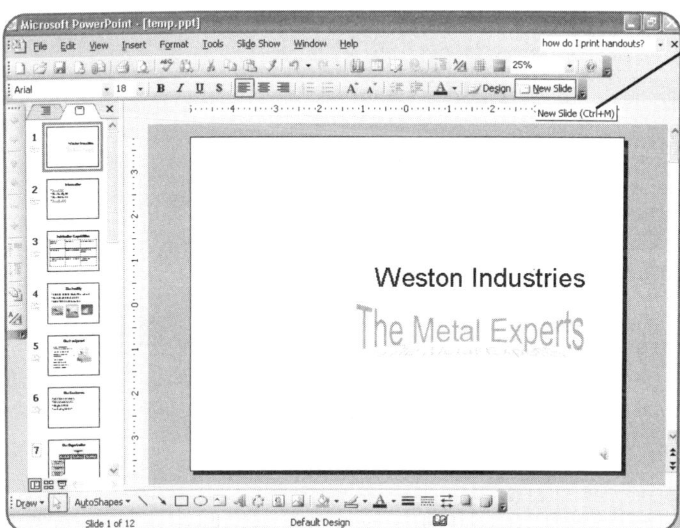

7. **Hold** the **mouse pointer** over a toolbar button. If a shortcut key is assigned to the command, it will appear in the ScreenTip.

Basic Shortcuts

Shortcut keys are easy to remember if you just start with a few shortcuts in the beginning. When you start using these few shortcuts without reverting to the mouse, add a few new shortcut keys. An easy way to start is to get into the habit of holding down the Ctrl key while pressing the S key (Ctrl+S) on a regular basis. This simple shortcut saves the document on which you are working. It's a good idea to save your work every few minutes.

The following table lists some other shortcut keys that will help you get your job done faster.

To execute this command...	Use this shortcut key
Start a new, blank presentation	Ctrl+N
Save a presentation	Ctrl+S
Close a presentation	Ctrl+W
Open a presentation	Ctrl+O
Spell check a presentation	F7
Print a presentation	Ctrl+P
Run a slideshow	F5

Working with the Help System

To display the Help task pane, press F1.

Working with the Outline Pane

In Chapter 4, "Organizing the Presentation Outline," you learned how to edit a presentation outline using the Outlining toolbar. The following table lists the shortcut keys you can use to make this job easier.

To execute this command...	Use this shortcut key
Insert a new slide	Ctrl+M
Demote an outline item	Tab
Promote an outline item	Shift+Tab
Move a paragraph down in the outline	Alt+Shift+Down Arrow
Move a paragraph up in the outline	Alt+Shift+Up Arrow
Show only the title for a selected slide	Alt+Shift+minus sign
Show all of the text for a selected slide	Alt+Shift+plus sign
Collapse an outline to show only the slide titles	Alt+Shift+1
Expand an outline to show all the text on all slides	Alt+Shift+9

Editing Text

As you are adding text to a presentation outline or to the slides, you'll want to try your hand at a few shortcut keys that will make it quicker to select and edit text.

To execute this command...	Use this shortcut key
Select one character to the right	Shift+Right Arrow
Select one character to the left	Shift+Left Arrow
Select from cursor to end of word	Ctrl+Shift+Right Arrow
Select from cursor to beginning of word	Ctrl+Shift+Left Arrow
Select from cursor to next line	Shift+Down Arrow
Select from cursor to previous line	Shift+Up Arrow
Delete selected text	Ctrl+X
Copy selected text	Ctrl+C
Paste text from the clipboard	Ctrl+V
Delete one character to the left	Backspace
Delete one word to the left	Ctrl+Backspace
Delete one character to the right	Delete
Delete one word to the right	Ctrl+Delete
Find text on a slide	Ctrl+F
Replace text on a slide	Ctrl+H
Undo editing changes	Ctrl+Z
Redo editing changes	Ctrl+Y

Formatting Text

Formatting text using shortcut keys is easy, and most of these shortcut keys are easy to remember. To format text, select the text and then use the appropriate shortcut keys. The following table lists the most common formatting shortcut keys.

To execute this command...	Use this shortcut key
Change the font of the selected text	Ctrl+Shift+F
Make the font larger	Ctrl+Shift+>
Make the font smaller	Ctrl+Shift+<
Make the text bold	Ctrl+B
Underline the text	Ctrl+U
Italicize the text	Ctrl+I
Center a paragraph	Ctrl+E
Left-align a paragraph	Ctrl+L
Right-align a paragraph	Ctrl+R

Moving Around in a Table or Slide Show

With the mouse, it's a snap to move from cell to cell in a table, or from slide to slide in a slide show. Just one click and you're there! Moving around with the keyboard isn't as intuitive. Use the following table to get around inside tables and slide shows.

To execute this command...	Use this shortcut key
Go to the next cell in a table	Tab
Go to the previous cell in a table	Shift+Tab
Move to the next row in a table	Down Arrow
Move to the previous row in a table	Up Arrow
Move to the next slide in a slide show	Spacebar
Go to the previous slide in a slide show	Backspace
Display a specific slide in a slide show	Type the slide number and press Enter
End the slide show	Esc

Glossary

3-D. Having or appearing to have three dimensions: width, height, and depth.

A

Accessibility. The ease of use and access to the program is enhanced to aid those with limited vision or impaired movement.

Agenda slide. A slide that lists items for the agenda or headings for main sections of your presentation.

Animation. The addition of special effects, such as movement or sound, to objects in your presentation.

Annotate. To draw or write on a slide during a presentation using the annotation pen.

Answer Wizard. Lets you formulate your question in your own words, and then automatically directs you to the proper place within Help for your answer.

AutoShape. A readymade shape for you to use in your presentations. The AutoShapes menu can be found on the Drawing toolbar.

B

Bitmap. A graphic file with its graphic information stored pixel by pixel. Bitmap images cannot be converted directly into PowerPoint images.

Bullet. A character, number, or graphic object used to delineate special sections of the text.

C

Callouts. These are text additions to the slide that point to specific items and give information about them. In PowerPoint, these are drawing objects that may be sized, rotated, and otherwise manipulated along with the information contained within them.

Caption. An alternative description of a picture, chart, or other graphic that may be used in a presentation to indicate the content of the picture, chart, and so on.

Chart. A graphic representation of a data array, such as a pie-shaped graphic sliced to show spending or budget contributions.

Clip art. The name applied to various graphics that are freely available for use in presentations.

Clip Organizer. This contains a large number of graphic objects and pictures that you can use to enhance and illustrate your slides.

Collapse. When you're working in Outline view, clicking on the minus sign (-) at the beginning of a major heading will hide the subheadings indented below the main heading. This can be used to show an Outline view that has only major headings.

Color scheme. A set of eight colors that you can use in combination within your presentation to give a uniform appearance.

Comments. Notes added to the slides by you, or perhaps others, that are not shown automatically with the slides in the presentation. They are separate from the slides and may be turned on or off.

Connector lines. There are three types of lines that you may use to connect objects: straight, angled, and curved. These remain attached to the object when it is moved, and may be reshaped by handles on the connector lines to make rearranging objects easier.

Crop. Trimming the horizontal and vertical edges of a picture using the cropping tool on the Picture toolbar.

D

Drag and drop. Moving or otherwise manipulating an object by clicking on the left mouse button and dragging the mouse pointer until the object is placed where desired.

Drawing object. A text box, WordArt drawing, AutoShape, or other clip art object that you can insert into a picture.

Duplicate. You can make more than one copy of a slide for the same presentation, or for use in other presentations, by selecting the object and then clicking on Duplicate on the Edit menu.

E

Embedded objects. Information inserted into a file from another file (source file) that becomes part of the file into which it is inserted (destination file) after it becomes embedded. Double-clicking on the embedded object launches the original application in which the object was created.

Emboss. A shadow effect available on the Drawing toolbar. Apply it to drawing objects to give them a 3-D effect.

Engrave. Effect on the Drawing toolbar that gives texture to drawing objects.

Expand. When you're working in the Outline view, clicking on the plus sign (+) beside a major heading in an outline will display the subheadings cascading down in outline format.

F

Fill. You can fill drawing objects with solid or shaded colors, textures, or even pictures.

Flip. You can rotate an object 90 degrees in either direction, and you can flip it horizontally or vertically.

Font. A family of type characters all of the same design, such as Garamond or Times New Roman.

Footer. The text at the bottom of every page that reflects the page number, the document name, or other similar information.

Format. The organized way in which objects and text are placed on a page or slide.

Freeform object. An object created by selecting a freeform shape from the AutoShapes menu and then dragging and reshaping it with the handles.

G

Gradient. A way of adding a pattern to an object to make it appear shaded.

Graph. A visual representation of an array of data organized to show trends.

Grayscale. A method that converts color images into black and white. Different amounts of black and white are combined to produce shades of gray that more closely represent the different shades of color in the image.

Grid. An area with evenly spaced lines (often invisible), in which objects may be dragged and then placed exactly by having their boundaries snap to a grid line.

Gridline. A line on a grid onto which drawing objects may be placed exactly by using the snap function.

Group. To assemble drawing objects and bind them, so that they can all be manipulated together and still maintain their positions relative to each other.

Guide. Helps you align objects and text on your slide.

H

Handle. A diamond-shaped handle is used to change the shape of most AutoShapes. There are also handles on the connecting lines to allow you to move drawing objects.

Header. A text box or graphic at the top of each page of a document, with information such as the company name, date, document title, or page number.

Hue. You can change the color of the shadow fills by clicking on the Shadow Style button on the Drawing toolbar and then clicking on Shadow Settings. On the Shadow Settings toolbar, click on the arrow next to Shadow Color.

Hyperlink. A link from a place in your document to another document (either in a separate file or on the Web), or to another place inside your document.

I

Import. To bring text or graphics into PowerPoint from other programs for inclusion as PowerPoint objects in a presentation, or to be stored in the PowerPoint clip art gallery.

K

Kiosk. A standalone computer that plays a presentation on a continuous basis. A kiosk is usually unattended or used as a part of a display, and the presentation is set up to move from slide to slide automatically.

L

Line art. Graphics that are redrawn on the screen from a set of vectors contained in a file, as opposed to a pixel-by-pixel graphic map such as a bitmap.

Linked objects. Objects (information) in a file that remain connected to, and receive updates from, the original application in which they were created.

M

Macro. A small script used to simplify repetitive tasks and reduce keyboard strokes.

Multimedia. Elements that you can add to your presentation, such as animation, music, and video.

N

Normal view. In Normal view, three panes are visible: the Outline pane, Slide pane, and Notes pane. It's helpful to be able to focus on all aspects of the presentation simultaneously. Dragging the pane borders can change the size of the different panes.

Notes Master. There are masters for both the Notes and Handouts. The master can contain the header and footer information or any picture or icon that you want to appear on all the Notes pages or handouts.

O

Office Assistant. A handy little piece of artificial intelligence that can help you sort through the Help files for the specific information you request. It also spontaneously offers help with tasks.

Organization chart. PowerPoint has a program that builds organization charts, offering tools and templates for you to create, edit, and modify the charts.

Outline view. A view of a document showing section headings and detailed subheadings in outline form. Text may be moved, and the overall order of elements changed, by dragging and dropping the outline heads in another spot in the document.

Overhead. A slide shown with an overhead projector on a screen.

P

Placeholder. A small, dotted-line box that marks the position of text or objects on a slide. You can add text by typing it into the placeholder.

Presentation. An organized collection of text and graphics displayed to an audience to orient, teach, advertise, market, and so on.

Presentation broadcasting. You can broadcast presentations over the Web and make them accessible to viewers in remote locations.

Preview. You may preview all your Web pages, as well as video and animation effects, before using them in a presentation.

R

Regroup. You may use the Drawing toolbar to reassemble objects that previously were grouped. Select Draw and then Regroup.

Rotate. To turn an object on its axis, such as rotating a picture or a graphic on a slide.

S

Scan. Pictures can be imported into PowerPoint from a scanner or a digital camera if the hardware is TWAIN-compatible.

Shadow. You can apply shadows to drawing objects by selecting the Shadow Style button on the Drawing toolbar.

Slide Master. This controls text characteristics, background color, and special effects, such as shadowing and bullet style. It also contains placeholders for text and layout attributes such as headers and footers.

Slide show. An ordered presentation of slides, often accompanied by narration or animation and other special effects.

Slide Sorter view. The whole presentation is shown in miniature. You can add slide transitions, rearrange slides, and preview them in this view.

Spell check. You may spell check your documents in PowerPoint as you do in other Office applications. You can have PowerPoint check your spelling as you type, or you can have the spell check done all at one time.

Style checker. PowerPoint automatically checks your presentation for consistency and style. The Office Assistant must be turned on to make this feature available.

Summary Slide. By clicking the Summary Slide button on the Slide Sorter toolbar, you can create a slide that contains all the agenda items for the presentation.

T

Table. Tables are handy ways of including data and other objects in your presentation. You can format a table of your own, or you can import tables from other programs, such as Microsoft Word.

Task pane. The pane to the right of the main window provides commands or options for certain activities, such as selecting a different design template or slide layout.

Text Box tool. You can enter text easily with the Text Box tool on the Drawing toolbar.

Transparent. You can set transparent areas in objects such as pictures. You can make the background of the picture transparent and just show certain objects in the picture, without the background.

U

Undo. The button on the Standard toolbar that's shaped like a left-curving arrow. You can undo any mouse or keyboard action, and its result, by clicking on the Undo button.

Ungroup. You can remove objects grouped in a drawing object by clicking on Ungroup, found in the Draw menu on the Drawing toolbar.

V

Voice-over narration. You can add voice-over narration to your presentation in PowerPoint. This narration can be archived and shown later, or it can be used as a Web presentation.

Z

Zoom. To move the viewer's perspective closer or farther away by either enlarging a detail (Zoom in) or displaying the complete object (Zoom out).

Index

D

G

H

I

J–K

L

P

U

V

W–Z